Law and Society
Recent Scholarship

Edited by Melvin I. Urofsky

A Series from LFB Scholarly

National Security in the Courts
The Need for Secrecy vs. the Requirement of Transparency

Derigan Silver

LFB Scholarly Publishing LLC
El Paso 2010

Library of Congress Cataloging-in-Publication Data

Silver, Derigan Almond.
  National security in the courts : the need for secrecy vs. the
requirement of transparency / Derigan Almond Silver.
      p. cm. -- (Law & society : recent scholarship)
  Includes bibliographical references and index.
  ISBN 978-1-59332-420-9 (hardcover : alk. paper)
  1. Freedom of the press--United States. 2. Freedom of information--
United States. 3. National security--Law and legislation--United States.
4. Censorship--United States. I. Title.
  KF4774.S57 2010
  342.7308'53--dc22
                                                2010022963

ISBN 978-1-59332-420-9

Printed on acid-free 250-year-life paper.

Manufactured in the United States of America.

For Alison,
with gratitude, respect and love

Table of Contents

Acknowledgements

This book is the culmination of a long effort and, thus, there are a great many people I need to thank for their help, support and encouragement. First, I am deeply grateful to Ruth Walden. For three years, I had the great pleasure of being her research assistant, teaching assistant and student. I am especially indebted to her for the support she gave my family during the tumultuous events that surrounded the beginning of this project. As a mentor, legal scholar, teacher and friend, she has few peers.

I am also deeply indebted to a number of others whose ideas and arguments have helped shaped my thinking on legal research and this book. They include: Lois Boynton, Ed Carter, Tori Ekstrand, Michael Hoefges, W. Wat Hopkins, Dan Kozlowski, William P. Marshall, Kathleen K. Olson, Kevin T. McGuire and Kyu Youm. These fine researchers and teachers have freely given their time to me whenever I needed it, and for that I am deeply thankful. I am also especially grateful to Cathy Packer. Her insights into legal theory and the way case law structures society continue to inspire me to do theoretically grounded work. I also deeply value her friendship.

In addition, I want to thank Rachel Davis Mersey and Peter Bobkowski for their friendship. I'd also like to thank the faculty of the Department of Media, Film and Journalism Studies at the University of Denver, particularly my chair, Renée Botta.

Finally, my family has provided me with mental and emotional support as well as a great deal of encouragement over the years. My children, Sydney, Roan, Noah and Joel, deserve my thanks for letting me work late nights, early mornings and weekends. They make our lives crazy and wonderful. I am the most grateful, however, to my wife, Alison. I wish I were a better writer so that I could effectively express my gratitude and love for her. There is no possible way I could finished even the most basic of tasks without her unwavering support and love.

CHAPTER 1

Introduction

In the years following the Sept. 11, 2001, terrorist attacks on New York and Washington, D.C., the U.S. government took numerous and extraordinary steps to increase secrecy in the name of national security. Although some authors assert that the administration of President George W. Bush was notably secretive even before the attacks,[1] in the years following 9/11 the government created secret military tribunals,[2] ordered court proceedings closed to the public,[3] claimed executive privilege in a wide variety of situations,[4] increased the use of the state secrets privilege to prevent the disclosure of national security information in court proceedings,[5] blocked access to the records of

---

[1] See, e.g., Jane E. Kirtley, *Transparency and Accountability in a Time of Terror: The Bush Administration's Assault on Freedom of Information*, 11 COMM. L. & POL'Y 479, 484-89 (2006); Peter M. Shane, *Social Theory Meets Social Policy: Culture, Identity and Public Information Policy After September 11*, 2 ISJLP i, iv (2006); Adam Clymer, *Government Openness at Issue as Bush Holds on to Records*, N.Y. TIMES, Jan. 3, 2003, at A1.

[2] Military Order, "Detention, Treatment, and Trial of Certain Non-Citizens in the War Against Terrorism," 66 Fed. Reg. 57833-57836, Nov. 13, 2001.

[3] Michael Creppy, Chief Immigration Judge of the United States, Memorandum: Cases Requiring Special Procedures, Sept. 21, 2001, *available at* http://fl1.findlaw.com/news.findlaw.com/hdocs/docs/aclu/creppy092101memo.pdf.

[4] See, e.g., Cheney v. United States District Court, 542 U.S. 367 (2004); George W. Bush, Memorandum: Disclosures to Congress, Oct. 5, 2001, *available at* http://www.fas.org/sgp/news/2001/10/gwb100501.html; George W. Bush, Memorandum for the Attorney General: Congressional Subpoena for Executive Branch Documents, Dec. 12, 2001, *available at* http://www.whitehouse.gov/news/releases/2001/12/20011213-1.html; PFIAB PLAYS SECRECY GAMES, Federation of American Scientists, SECRECY NEWS, vol. 2002, no. 77, Aug. 15, 2002, *available at* http://ftp.fas.org/sgp/news/secrecy/2002/08/081502.html.

[5] William G. Weaver & Robert M. Pallito, *State Secrets and Executive Power*, 120 POLI. SCI. Q. 85, 86 (2005). The state secrets privilege, a judicial creation, is most often used by executive branch officials in civil court cases to protect against subpoenas, discovery motions and other judicial requests for

former presidents,[6] refused to provide documents in response to congressional inquiries,[7] kept secret the National Security Agency's (NSA) surveillance of citizens,[8] reclassified previously unclassified documents,[9] created additional exemptions to the federal Freedom of Information Act (FOIA) for critical infrastructure information,[10] and banned media coverage of the arrival of the bodies of military personnel killed in the Iraq War.[11] In addition, the Bush Administration oversaw an amazing increase in the production of classified documents. The U.S. government classified 11.3 million documents in 2002 and 14.2 million the next year.[12] By 2004 the federal government created 15.6 million classified documents, or 81 percent more than in 2000, the year before the terrorist attacks.[13] Whether this increased government secrecy was a sincere effort by well-meaning but overzealous officials to protect the nation or an intentional abuse of power to manipulate public debate, the amount of secrets the U.S. government was keeping should be alarming to anyone concerned with self-government.

Yet, as alarming as this trend might be, government secrecy was not created by the war on terror, nor did it disappear when George W.

---

information. See *United States v. Reynolds* 345 U.S. 1 (1953) for the genesis of the privilege.

[6] Exec. Order No. 13,233 (2001) "Further Implementation of the Presidential Records Act," 66 Fed. Reg. 56025-56029.

[7] *See, e.g., The FBI's Handling of Confidential Informants in Boston: Will the Justice Department Comply with Congressional Subpoenas? Hearing Before the Committee on Oversight and Government Reform,* 107th Cong. (2001) (statement of Rep. Henry Waxmen, Chairman, House Comm. on Oversight and Government Reform).

[8] James Risen & Walter Lichblau, *Bush Lets U.S. Spy on Callers Without Courts,* N. Y. TIMES, Dec. 16, 2005, at A01.

[9] Kirtley, *supra* note 1, at 495. *See also* Scott Shane, *U.S. Reclassifies Many Documents in Secret Review,* N.Y. TIMES, Feb. 21, 2006, at A1.

[10] 6 U.S.C. § 214(a)(1)(A) & (E) (2005).

[11] Dana Milbank, *Curtains Ordered for Media Coverage of Returning Coffins,* WASH. POST, Oct. 21, 2003, at A23.

[12] David Nather, *Classified: A Rise in 'State Secrets,'* 63 CQ WEEKLY 1958, 1960 (2005).

[13] Kenneth Jost, *Government Secrecy,* 15 CQ RESEARCHER 1007, 1008 (2006).

Bush left office.[14] Government secrecy is as old as government itself. The tendency of those in power to suppress information that might be dangerous, damaging, or politically embarrassing is part of our political heritage, long predating the rise of democracy. However, once the relationship between the governed and government began to change— once those in power were viewed as receiving the right to govern through the consent of those they governed rather than by divine right or military power—the conflict between government secrecy and transparency took on new meaning.[15]

Under new ideas proposed by social contract philosophers and liberal democratic theorists, government secrecy was seen as conflicting with self-government because it prevented a fully informed electorate from making fully informed decisions.[16] Focusing on the role a free press plays in a democracy, historian Fredrick S. Siebert wrote, "As democratic forms superseded the ancient relationship between the government and its constituents, the press as a necessary corollary took on an extra-legal function, that of an informant and a watch-dog of public affairs."[17] Thus, while not as old as secrecy, transparency is also part of our political heritage. As one scholar noted, transparency in government was promoted in the classical liberalism of John Locke, John Stuart Mill and Jean-Jacques Rousseu as well as the moral philosophy of Jeremy Bentham and Immanuel Kant, the political and ethical philosophers who had the greatest impact on western democracy.[18]

---

[14] The administration of President Barrack Obama has received mixed reviews for its handling of government secrecy. *See, e.g.*, Amanda Becker, *Obama's Transparency Efforts Achieve Mixed Results*, 34 NEWS MEDIA & THE LAW 12 (2010).

[15] *See generally* LEONARD W. LEVY, EMERGENCE OF A FREE PRESS (1985); FREDRICK SEATON SIEBERT, FREEDOM OF THE PRESS IN ENGLAND 1476-1776 (1965).

[16] *See generally* DAVID HELD, MODELS OF DEMOCRACY (2006). Concerned primarily with the protection of individual rights and the maintenance of a democratic system of government, liberal democratic theory is the dominant philosophical tradition in U.S. political thought.

[17] SIEBERT, *supra* note 15, at 10.

[18] Mark Fenster, *The Opacity of Transparency*, 91 IOWA L. REV. 885, 896 (2007).

Therefore, even in a democratic society, transparency and the benefits it brings must be balanced with an important countervailing interest: the occasional, legitimate need for government secrecy. Even authors who warn that a predilection for secrecy poses a threat to the First Amendment acknowledge that a certain amount of secrecy is necessary in the areas of executive privilege, foreign affairs, and national security.[19] Secrecy in these areas is seen as a necessary tool to advance legitimate functions of government under democratic theory. As one scholar noted, in Lockean philosophy government's central purpose is to protect each individual's rights against invasion *and* to protect "the entire society from having the rights of its members robbed from them by another nation's war-launching invasion."[20] First Amendment theorists also generally agree that two essential ingredients of a healthy democracy are a free press and national security. Thus, under democratic theory, both government secrecy and transparency have their places. However, sometimes it is very difficult—perhaps impossible—to have one without jeopardizing the other.

Conflicts between secrecy based on national security concerns and transparency raise extremely important questions all democratic societies must answer. How should the conflicts be settled? Which branch of government is best suited to address concerns over government secrecy? What rationales should be use to reach—or ex post facto justify—decisions? What is the proper balance between government secrecy and transparency? Does the proper balance change with societal conditions? In America, the federal court system is often called upon to balance these two important interests and decide which interest shall carry the day.[21] This book explores the reasoning and

---

[19] *E.g.*, David H. Topol, Note, United States v. Morison: *A Threat to the First Amendment Right to Publish National Security Information*, 43 S. C. L. REV. 581, 593 (1992).

[20] Thomas B. McAffee, *Restoring the Lost World of Classical Legal Thought: The Presumption in Favor of Liberty Over Law and the Court Over the Constitution*, 75 U. CIN. L. REV. 1499, 1507 (2007).

[21] Even when courts defer to the executive in areas of national security or rule that an issue is a political question rather than one that can be adjudicated, they are answering the question of what branch of government should balance government secrecy and transparency.

justifications used by federal courts to answer questions about transparency and secrecy.

By examining both how federal courts identify the main legal issues present in a case, or "frame" the legal arguments of a case, and the legal factors or modes of legal analysis—such as precedent, framers' intent/originalism, or textualism—they use to reach or justify their conclusions this book explores the legal, theoretical, and public policy arguments used by federal courts when they address the conflict between government secrecy and transparency. In addition, it compares national security/transparency cases to a parallel area in order to offer a "control" set of cases. Because some scholars have argued that national security is, or should be, a unique area of information control or judicial decision making, it is important to compare national security information cases to a similar set of cases in which national security is not an issue. Therefore, each chapter first explores how courts frame the conflict between secrecy and transparency in cases involving national security and identifies the factors used by the courts to reach and justify their decisions. Next, each chapter compares the frameworks and factors used in national security/transparency cases to those in judicial process/transparency cases. Thus, the book describes how courts balance transparency and national security and compares the frameworks and factors used to an area of law that does not involve national security in order to provide a deeper understanding of the courts' decisions and the perhaps unique nature of national security information cases.

Based on these cases, in the final chapter, the book explains how the majority of national security/transparency cases are as much—if not more—about separation of powers issues as they are about balancing transparency with national security. The opinions often discuss the inherent power of the courts vis-à-vis the executive or legislative branch or grapple with how much deference the courts should give to the executive branch when dealing with national security information. In addition, while the research supports previous scholarship that has emphasized the importance of precedent in judicial decision making, the cases also demonstrate that jurists often use First Amendment and democratic theory to support or justify their decisions. Finally, the book concludes that the ability to frame cases and selectively rely on some legal factors or rhetorical devices while ignoring others gives courts a great deal of flexibility to mold law regarding national security information as they see fit. To understand how these findings fit into the larger framework of government transparency, national security and judicial decision making, however, this chapter begins with an examination of the historical and theoretical foundations of these topics that form the basis for the subsequent chapters.

Liberal Democratic Theory and the First Amendment
The term social contract describes a broad class of philosophical theories addressing the implied agreements by which people form nations and maintain a social order.[22] Social contract theory provides the rationale behind the historically important notion that legitimate state authority must be derived from the consent of the governed. According to political scientists David Boucher and Paul Kelly, civil contractarianism is "that form of social compact, whether historical or hypothetical, whose role is either to legitimize coercive political authority, or to evaluate coercive constraint."[23] The "first and most obvious element" of social contract theory is that the foundation of any authentic body politic is a pact or agreement made by and between all individuals who are to compose it.[24]

Social contract theory forms the foundation of modern liberal democratic theory. Concerned primarily with the protection of individual rights and the maintenance of a democratic system of government, liberal democratic theory is the dominant philosophical tradition in U.S. political thought.[25] Social contract and classic liberal democratic theory can both be traced, at least partially, to the works of

---

[22] *See generally* THE SOCIAL CONTRACT FROM HOBBES TO RAWLS (David Boucher & Paul Kelly eds., 1994); JULES STEINBERG, LOCKE, ROUSSEAU, AND THE IDEA OF CONSENT (1978). Social contract theories fall into three broad categories: moral theories, civil theories, and constitutional theories. David Boucher & Paul Kelly, *The Social Contract and Its Critics: An Overview* in THE SOCIAL CONTRACT FROM HOBBES TO RAWLS 1, 1 (David Boucher & Paul Kelly eds., 1994).
[23] Boucher & Kelly, *supra* note 22, at 4.
[24] Murray Forsyth, *Hobbes's Contractarianism*, in THE SOCIAL CONTRACT FROM HOBBES TO RAWLS 35, 37 (David Boucher & Paul Kelly eds., 1994).
[25] *See generally* HELD, *supra* note 16.

John Locke,[26] who had perhaps more influence on the formation of America's government and its protection of free expression than any other political philosopher.[27] Liberal democratic theory, in particular, provided the "philosophical foundation" for our society's comprehensive understanding of speech rights.[28] Thus, social contract and democratic theories are important when considering transparency and government secrecy in the United States because together they serve as the foundation for the American concepts of free speech and free press.

The development of the social contract—a concept first proposed by religious groups such as the Levellers—was intrinsically linked to the emergence of the twin ideas of man's ability to reason and the equality of human beings first proposed during the Protestant Reformation.[29] The Levellers, members of a political movement in Seventeenth Century England named for the belief in society everyone should be equal or "level," were particularly important to the development of the social contract as it pertains to this book because of their early and enthusiastic support for press freedom.

Historian Leonard W. Levy credited Leveller leaders, such as John Lilburne, William Walwyn and Richard Overton, as being the facilitators of the first great outburst of democratic thought in history.[30] Levy wrote that almost all Leveller tracts of the 1640s contained passages condemning censorship and arguing that freedom of speech and the press were essential elements of both a free government and individual liberty.[31] Siebert credited Lilburne, Walwyn and Overton with a number of original contributions to political theory in England, including the need for a written constitution, the importance of limited governmental powers, the benefits of separation of political powers

---

[26] *See generally* JOHN LOCKE, SECOND TREATIES OF GOVERNMENT (Hackett Publishing Company, Inc. 1980) (1690).

[27] DAVID A. COPELAND, THE IDEA OF A FREE PRESS 91 (2006).

[28] Laura Stein, *Understanding Speech Rights: Defensive and Empowering Approaches to the First Amendment*, 26 MEDIA, CULTURE & SOC'Y 102, 104 (2004).

[29] COPELAND, *supra* note 27, at 79.

[30] LEVY, *supra* note 15, at 91.

[31] *Id.*

and, finally, freedom of the press.[32] Siebert concluded that the Levellers were significant not only for being one of the first groups to argue for press freedom but also one of the most eloquent and powerful. He wrote, "Nowhere in the literature of liberty can be found a more comprehensive or more logical statement of the argument for liberty of the press" than the Levellers' petitions to Parliament.[33]

Unfortunately for the Levellers, England was not ready to embrace their radical ideas. Historians David Copeland, Levy and Siebert all concluded that the ideas proposed by Lilburne, Walwyn and Overton did not catch on with Parliament or the common man. As Siebert noted, Parliament's response to Lilburne's argument for liberty of the press was to charge him with treason in 1645, although he was eventually released because a jury refused to convict him.[34] Copeland noted that even though the Levellers continued to write, their work "could not convince most Britons, upper, middle or lower class, that a level society was in the country's best interests."[35] Ultimately, by 1649 the English Civil War and the establishment of Cromwell as the military dictator of the country had drowned out the Levellers' calls for a free press. However, the radical ideas of the group would influence a different group of writers, political philosophers who eventually had a profound impact on the foundation of American government.

Thomas Hobbes, the great English political philosopher, defined his concept of the social contract in *Leviathan*, his treatise on government.[36] Written in 1651, eleven years after he fled England for France because of his support for the monarchy prior to the English Civil War, *Leviathan* established Hobbes as "the first great theorist of the social contract."[37] His conceptualization of the social contract was "the dramatic culmination of a step-by-step process of developing human rationality."[38] Like most political theorists of the seventeenth

---

[32] SIEBERT, *supra* note 15, at 200.
[33] *Id.* at 201.
[34] *Id.* at 87.
[35] COPELAND, *supra* note 27, at 89.
[36] THOMAS HOBBES, LEVIATHAN (Edwin Curley ed., 1994) (1651). The title refers to Job 41 in which Leviathan is a sea monster. *See id.* at 27.
[37] Forsyth, *supra* note 24, at 35.
[38] *Id.* at 43.

and eighteenth centuries,[39] Hobbes began his arguments by hypothesizing about the state of nature, writing that prior to the establishment of governments, man existed in a state of nature that was "solitary, poor, nasty, brutish and short."[40] To avoid harm and the risk of death, man willingly entered into the social contract and formed government.[41] At the heart of Hobbes's notion of the social contact was an act by which a multitude united for safety and protection.[42] Hobbes wrote that a commonwealth, or government, is formed "when men, coming together voluntarily, agree, every one with every one, that they will obey whatever man or assembly the greater part, by their votes, shall give the right of bearing the person of them all."[43]

Like Hobbes, John Locke wrote that the establishment of political institutions followed a state of nature[44] in which man had natural rights. Locke was also concerned with what form a legitimate government should take and how to establish the conditions necessary for peace and security. However, unlike Hobbes, Locke was also greatly concerned with individual liberty, and the social contract he argued for in *Second Treatise of Government*, first published in 1690,[45] was vastly different than the one proposed by Hobbes. Although Locke never mentioned Hobbes or *Leviathan* by name, the *Second Treatise* explicitly rejected the idea that people could only find peace and tranquility by subjecting themselves to the dictates of a single indivisible authority.[46] Copeland

---

[39] *See* C.B. Macpherson, *Introduction* to JOHN LOCKE, SECOND TREATISE OF GOVERNMENT vii, viii (C.B. Macpherson, ed., 1980) 1690.

[40] HOBBES, *supra* note 36, at 76.

[41] The Hobbesian state of nature is not the description of a particular historical period or a generalization of historical tendencies that attempts to describe how most states materialize. It is a hypothetical "thought experiment." *See* HELD, *supra* note 16, at 60; Forsyth, *supra* note 24, at 44.

[42] HOBBES, *supra* note 36, at 106-26.

[43] *Id.* at 110.

[44] Locke, like Hobbes, introduced the state of nature not as a historical condition, but as a logical abstraction given the nature of man.

[45] LOCKE, *supra* note 26. Locke's work was originally published as one volume, *Two Treatise on Government*, but the *Second Treatise* was meant to be a self-contained work. The *First Treatise* was directed against the divine right of kings as argued by Sir Robert Filmer. *See* Macpherson, *supra* note 39, at viii.

[46] LOCKE, *supra* note 26, at 8.

noted that while Locke and Hobbes agreed that people needed to form a social contract, Locke emphasized the rights of individuals within the collective and proposed a society based on the consent of the governed.[47]

Locke focused on the restriction of state power to create private spheres of civil liberty. Locke based his understanding of the social contract on the pre-existing rights of the individual, which were retained even when the individual entered into the collective. Hobbes, the first modern philosopher to articulate a detailed contract theory, gave the right to censor subversive writings to the government, whereas Locke did not. Although Hobbes wrote of the natural rights of man, he was clear that anything that might usurp the commonwealth or cause it to be disbanded was morally wrong. To Locke, because government existed solely based on the consent of the governed, the government could not take away pre-existing rights, such as the right to free expression. Siebert argued that to Locke a free and open press was the best way to guarantee citizens protection from government tyranny that may impinge on these natural rights.[48] According to Copeland, it was on this point that revolutionary America rejected Hobbes and looked instead to Locke for his blend of individualism and common concern.[49]

According to Copeland, by 1730 Americans had adopted the idea of the social contract.[50] Copeland based his argument on the work of a group of writers he referred to as the "newspaper polemicists,"[51] who "took the concepts of (John) Milton, Locke and others and synthesized their thinking for all levels of society that had access to what they wrote."[52] Chief among these was "Cato," the pseudonym of two English writers, John Trenchard and Thomas Gordon. While most Americans in the middle of the eighteenth century would not have heard of John Locke, they would have known of Cato.[53] Beginning in 1720, Trenchard and Gordon published a series of essays focusing on

---

[47] COPELAND, *supra* note 27, at 91.
[48] SIEBERT, *supra* note 15, at 261.
[49] COPELAND, *supra* note 27, at 90. *See also* HELD, *supra* note 16, at 59.
[50] *Id.* at 88.
[51] *See id.* at 95-102.
[52] *Id.* at 94.
[53] *Id.* at 95.

Locke's idea of government being founded on the consent of the governed and John Milton's marketplace of ideas concept. The essays first appeared in the *London Journal*, and by 1723 the two had written 138 essays supporting free speech and advancing Locke's ideas.[54]

University of Texas law professor David A. Anderson has credited Cato with helping to develop the idea that the press played a structural role in a democracy by introducing the phrase "bulwark of liberty" to the framers of the Constitution.[55] According to Anderson, the phrase— a metaphor for the ability of the press to provide a check on government—was first used in one of Cato's essays and became widely popular and quoted.[56]

> Cato touted freedom of speech, not for its own sake, but for its value in combating governmental oppression and tyranny. . . .
> That Cato described speech, not press, as the bulwark of liberty apparently was not important to those who borrowed the metaphor. The early press clauses drew heavily on both the phrase and the idea.[57]

Anderson concluded, "[A] press clause was necessary, not to induce the press to provide a check on government power, but because it was universally assumed that the press would indeed provide such a check and that government therefore would seek to suppress it."[58]

This interpretation of the function of the press depicts a government system in which the people must have information in order to both effectively govern themselves and keep their government accountable. Based on the work of Locke and subsequent political theorists, liberal democratic theory encompasses two fundamental concerns: first, the protection of individual autonomy and, second, the maintenance of political systems that allow citizens to engage in democratic self-

---

[54] *Id.* at 97.
[55] David A. Anderson, *The Origins of the Press Clause*, 30 UCLA L. REV 455, 491 (1983).
[56] *Id.*
[57] *Id.* at 491-92.
[58] *Id.* at 491.

government.[59] Thus, to democratic theorists, speech rights are both an important individual liberty and a way to promote self-governance.[60] Perhaps the most famous modern First Amendment theorist to argue that freedom of expression was essential to self-governance was Professor Alexander Meiklejohn, who published several seminal works on freedom of expression in the 1940s. To Meiklejohn the primary purpose of the First Amendment was to ensure that all political speech relevant to democratic debate be heard.[61] Meiklejohn addressed the question of whether the clear and present danger doctrine, or any other test, could constitutionally sustain legislation punishing political speech on the grounds of national security concerns.[62] He concluded that the First Amendment "established an absolute, unqualified prohibition of the abridgement of the freedom of speech."[63] However, Meiklejohn extended this absolute protection only to speech related to self-government. Meiklejohn wrote that the purpose of protecting political speech was to "give to every voting member of the body politic the fullest possible participation in the understanding of those problems with which the citizens of a self-governing society must deal."[64] Meiklejohn relied heavily on the concept of the social contract to develop his ideas of free speech protected by the U.S. Constitution.[65] He argued the First Amendment was best understood in relation to the overall function of the Constitution as a means to establish self-government.[66] Because the overall purpose of the Constitution was to establish a democratic form of government, the purpose of the First

---

[59] *See* HELD, *supra* note 16, at 77-79.

[60] Stein, *supra* note 28, at 105.

[61] ALEXANDER MEIKLEJOHN, FREE SPEECH AND ITS RELATION TO SELF-GOVERNMENT 21-27 (1948).

[62] ALEXANDER MEIKLEJOHN, POLITICAL FREEDOM 20 (1948). See also MEIKLEJOHN, *supra* note 61, at 28-56 for further discussion of the clear and present danger test.

[63] MEIKLEJOHN, *supra* note 61, at 20.

[64] *Id.* at 88-89. For development of the argument that this limitation is appropriate, see Lillian R. BeVier, *The First Amendment and Political Speech: An Inquiry Into the Substance and Limits of the Principle*, 30 STAN. L. REV. 299 (1978); Robert Bork, *Neutral Principles and Some First Amendment Problems*, 47 IND. L.J. 1 (1971).

[65] *E.g.*, MEIKLEJOHN, *supra* note 61, at 14.

[66] *Id.* at 15.

Amendment was to facilitate public participation in government. Meiklejohn's focus on self-government is echoed in the works of other scholars and in Supreme Court decisions. As law professor Lillian BeVier wrote, in First Amendment theory, there is "one area which both commands widespread agreement and is derived from constitutional structure: the core first amendment value is that of the democracy embodied in our constitutionally established processes of representative self-government."[67]

Meiklejohn also emphasized the role of the listener, or the person who was to receive the information. What was important to him was not that everyone had a right to speak or to be heard, but that all ideas worth hearing were heard. The meaning of the First Amendment, he contended, was derived from the necessity of citizens to have access to all relevant ideas so that they could engage in effective self-government. This required that all political speech relevant to democratic debate be heard, even if that information was deemed to be dangerous to national security.[68]

Unlike Meiklejohn, most other First Amendment theorists have taken more nuanced approaches to national security and transparency and have called for a balance between the two. Law professor and First Amendment scholar Vincent Blasi, for example, advocated for a great deal of protection for the press, but limited this protection when national security was involved. [69] In 1977, Blasi, who primarily advocated a free press as a check on the government, wrote that the First Amendment should be given "preferential" treatment when evidence of government misconduct was presented by the press, but it was also important to balance government secrecy with a free press. [70]

According to Blasi, by providing information to the public— especially information the government does not want revealed—the press plays an important role in revealing governmental abuses, incompetence, and malfeasance.

---

[67] Lillian R. BeVier, *An Informed Public, an Informing Press: The Search for a Constitutional Principle*, 68 CAL. L. REV 482, 502 (1980).

[68] MEIKLEJOHN, *supra* note 61, at 25.

[69] Vincent Blasi, *The Checking Value in First Amendment Theory*, 1977 AM. B. FOUND. RES. J. 521 (1977).

[70] *Id.* at 609-11.

But for the tradition of a free press, the crimes and abuses of
Watergate might never have been uncovered. . . . In the last
decade, the First Amendment has had at least as much impact
on American life by facilitating a process by which
countervailing forces check the misuse of official power as by
protecting the dignity of the individual, maintaining a diverse
society in the face of conformist pressures, promoting the
quest for scientific and philosophic truth, or fostering a regime
of "self-government" in which large numbers of ordinary
citizens take an active part in political affairs.[71]

Blasi traced the source of his powerful new First Amendment value—
the checking function—to the long history of public officials abusing
their political trust[72] and noted that the writings and speeches of both
James Madison and Thomas Jefferson viewed the liberty of the press in
terms of its checking value.[73]

Blasi was clear that the checking function was directly tied to the
press's role as an institution. Blasi argued that the "inevitable size and
complexity" of modern government called for "well-organized, well-
financed, professional critics to serve as a counterforce to
government."[74] To Blasi, the press was important in a democracy for
its ability to serve as a professional critic and its capacity to
disseminate information to the public.[75] Thus, Blasi argued the
checking function of the press as an institution would support claims
against government control of information.[76]

However, Blasi also wrote that there were situations in which the
checking function must give way to government secrecy. Blasi said
that although classification systems can have the effect of covering up
government wrongdoing, they also can serve legitimate government
interests.[77] While Blasi wrote that it was difficult to imagine sufficient

---

[71] *Id.* at 527.
[72] *Id.* at 529-32.
[73] *Id.* at 535-38.
[74] *Id.* at 541.
[75] *Id.*
[76] *Id.* at 566.
[77] *Id.* at 608.

justification for any order that would prohibit a source under government control from having contact with the press, he also noted that not all restrictions on communication between sources under government control and reporters were inconsistent with the First Amendment.[78] However, Blasi reasoned that because punishment of "leakers" should be thought to raise serious First Amendment concerns under the checking value, punishment would be consistent with the checking value only if the disclosure of information could "be shown to create a serious risk of harm to the implementation of government policy."[79]

Like Meiklejohn, famed First Amendment scholar and Yale law professor Thomas Emerson also wrote that a system of free expression is necessary as a method of securing participation by the members of a democratic society in political decision making.[80] Freedom of expression "in the political realm is usually a necessary condition for securing freedom elsewhere," Emerson wrote in 1963.[81] To meet the core objective of democratic government, individuals—or their representatives in the press—need access to information. This would suggest that any system of free expression designed to advance political communication would necessarily have to protect the gathering of information. As BeVier noted, "It is a truism that we cannot responsibly exercise our franchise unless we have sufficient knowledge about governmental affairs, operations, and polices to make informed choices."[82] Therefore, in addition to advocating a broad First Amendment theory, in 1976, Emerson wrote specifically about the relationship between democracy, government secrecy and access to information in his work on the public's "right to know."[83]

---

[78] *Id.*

[79] *Id.* at 609.

[80] Thomas I. Emerson, *Toward a General Theory of the First Amendment*, 72 YALE L.J. 877, 878 (1963).

[81] *Id.*

[82] BeVier, *supra* note 67, at 483. BeVier noted that while a right to know does encompass many of the same principles as the right to publish, it is in principle a different type of right. *See id.* at 498.

[83] Thomas I. Emerson, *Legal Foundations of the Right to Know*, 1976 WASH. U.L.Q. 1, 3 (1976).

The general term "right to know" or "right to receive information" can refer to numerous concepts, including both the audience's right to receive expression and the right to gather information for dissemination to the public.[84] The public's general right to be informed about the operations of the government, the right to compel the government to produce records and documents, and the right to access government meetings and judicial proceedings can all be considered different aspects of a general "right to know." As it relates to this book, the right to know is the right of the people "to have access to information controlled by the government"[85] so that they might be better informed in order to better participate in self-government.[86] In this sense, the term "right to know" has been a traditional rallying cry for scholars, journalists and public interest groups arguing for a right of access to government information.[87]

Emerson defined the right to know as "the right to read, to listen, to see, and to otherwise receive communications . . . and the right to obtain information as a basis for transmitting ideas or facts to others."[88] He described the right as "obscure" and noted that although the Supreme Court had, on a number of occasions, recognized the right to know, it had also failed to "give weight" to the right on occasion.[89] Although Emerson appeared to be a vocal advocate of the right to know, it is important to note that there are a number of contradictions in his writings, and he greatly limited the amount of information that should be available to the public.

---

[84] *See* William E. Lee, *The Supreme Court and the Right to Receive Expression*, SUP. CT. REV. 303, 307 n. 14 (1988).

[85] BeVier, *supra* note 67, at 484 n. 10. *See also*, Saxbe v. Washington Post Co., 417 U.S. 843, 860 (1974) (Powell, J., dissenting).

[86] The right to compel the government to produce records is embodied in the federal Freedom of Information Act (FOIA). The statute allows individuals to obtain federal agency records. 5 U.S.C. § 552 (2005).

[87] *See generally* HERBERT M. FOERSTEL, FREEDOM OF INFORMATION AND THE RIGHT TO KNOW (1999).

[88] Emerson, *supra* note 83, at 2.

[89] *See id.* at 3 (contrasting the Supreme Court's holdings in Lamont v. Postmaster General, 381 U.S. 301 (1965), Stanley v. Georgia, 394 U.S. 557 (1969), and Red Lion Co. v. FCC, 395 U.S. 367, 390 (1969) with Zemel v. Rusk, 381 U.S. 1 (1965) and Kleindienst v. Mandel, 408 U.S. 753 (1972)).

Early in his article on the right to know, Emerson stated the right should be given near absolute protection. Emerson's reason for adopting this strict standard—when other First Amendment doctrines called for balancing tests—was "the right to read, listen, or see is so elemental, so close to the source of all freedom, that one can hardly conceive of a system of free expression that does not extend it full protection."[90] Emerson appeared to advocate that a great deal of information should be available to citizens.

One would seem to be on solid ground, therefore, in asserting a constitutional right in the public to obtain information from government sources necessary or proper for the citizen to perform his function as ultimate sovereign. Furthermore, this right would extend, as a starting point, to all information in the possession of the government. It is hard to conceive of any government information that would not be relevant to the concerns of the citizens and taxpayers.[91]

In addition, Emerson also wrote that in a democracy the government should have no power to control the dissemination of information by its employees and former employees through leaks, books, speeches and articles except in the "narrow sense of conveying sensitive national defense information to a foreign country with intent to injure the United States."[92] Again, Emerson cited the concept of self-government to justify his argument. He was concerned that granting the government the ability to control leaks allowed it to control information, which in turn would allow it to control public debate and cover up questionable government practices.[93] Finally, Emerson also argued that one branch of government should not, as a general principle, be able to keep information from another branch. He argued that "the power of Congress to force the executive to produce materials necessary to the congressional function cannot be doubted."[94]

---

[90] *Id.* at 7.
[91] *Id.* at 16.
[92] *Id.* at 18.
[93] *Id.*
[94] *Id.* at 15.

However, as noted above, despite this strong rhetoric in favor of access to government sources and information, Emerson wrote that "some exceptions would have to formulated" to any theory of the right to know.[95] Although he contended that "[i]n theory these exceptions should be scrupulously limited to those that are absolutely essential to the effective operation of government institutions," he listed an extremely wide range of information that could be kept secret by government, including "sensitive national security data" and information that would protect "the right of executive officials to receive full and frank advice from subordinates and colleagues—that is, executive privilege."[96] Emerson was willing to grant exemptions to information related to tactical military movements, design of weapons, operation of espionage or counterespionage, diplomatic and collective bargaining negotiations, criminal investigations, uncompleted litigation, trade secrets, executive privilege, and individual privacy.[97] Emerson made no attempt to reconcile the contradictions in his arguments, nor did he provide a framework for balancing competing interests.

In sum, for hundreds of years philosophers and scholars have recognized the relationship between self-government and transparency. Social contract theory and liberal democratic theory exerted a strong influence on both the framers of the U.S. Constitution and later First Amendment philosophers. In addition, modern scholars almost always tie justifications for government transparency to notions of democracy. They advocate transparency as means to advance self-government as well as a tool for checking abuses of power by those selected to govern. However, the literature also reflects a countervailing emphasis on the occasional need for government secrecy, and even the most ardent supporters of a right to know recognize limitations and exceptions.

---

[95] *Id.* at 16.
[96] *Id.* at 16-17.
[97] *Id.*

Government Secrecy and National Security

Although there were some objections by various framers, the Constitution itself was drafted in secret.[98] However, the Constitution has only one textual reference to secrecy. Article I, section 5, states:

> Each House shall keep a Journal of its Proceedings, and from time to time publish the same, excepting such Parts as may in their Judgment require Secrecy; and the Yeas and Nays of the Members of either House on any question shall, at the Desire of one fifth those Present, be entered on the Journal.[99]

Furthermore, there is no evidence the founding fathers discussed whether the First Amendment imposed any limitations on the power of the government to keep information secret.[100] Indeed, according to Benjamin S. DuVal Jr., a project director at the American Bar Association, there was little discussion of the First Amendment aspects of government secrecy until late in the twentieth century.[101]

DuVal noted that although the Supreme Court said relatively early in the century that the government could prevent publication of "the sailing dates of transports or the number and location of troops,"[102] it was not until 1971 that the High Court ruled on the press's ability to publish classified government documents in the famous *Pentagon Papers Case, New York Times v. United States*.[103] In that case, the Supreme Court, on a 6-3 vote, set a very high standard for preventing the press from publishing government information. In a per curiam opinion accompanied by nine concurring and dissenting opinions, the

---

[98] For a further discussion of the decision to draft the Constitution in secret, see Vasan Kesavan & Michael Stokes Paulsen, *The Interpretive Force of the Constitution's Secret Drafting History*, 91 GEO. L.J. 1113 (2003); Heidi Kitrosser, *Secrecy and Separated Powers: Executive Privilege Revisited*, 92 IOWA L. REV. 489, 522 (2007).

[99] U.S. CONST. art. I, § 5, cl. 3.

[100] *See generally* DANIEL HOFFMAN, GOVERNMENTAL SECRECY AND THE FOUNDING FATHERS (1981).

[101] Benjamin S. DuVal, Jr., *The Occasions of Secrecy*, 47 U. PITT. L. REV. 579, 581-82 (1986).

[102] Near v. Minnesota, 283 U.S. 697, 716 (1931).

[103] 403 U.S. 713 (1971).

Court refused to grant the government's request for an injunction to prevent the *New York Times* and the *Washington Post* from printing a classified study of U.S. involvement in Vietnam. The Court held that any government attempt to prevent publication carried a heavy presumption of unconstitutionality.[104] However, in dicta, some of the justices indicated that the newspapers could be prosecuted under the Espionage Act even if the government could not prevent them from publishing the documents.[105] Today, more than thirty-five years after the *Pentagon Papers Case*, how the judiciary should deal with attempts to punish the publication of national secrets is still debated. DuVal wrote: "Despite a rapidly growing body of case law, . . . the Court's decisions fail to deal in any comprehensive fashion with the issue. More seriously, the Court has failed to come to grips with the distinctive character of the secrecy issue."[106]

Scholarship has noted that notwithstanding the Court's strong language condemning prior restraints in the *Pentagon Papers Case* national security concerns often outweigh any arguments in favor of transparency or free expression. Constitutional scholar and prolific author Frederick Schauer wrote: "The interest in the security of the nation is often thought to be a trump card in free speech disputes. Whatever the strength of the Free Speech Principle, a threat to national security is commonly held to be a danger of sufficient magnitude that the interest in freedom of speech must be subordinated."[107] Professor of public policy Alasdair Roberts stated, "Arguments for more open government that are powerful in other circumstances seem

---

[104] *Id.* at 713 (per curiam) "'Any system of prior restraints of expression comes to this Court bearing a heavy presumption against its constitutional validity.' The Government 'thus carries a heavy burden of showing justification for the imposition of such a restraint.' The District Court for the Southern District of New York in the *New York Times* case and the District Court for the District of Columbia and the Court of Appeals for the District of Columbia Circuit in the *Washington Post* case held that the Government had not met that burden. We agree." *Id.* (citations omitted).

[105] *Id.* at 735 (White, J., concurring); *id.* at 743 (Marshall, J., concurring); *id.* at 752 (Burger, J., dissenting); *id.* at 754 (Harlan, J., dissenting); *id.* at 759 (Blackmun, J., dissenting).

[106] DuVal, *supra* note 101, at 582.

[107] FREDERICK SCHAUER, FREE SPEECH: A PHILOSOPHICAL ENQUIRY 197 (1982).

insubstantial, or even reckless in matters of national security."[108]   Eric
E. Ballou and Kyle E. McSlarrow argued that while government
secrecy might clash with the important American values of open
government, an educated and enlightened people, and an unfettered
press, it was a necessary evil.[109]   Roberts warned that the tendency to
defer to secrecy was especially strong in times of fear and uncertainty:

> Many well-established democratic states, facing uncertain but
> potentially fundamental threats to their security, resort to the
> use of extraordinary police powers and an assertion of
> executive authority. . . .   In moments of crisis, when the
> severity of the threat remains uncertain, it is difficult for
> citizens to resist these calls for stronger state powers.[110]

Polling research supports these points, suggesting that when access
issues are framed as matters of national security, public support for
openness drops.[111]

Cass Sunstein, a law professor at Harvard University who is
currently working for the Obama Administration, argued in 2002 that in
America this tendency is more pronounced now than before the
terrorist attacks of September 11, 2001, when Americans entered "a
new and frightening geography where the continents of safety and
danger were forever shifted."[112]   Sunstein posited that the intense
emotions of September 11 caused people to focus on adverse outcomes
rather than on their likelihood.[113]   This focus, which Sunstein called
"probability neglect," allows political actors to promote attention to

---

[108] Alasdair Roberts, *National Security and Open Government*, 9 GEO. PUB.
POL'Y REV. 69, 70 (2004).

[109] Eric E. Ballou & Kyle E. McSlarrow, Note, *Plugging the Leak: The Case
For A Legislative Resolution of the Conflict Between the Demands of Secrecy
and the Need for an Open Government*, 71 VA. L. REV. 801, 823-34 (1985).

[110] Roberts, *supra* note 108, at 80.

[111] *See* The Bush Administration's Secrecy Policy: A Call to Action to Protect
Democratic Values, Oct. 25, 2002, available at
http://www.ombwatch.org/article/articleview/1145/1/253.

[112] Cass R. Sunstein, *Probability Neglect: Emotions, Worst Cases, and Law*,
112 YALE L. J. 61, 61 (2002).

[113] *Id.*

problems that may not deserve public concern and to enact laws and promote policies that may not be in the best interests of the public.[114]

Currently, according to law professor Heidi Kitrosser, the ability of the executive to keep information secret manifests itself in both "a staggeringly large (and growing) system of information classification and in case-by-case refusals to disclose information" sought by Congress, the courts, or persons or agencies empowered by Congress to seek information.[115]   In 1997, the Commission on Protecting and Reducing Government Secrecy reported that there were five categories of information that the president could keep secret: (1) national defense information; (2) information concerning foreign affairs and diplomatic service; (3) information developed by law enforcement agencies; (4) proprietary information related to commercial advantage; (5) personally private information.[116]   Only the first two categories are relevant to national security information.

Military information, including contingency plans, the nature, location and characteristics of weapons, and the strength and deployment of forces in peace and war, is often listed as information our society needs to protect. At the core of this type of information lie military plans that have not yet been fully executed.[117] Another secrecy concern related to national security is the protection of intelligence information, including raw data, information-gathering methods, sources and covert operations.[118] Disclosure of the identities of agents and sources impairs the ability of the government to gather information[119] and endangers lives.[120]

Scientific and technological information related to national security may be information with exclusively military applications, information with both military and civilian applications, or information

---

[114] *Id.*

[115] Kitrosser, *supra* note 98, at 491. *See also*, Christina E. Wells, *"National Security" Information and the Freedom of Information Act*, 56 ADMIN. L. REV. 1195, 1201-02 (2004).

[116] U.S. Senate, Report of the Commission on Protecting and Reducing Government Secrecy, 105th Congress, 2nd session, Senate Doc. 105-2, 1997, 5.

[117] DuVal, *supra* note 101, at 591.

[118] *Id.* at 598; Ballou & McSlarrow, *supra* note 109, at 805.

[119] *E.g.,* Ballou & McSlarrow, *supra* note 109, at 801.

[120] *Id.* at 825; DuVal, *supra* note 101, at 598.

with no known military application.[121] One of the principal justifications for restricting information regarding military technology is to prevent other governments from using that technology against the United States.[122] For example, there has always been a great deal of concern over the publication of information related to atomic and nuclear weapons, even when the information did not come from the government.[123] Commentators have also argued that secrecy is important in conducting international affairs and diplomacy. In the *Pentagon Papers* case, Justice Potter Stewart asserted: "[I]t is elementary that the successful conduct of international diplomacy . . . require[s] both confidentiality and secrecy. Other nations can hardly deal with this Nation in an atmosphere of mutual trust unless they can be assured that their confidences will be kept."[124]

Scholarship supporting the executive branch's power to keep information secret focuses on the president's need for candid advice and for great, almost unconditional, deference to the executive in matters of national security and foreign policy.[125] According to Adam Samaha, a professor at the University of Chicago Law School, "Effective executive power and the president's commander-in-chief status sometimes depend on discretion to withhold information from general circulation. Deliberation, diplomacy, and military victory can be jeopardized when the executive cannot control information."[126] Mark J. Rozell, a professor of public policy who has written extensively about executive privilege, has argued that the ability of the executive to keep information secret is supported by history, emphasizing the writings and behavior of the framers of the

---

[121] For a discussion of academic research on biosecurity in the context of federal secrecy policy, see Brian J. Gorman, *Biosecurity and Secrecy Policy: Problems, Theory, and a Call for Executive Action*, 2 ISJLP 53 (2006).

[122] DuVal, *supra* note 101, at 606.

[123] *See, e.g., United States v. Progressive*, Inc., 467 F.Supp. 990 (W.D. Wis. 1970).

[124] New York Times Co. v. United States, 403 U.S. 713, 728 (1971) (Stewart, J., concurring).

[125] *See generally* MARK J. ROZELL, EXECUTIVE PRIVILEGE: PRESIDENTIAL POWER, SECRECY, AND ACCOUNTABILITY (2002).

[126] Adam M. Samaha, *Government Secrets, Constitutional Law, and Platforms for Judicial Intervention*, 53 UCLA L. REV 909, 933 (2006).

Constitution, who envisioned a strong executive with the capacity to keep secrets.[127]

There are currently a number of statutes designed to protect information related to national security information and a large body of scholarship has addressed the nature of these statutes and their relationship to government transparency. For example, Federal Judge Richard A. Posner of the Court of Appeals for the Seventh Circuit has been highly critical of current U.S. law in his academic writings, arguing that no federal statutes constituted an effective prohibition of dissemination of properly classified material.[128] Posner concluded that because the Espionage Act of 1917[129] requires that the individual has reason to believe information he passes on could be used to injure the United States or advantage a foreign nation, it could not be used to punish the press.[130] In addition, Posner concluded that no other statutes explicitly authorize punishing journalists for the publication of illegally leaked classified information.[131] Unlike Posner, DuVal found that the Espionage Act, "while arguably not so intended, can be read to cover a reporter who knowingly publishes a classified document."[132] However, in the end, DuVal concluded the Espionage Act "is of uncertain applicability against disclosures made for the purpose of public debate."[133]

Ballou and McSlarrow analyzed the case for creating a new, comprehensive statutory solution that would allow criminal punishment of the press for the possession and publication of classified information.[134] While the authors concluded that Congress may proscribe the disclosure of national security information without

---

[127] ROZELL, *supra* note 125, at 19-28. *But see* RAOUL BERGER, EXECUTIVE PRIVILEGE: A CONSTITUTIONAL MYTH, 49-59 (1974) (arguing that the founders feared a too-powerful executive and therefore would not have empowered the position to keep information secret).

[128] RICHARD A. POSNER, NOT A SUICIDE PACT: THE CONSTITUTION IN A TIME OF NATIONAL EMERGENCY 108 (2006).

[129] 18 U.S.C. § 793-798 (2005).

[130] POSNER, *supra* note 128, at 108.

[131] *Id.*

[132] DuVal, *supra* note 101, at 671.

[133] *Id.* at 673.

[134] Ballou & McSlarrow, *supra* note 109.

infringing on First Amendment rights,[135] current laws are too narrow in their definitions and do not provide adequate means to stop the leaking of national security information.[136] "Under current United States law, the federal government is largely unable to prevent or to punish leaking and publishing of classified government information," they wrote.[137] Although Ballou and McSlarrow focused much of their attention on expression by government employees, they also addressed cases involving the press. Regarding post-publication punishments, the authors concluded that while the Supreme Court has never decided such a case, *Haig v. Agee*[138] suggested that with the proper statutory tools the government could impose post-publication sanctions on the press without offending the First Amendment.[139] William E. Lee, a First Amendment scholar and journalism professor at the University of Georgia, explored the link between the manner in which journalists obtain information and the First Amendment's protection of the information's publication.[140] Lee concluded that courts usually regard information-gathering techniques as irrelevant when analyzing the constitutionality of prior restraints, but they do consider how information was obtained when considering post-publication punishments.[141]

A large body of scholarship has also examined the complex relationships between government secrecy, political theory and democratic processes and institutions. For example, recent scholarship by political scientists Robert M. Pallitto and William G. Weaver has examined presidential secrecy and its effect on democracy.[142] They concluded that changes to the institution of the presidency were resulting in vast changes in American democracy. "Increasingly, our governmental institutions are unable to hold the president accountable

---

[135] *Id.* at 829-49.
[136] *Id.* at 804.
[137] *Id.*
[138] 453 U.S. 280 (1981).
[139] Ballou & McSlarrow, *supra* note 109, at 845-47.
[140] William E. Lee, *The Unusual Suspects: Journalists as Thieves*, 8 WM. & MARY BILL RTS. J. 53 (2000).
[141] *Id.* at 58.
[142] ROBERT M. PALLITTO & WILLIAM G. WEAVER, PRESIDENTIAL SECRECY AND THE LAW (2007).

for actions undertaken in secret in the name of national security. In a subtle but sweeping way, this failure is working detrimental changes in our federal governmental institutions."[143] Their research focused on three issues: first, the increasing institutionalization of executive secrecy—"how massive presidential power accrued to permit a wide range of questionable activity without fear of congressional oversight or judicial interference"; second, the abdication of judicial responsibility for oversight of the executive branch and the failure of the judiciary to maintain the separation of powers called for in the Constitution in the area of national security; and finally, the inability of Congress as an institution to maintain oversight and control of executive national security activity. The two argued, "[A]ggressive action to control executive branch abuse of secrecy should not come from Congress but from the courts, which are in a position to provide the scrutiny necessary to discourage presidential abuse of secrecy powers."[144]

Political science literature has also developed the concepts of shallow and deep secrecy to help explore issues of political accountability and secrecy in a democracy. A "shallow secret" is a secret whose existence is known although the secret itself remains unknown. A deep secret is a secret whose very existence is a secret.[145] Kitrosser argued that the notions of shallow and deep secrecy are useful because of the importance of maintaining political accountability when secrecy is necessary. Kitrosser used the concepts of deep and shallow secrecy to examine executive privilege and the role of the judiciary in settling disputes between the other two branches of government. She concluded, "Secrecy in government sometimes is a necessary evil, but secrecy within the political branches must, to be legitimate, remain a politically controllable tool of the people."[146] Based on the Constitution's special treatment of information and historical examples of abuses of executive secrecy, Kitrosser was highly critical of judicial

---

[143] *Id.* at 16.
[144] *Id.* at 223.
[145] *E.g.*, AMY GUTMANN & DENIS THOMPSON, DEMOCRACY AND DISAGREEMENT 121-26 (1996); Kitrosser, *supra* note 98, at 493; Dennis F. Thompson, *Democratic Secrecy*, 114 POL. SCI. Q. 181, 183 (1999).
[146] Kitrosser, *supra* note 98, at 493.

deference to the executive in areas of national security information, and she argued for a much a stronger role for the judiciary in determining secrecy issues.

Kitrosser also wrote about the special role information has in the constitutional framework and the function of information in democratic theory.[147] Kitrosser contended that information and information control have very special constitutional significance:[148] "[I]nformation is not, for constitutional purposes, like any other tool of power. Rather, constitutional analysis suggests that government secrecy, while sometimes necessary, must be kept on a tight leash to prevent it from becoming a tool of tyranny."[149] Kitrosser wrote:

> [C]onstitutional text and structure suggest a faith in openness between the political branches and between such branches and the people. At the same time constitutional structure, text, and history also suggest an understanding that government secrecy sometimes is a necessary evil. Ultimately, text, structure, and history suggest the means of reconciling these points is to ensure that any government secrecy remain a politically controllable tool of the people and their representatives. Specifically, text, structure, and history suggest that, to keep government secrecy within the ultimate control of the people and hence non-tyrannical, the very fact of such secrecy must remain shallow and politically checkable.[150]

Samaha addressed the issue of leaks and confidential news sources in a democratic system.[151] Samaha described the press as playing a role in "an active informal system of information access" that makes transparency possible.[152] Samaha contended that because courts are usually "happy" to protect the dissemination of truthful information about the government by the press, the press provides an important tool

---

[147] *Id.* at 510-27.
[148] *Id.* at 513.
[149] *Id.* at 510.
[150] *Id.* at 513-14.
[151] Samaha, *supra* note 126.
[152] *Id.* at 919.

for government officials to disseminate information to the public.[153]
Thus, although Samaha did not delve into the case law at any depth, he
did note that laws concerning investigative reporting and source
confidentiality or protection for government employees who leak
information to the press are important components of any system of
public access to information in a democracy.[154]

Law professor Mark Fenster presented an analysis of open
government laws that included a discussion of liberal democratic theory
but reached very different conclusions than Weaver and Pallitto,
Kittrosser or Samaha.[155] Fenster was highly critical of current laws, the
press and the judiciary's role in transparency. Noting that
"contemporary transparency advocates typically draw connections
between their efforts and liberal democratic theory,"[156] he examined
"transparency theory" and its relation to self-government. He
concluded that conceptions of transparency fail to take into account
"the complexities of bureaucracy, communication, and the public."[157]
According to Fenster, because transparency proponents and open
government laws are overly broad, they are forced to concede a
substantial set of exceptions to disclosure when confronted with
information regarding national security.[158] Fenster argued, "To
calibrate an optimal practice of open government, transparency theory
must abandon equating the best government with the one that is the
most open—or, more precisely, with the one that appears most open on
the face of its formal commitment to transparency requirements."[159]

Fenster contended that government information should be made
available only when "normative and consequential" governmental gains
outweigh the "costs" of disclosure. To Fenster, the costs of
transparency included "harm to national security, military actions, and
law enforcement," the inhibition of "deliberative decision making,"
"the administrative costs incurred through opening meetings and

---

[153] *Id.* at 946.
[154] *Id.* at 948.
[155] Fenster, *supra* note 18.
[156] *Id.* at 894.
[157] *Id.*
[158] *Id.* at 892.
[159] *Id.*

disclosing documents," and the "reputation costs (and perhaps legal liability)" incurred by public officials from "the disclosure of failed or unpopular policies and decisions."[160] In addition, unlike Pallitto and Weaver and Kitrosser who all called for greater judicial oversight, Fenster concluded that because the judiciary had proven ineffective in resolving access issues, conflicts between secrecy and transparency would best be settle through political means.[161] Fenster argued that conflicts between transparency and secrecy would be best served by "more effective open government laws [that] would create and vest authority in non-judicial institutions that can develop expertise in overseeing informational disputes between members of the public and government agencies."[162]

Finally, Fenster was highly critical of the press's role in transparency. Fenster noted that media institutions are "gatekeepers of information that select and present news within organizational, professional, economic, and ideological constraints."[163] He further contended that because a media company's objectives are to seek financial gain, compete with each other, and further political objectives, this often keep news organizations from informing the public.[164]

These objectives, and the discipline that attempting to meet them imposes, may in some instances lead news organizations to serve as a conduit of information that would help create an informed deliberative public. But more often, they will incline the media towards creating and finding political scandal rather than focusing on and explaining political issues and development[s], and towards producing depoliticized, risk-averse, and entertainment-focused content. Contemporary politicians and officials recognize these tendencies and exploit them by strategically disclosing "information" through

---

[160] *Id.*
[161] *Id.* at 945-46.
[162] *Id.* at 946-47.
[163] *Id.* at 926.
[164] *Id.*

coordinated public relations campaigns that produce pre-packaged, tightly controlled "news."[165]

Fenster concluded, "Merely requiring disclosure of more information might have little effect in the face of efforts to manipulate such information through false or misleading statements."[166]

Thus, there is obviously a great deal of literature that has examined government secrecy in the area of national security. However, much of this scholarship is normative rather than empirical. While numerous authors have suggested the judiciary should treat government secrecy differently than it currently does, little research actually examines judicial decision making in the area of national security. This book, however, attempts to move beyond normative discussions of secrecy and toward empirical observations of judicial decision making in the area of government secrecy and national security information. Rather than argue for or against judicial intervention or analyze statutes or scrutinize them under First Amendment standards, the purpose of this book is to examine how the judiciary decides cases involving the need to balance transparency and free expression against government secrecy and national security. Therefore, the next portion of this chapter addresses political science and legal literature related to the judicial decision making process.

Judicial Decision Making
Faced with the difficult task of balancing transparency with national security, judges are called upon to make decisions and to interpret and create law that affects the flow of information in our democracy. Most of the scholarship on judicial decision making is based on one of two presumptions: that the law decides cases—the legal model—or that the policy preferences of individual judges best predict and explain courts' decisions—the attitudinal model. [167]

---

[165] *Id.*
[166] *Id.* at 929-30.
[167] See JEFFERY A. SEGAL & HAROLD J. SPAETH, THE SUPREME COURT AND THE ATTITUDINAL MODEL REVISITED 44-48 (2002) for a discussion of models and judicial decision making.

According to legal scholars Lee Epstein and Joseph F. Kobylka, legalism assumes that jurists derive rules from precedents, statutes and the Constitution and then apply them to specific cases to reach decisions.[168] Mechanical jurisprudence, also called legal formalism, holds that there is one "correct" answer to a legal question, which can be "discovered" by a judge.[169] This approach views judges as "reasoning from determinate premises to determinate results."[170] Mechanical jurisprudence was a popular theory in the legal literature and law schools prior to and right after the beginning of the twentieth century. However, according to constitutional law scholar Erwin Chemerinsky, while Supreme Court opinions are still written in the style of mechanical jurisprudence, few, if any, scholars still hold this view of legal decision making.[171] According to Chemerinsky, mechanical jurisprudence was "put to rest" by the legal realists of the early twentieth century.[172]

One aspect of interpreting the law under the legal model is plain meaning or textualism. Plain meaning or textualism dictates that the meaning of the Constitution and statutes should be construed from the "plain meaning of the words." As a mode of constitutional interpretation,[173] a texualist approach holds that justices should create

---

[168] LEE EPSTEIN & JOSEPH F. KOBYLKA, THE SUPREME COURT AND LEGAL CHANGE: ABORTION AND THE DEATH PENALTY 10-11 (1992).

[169] *See e.g.* KENT GREENAWALT, LAW AND OBJECTIVITY (1992); RICHARD S. MARKOVITS, MATTERS OF PRINCIPLE: LEGITIMATE LEGAL ARGUMENT AND CONSTITUTIONAL INTERPRETATION (1998).

[170] Erwin Chemerinsky, *The Rhetoric of Constitutional Law*, 100 MICH. L. REV. 2008, 2012 n. 24 (2002).

[171] *Id.* at 2012. *See also* Frank Cross, *Political Science and the New Legal Realism: A Case of Unfortunate Interdisciplinary Ignorance*, 92 NW. U. L. REV. 251, 255 (1997).

[172] Chemerinsky, *supra* note 170, at 2012. For a summary of the legal realists' critiques of formalism, see MORTON J. HORWITZ, THE TRANSFORMATION OF AMERICAN LAW, 1870-1960, 182-230 (1992).

[173] *See* PHILIP BOBBITT, CONSTITUTIONAL INTERPRETATION 12-13 (1991) (identifying the dominant modes of constitutional interpretation as historical, textual, structural, doctrinal, ethical and prudential); Glenn A. Phelps & John B. Gates, *The Myth of Jurisprudence: Interpretive Theory in the Constitutional Opinions of Justices Rehnquist and Brennan,* 31 SANTA CLARA L. REV 567,

no new rights that are not explicitly guaranteed by the Constitution. As a mode of statutory interpretation, textualism suggests judges should defer to the text of a statute without resorting to extrinsic interpretive aids such as legislative histories.[174]

The key problem with relying on plain meaning is that, as political scientists Jeffery A. Segal and Harold J. Spaeth pointed out, English as a language lacks specificity and many words in the Constitution and Bill of Rights are not explained in great detail.[175] For example, what does the word "liberty" in the Fifth and Fourteenth Amendment mean? What is "cruel and unusual" punishment? Chemerinsky noted that interpreting textual provisions "inevitably requires value choices as to their meaning."[176] In addition, Chemerinsky wrote that the Supreme Court often decides cases in which there are no textual provisions to interpret.[177] For example, the Court has been asked to decide if executive privilege exists and, if so, its scope without any reference to such a privilege in the Constitution.[178] Plain meaning interpretations also encounter problems because statutes, like the Constitution, do not always do a perfect job explaining what is covered by a term.[179] These problems have led some scholars to conclude that it is difficult to use plain meaning or textualism to reliably predict Supreme Court decisions. In addition, because the meaning of a word is subject to multiple interpretations, it is possible that plain meaning or textualism is simply a tool used to advance policy preferences.[180]

Closely tied to textualism is "originalism" or "original intentalism," a mode of constitutional interpretation which focuses on

---

581-84 (1991) (classifying the types of constitutional interpretive arguments as textual, structural, doctrinal, extrinsic, and historical/intentional).

[174] *See, e.g.*, William N. Eskridge Jr., *The New Textualism*, 37 UCLA L. REV. 621 (1990); Fredrick Schauer, *Statutory Construction and the Coordinating Function of Plain Meaning*, 1990 SUP. CT. REV. 231.

[175] SEGAL & SPAETH, *supra* note 167, at 54.

[176] Chemerinsky, *supra* note 170, at 2011.

[177] *Id.*

[178] *Id.* See United States v. Nixon, 418 U.S. 683 (1974) for a discussion of the existence and scope of executive privilege.

[179] *See, e.g.*, New York Times v. United States, 403 U.S. 713, 721 (1971) (Douglas, J., concurring).

[180] *See, e.g.*, SEGAL & SPAETH, *supra* note 167, at 58-59.

the framers of the Constitution. Under originalism, judges should construe statutes and the Constitution "according to the preference of those who originally drafted and supported them."[181] Originalists are "committed to the view that original intent, or original meaning is not only relevant but also authoritative; that we are in some sense obligated to follow the intent, or plain meaning, of the framers."[182] According to Chemerinsky, originalism has the appeal of making it seem that judicial decisions are not based on judges' personal preferences but rather are solely the product of following the framers' wishes.[183] Current Supreme Court Justice Antonin Scalia has offered a variant of this idea, which he has described as "original meaning," or, as other scholars have described it, "public-meaning originalism."[184] According to Scalia, when interpreting the Constitution judges should focus on the practices at the time of the framing or attempt to discern what a rational person at the time of the framing of the Constitution would have taken the words of the Constitution to mean.[185] As with textualism, originalism holds that judges should add no new rights to the Constitution that were not expressly intended by the framers. As applied to statutes, this mode of interpretation is best described as intentionalism or the idea that when interpreting statutory meaning, courts should defer to legislative intent as evidenced in the legislative record or committee reports.[186]

Normative debates for and against binding judicial interpretation of the Constitution to the intent of the framers became increasingly popular in the years following the Court's decisions in abortion cases and comments made by then Attorney General Edwin Meese in the

---

[181] *Id.*, at 60.
[182] Pamela C. Corley, Robert M. Howard & David C. Nixon, *The Supreme Court and Opinion Content: The Use of the Federalist Papers*, 58 POL. RES. Q. 329, 331 (2005).
[183] Chemerinsky, *supra* note 170, at 2012.
[184] *See* Larry Kramer, *Panel on Originalism and Pragmatism* 153, *in* ORIGINALISM: A QUARTER-CENTURY OF DEBATE (Steven G. Calabresi, ed. 2007).
[185] *See generally* ANTONIN SCALIA, A MATTER OF INTERPRETATION: FEDERAL COURTS AND THE LAW (1997).
[186] *See* Eskridge, *supra* note 174, at 630.

1980s.[187] Justice William J. Brennan, Jr., for example, was highly critical of originalism, writing that because the text of the Constitution is unclear and requires interpretation, efforts to discern its authors' intentions were "little more than arrogance cloaked as humility."[188] Brennan wrote, "It is arrogant to pretend that from our vantage we can gauge accurately the intent of Framers on application of principles to specific, contemporary questions."[189]

A number of scholars have also made compelling cases against originalism, pointing out problems with using originalism or legislative intent to predict and explain judicial decisions. [190] First, the judiciary is often presented with novel situations that the framers of the Constitution—or other lawmakers—would not have had to consider.[191] For example, it would be difficult to determine exactly what the framers would have thought of wire tapping or bloggers because neither existed at the time of the framing of the Constitution.[192]

Second, for many reasons it is difficult to determine exactly whose intent should be controlling. Chemerinsky noted that originalism inherently involves judges making decisions "about who counts as a Framer, what they thought and at what level of abstraction to state their views."[193] There were multiple framers of the Constitution, and

---

[187] *See* Edwin Meese, III, *Speech Before the American Bar Association* 53, in ORIGINALISM: A QUARTER-CENTURY OF DEBATE (Steven G. Calabresi, ed. 2007).

[188] William J. Brennan, Jr., *Speech to the Text and Teaching Symposium* 58, *in* ORIGINALISM: A QUARTER CENTURY OF DEBATE (Steven G. Calabresi, ed. 2007).

[189] *Id.*

[190] *See, e.g.*, Paul Best, *The Fundamental Rights Controversy: The Essential Contradictions of Normative Constitutional Scholarship*, 90 YALE L.J. 1063 (1982); Jeffery Shaman, *The Constitution, the Supreme Court and Creativity*, 9 HASTINGS CONST. L.Q. 257 (1982); Larry G. Simon, *The Authority of the Framers of the Constitution: Can Originalist Interpretation Be Justified?* 73 CAL. L. REV.1482 (1985).

[191] SEGAL & SPAETH, *supra* note 167, at 66.

[192] *See, e.g.,* Berger v. New York, 388 U.S. 41, 78-88 (1967) (Black, J. dissenting) (arguing that the framers obviously did not intend for the Fourth Amendment to prohibit wiretapping and it was not up to the Court to update the Constitution to keep up with modern technology).

[193] Chemerinsky, *supra* note 170, at 2013.

obviously, it is highly unlikely that all of them had the exact same intent in mind when they crafted provisions of the Constitution. Segal and Spaeth wrote:

> [W]ho were the Framers? All fifty-five of the delegates who showed up at one time or another in Philadelphia during the summer of 1787? Some came and went. Only thirty-nine signed the final document. Some probably had not read it. Assuredly, they were not all of a single mind. Apart from the delegates who refused to sign, should not the delegates to the various state conventions that were called to ratify the Constitution also be counted as Framers?[194]

Because there were multiple framers with various views of the Constitution and Bill of Rights, judges are able to strategically use originalism to advance their policy preferences and insulate their decisions from criticism.[195] For example, Pamela Corley, Robert Howard and David Nixon found that justices often cited the Federalist Papers to come to divergent conclusions.[196] According to Corley, Howard and Nixon's content analysis of Supreme Court decisions, justices used strategic citations to the Federalist Papers to advance policy preferences, insulate the Court from criticism and controversy, and sway their colleagues on the bench.[197] The research of John Gates and Glenn Phelps demonstrated that justices used the arguments of the same framer, James Madison, to come to divergent conclusions in the same case.[198] Gates and Phelps showed that in the same case, *Marsh v. Chambers*,[199] Chief Justice Warren E. Burger and Associate Justice Brennan both cited writings by Madison to justify their conclusions.

> Brennan went to some length to argue that the views of Madison the elder statesman were more historically valid than

---

[194] SEGAL & SPAETH, *supra* note 167, at 68 (citations omitted).
[195] Corley, Howard & Nixon, *supra* note 182, at 338-39.
[196] *Id.*
[197] *Id.* at 335-39.
[198] John B. Gates & Glenn A. Phelps, *Intentionalism in Constitutional Opinions*, 49 POL. RES. Q. 245 (1996).
[199] 463 U.S. 783 (1983).

the views of Madison the congressmen. This difference was significant because Chief Justice Burger's majority opinion, utilizing an intentionalist reading of the First Amendment, had noted with favor Madison's legislative actions.[200]

Gates and Phelps concluded that citing "Madison the framer" or "Madison the legislator" or "Madison the elder statesmen" all supported different results and the justices' strategic citation to historical support was driven largely by their "competing visions of a constitutional order."[201]

Using original intent to discern the meaning of the First Amendment is particularly difficult because of the lack of debate surrounding the actual meaning of the Amendment. According to Anderson, Congress never debated the merits or meaning of the First Amendment[202] and the final wording of the Amendment was decided upon by the First Senate, which did not keep a record of its meeting.[203] Although Justice Scalia argued that his judicial philosophy of "original meaning" corrected many of the problems associated with originalism and constitutional interpretation, scholars have criticized this approach as well.[204]

As a mode of statutory interpretation, intentionalism has also attracted critics. Like the Constitution itself, statutes are enacted by groups rather than by a single legislator. It is impossible to say what the overriding intent behind a statute was or even if all the motivations for passing a statute were the same. This problem has been brought up in a First Amendment context by at least one justice, Scalia. In stinging criticisms of using legislative intent as a mode of statutory analysis,

---

[200] Gates & Phelps, *supra* note 198, at 254.

[201] *Id.* at 255.

[202] Anderson, *supra* note 55, at 485.

[203] *Id.* at 480. Sessions of the Senate were closed throughout the period during which the Bill of Rights was being drafted. The Senate Journal and the History of the Proceedings and Debates recorded only actions taken. *Id.*

[204] For a critique of original meaning see Erwin Chemerinsky, *The Jurisprudence of Justice Scalia: A Critical Appraisal*, 22 U. HAW. L. REV. 385, 391-401 (2000). For a methodological criticism of original meaning originalism see Saul Cornell, *The Original Meaning of Original Understanding: A Neo-Blackstonian Critique*, 67 MD. L. REV. 150 (2007).

Scalia has pointed out that a great number of motivations are behind decisions to pass statutes and it is impossible to focus on only one.[205]

A third aspect of the legal model of judicial decision making is rooted in the legal concept of stare decisis, which means "stand by the decision" and holds that basing decisions on precedent allows for the law to develop a quality of connectedness and appearance of stability. Precedent can appear to be a powerful predictor of judicial decisions. According to Segal and Spaeth, the frequency with which courts based decisions on precedent far surpasses any other aspect of the legal model.[206] The Court often appears to be very reluctant to overturn precedent, and at times the justices go to great lengths to avoid doing so.[207] According to Segal and Spaeth's research, the Supreme Court overruled its own precedents only 128 times between 1953 and 2000, a period of time during which the Court ruled four times as many statutes unconstitutional.[208] Chemerinsky contended: "The rhetorical force of precedent is seen in how the Court writes its opinions when it does overrule earlier decisions. The Court describes the earlier rulings as aberrations and its current interpretation as the long-standing approach, even when that is not at all the case."[209] In addition, when the Court does overturn precedent, Segal and Spaeth's research has shown it is often done *mirabile dictu*, or on the basis of a different precedent.[210] Chemerinsky also noted that opinions are written to appear consistent with precedent even when they are not.[211] For example, *Brandenburg v. Ohio*,[212] a case involving a Ku Klux Klan leader in rural Ohio, the Court clearly tried to present the First Amendment incitement test used in the case as being well established law when, in fact, *Brandenburg* created a new standard.[213]

---

[205] *See* Edwards v. Aguillard, 482 U.S. 578, 610-39 (1987) (Scalia, J. dissenting). *See also*, Naturalization Serv. v. Cardoza-Fonseca, 480 U.S. 421, 452-55 (1987) (Scalia, J., concurring).
[206] SEGAL & SPAETH, *supra* note 167, at 76.
[207] Chemerinsky, *supra* note 170, at 2017.
[208] SEGAL & SPAETH, *supra* note 167, at 83.
[209] Chemerinsky, *supra* note 170, at 2018.
[210] SEGAL & SPAETH, *supra* note 167, at 84.
[211] Chemerinsky, *supra* note 170, at 2015-19.
[212] 395 U.S. 444 (1969).
[213] Chemerinsky, *supra* note 170, at 2017.

However, there are a number of other weaknesses inherent in trying to predict judicial decisions based solely on precedent. Spaeth and Segal's research on precedent and stare decisis concluded that dissenting justices, even ones who elsewhere wrote of respecting precedent, rarely switched sides in later cases to support earlier majority opinions.[214] Rather, the justices continued to support their losing positions. In addition, in almost all cases there is some precedent to support either side of a case.[215] Segal and Spaeth wrote:

> Because the facts in two appellate cases invariably differ, and the degree of factual similarity and dissimilarity between any two cases involves intensely personal and subjective judgment, judges may pick and choose among precedents to find those that accord with their policy preferences, while simultaneously asserting that these are also the ones that best accord with the facts of the case at hand.[216]

Furthermore, judges are able to distinguish precedent without having to actually overrule a precedent. All a judge must do is assert that the facts of the present case differ from the facts of the precedent. Judges often spend the first part of a decision discussing why the present case is similar to or different from preceding cases or alternative lines of precedent. Chemerinsky wrote, "A significant portion of almost every Supreme Court opinion is about how the decisions fit within, and flow from, the earlier case."[217]

---

[214] *See generally* HAROLD J. SPAETH & JEFFREY A. SEGAL, MAJORITY RULE OR MINORITY WILL: ADHERENCE TO PRECEDENT ON THE U.S. SUPREME COURT (1999); SEGAL & SPAETH, *supra* note 167, at 76-85; Jeffery A. Segal & Harold J. Spaeth, *The Influence of Stare Decisis on the Votes of U.S. Supreme Court Justices*, 40 AM. J. POL. SCI. 971 (1996).

[215] SEGAL & SPAETH, *supra* note 167, at 77. *See also* Linda Greenhouse, *Precedent for Lower Courts: Tyrant or Teacher*, N.Y. TIMES, Jan. 29, 1988, at A12 (quoting judges from the U.S. Court of Appeals for the First and Seventh Circuits who argued that if precedent clearly governed a case, no litigant would ever appeal a lower court's decision).

[216] *See* SEGAL & SPAETH, *supra* note 167, at 80.

[217] Chemerinsky, *supra* note 170, at 2019.

In sum, while "legalism" is the primary way courts frame and explain their opinions and is often the focus of political science and legal scholarship, the legal model of judicial decision making has numerous weaknesses as a predictive and explanatory tool. Noting these weaknesses, positivist legal scholars put forth a competing model of judicial behavior that assumes the personal policy preferences of jurists can explain most, if not all, of their decisions.

The attitudinal model was described by Segal and Spaeth as a combination of legal realism, political science, psychology and economics.[218] Legal realism, first advanced in the early twentieth century, held that law is vague, internally inconsistent, and revisable.[219] Near the turn of the century, Justice Oliver Wendell Holmes was one of the first jurists to suggest that law was not a formal process of neutral application or logical deduction but a process of choosing among competing values.[220] In 1931, Karl Llewellyn, an extremely influential legal scholar, wrote that legal realism recognizes that "the law is in flux" and "moving," and that judges create law.[221] Segal and Spaeth, building upon legal realism and the work of political scientists such as Glendon Schubert,[222] have consistently argued that policy preferences are the only factor that needs to be considered when attempting to predict and explain Supreme Court decision making. In 2002 they argued, "Simply put, Rehnquist votes the way he does because he is extremely conservative; Marshall voted the way he did because he was extremely liberal."[223]

Influenced by legal realists and applying "notions of rationality" developed in economics to judicial decision, positivist legal scholars such as Spaeth and David Rhode put forward a number of reasons why

---

[218] SEGAL & SPAETH, *supra* note 167, at 86.

[219] Howard Gillman, *What's Law Got to Do With It? Judicial Behavorialists Test the "Legal Model" of Judicial Decision Making*, 26 LAW & SOC. INQUIRY 465, 468-69 (2001).

[220] *See, e.g.,* Oliver Wendell Holmes, *The Path of Law*, 10 HARV. L. REV. 457 (1897).

[221] Karl N. Llewellyn, *Some Realism About Realism—Responding to Dean Pound*, 44 HARV. L. REV. 1222, 1237 (1931). *See also*, Karl N. Llewellyn, *A Realistic Jurisprudence—The Next Step*, 30 COLUM. L. REV. 431 (1930).

[222] GLENDON SCHUBERT, THE JUDICIAL MIND REVISITED (1974).

[223] SEGAL & SPAETH, *supra* note 167, at 86.

Supreme Court justices are in an excellent position to make decisions based solely on policy preferences. [224] Segal and Spaeth wrote, "The Supreme Court's rules and structures, along with those of the American political system in general, give life-tenured justices enormous latitude to reach decisions based on their personal policy preferences."[225] First, Supreme Court justices are politically isolated. They are granted lifetime appointments, and while they can be impeached, one has never been removed from office.[226] Second, justices cannot be overruled and have little fear of their policy preferences being overturned by the actions of one of the other branches of government. According to Segal and Spaeth, the fractured nature of Congress makes statutory changes unlikely once the Court has ruled, and the supermajority requirement for adoption of constitutional amendments makes passing one extremely difficult, as evidenced by the relatively few that have passed in the last 200-plus years.[227] Third, because the Supreme Court can choose its own docket, it has a great deal of power to control which cases it will hear. According to Segal and Spaeth, this gives justices the ability to advance their policy making in cases of their choosing.[228] In addition, Segal and Spaeth noted that the Supreme Court does not typically decide routine cases that have obvious answers. This lets the justices decide cases on personal or extra-legal factors. Finally, Segal and Spaeth argued that the justices typically do not have any goals of higher office.[229] The power, prestige, intellectual stimulation, and relatively easy workload of a modern justice make the job a highly desirable one, and few would want any other job in or out of government. Although the absence of some of these factors may inhibit the policy making ability of lower court judges, the attitudinal model does not suggest that lower court judges do not attempt to advance their policy preferences, only that they may be more constrained in doing so than Supreme Court justices.

---

[224] DAVID W. ROHDE & HAROLD J. SPAETH, SUPREME COURT DECISION MAKING 71 (1976).

[225] SEGAL & SPAETH, *supra* note 167, at 92.

[226] Only one justice has been impeached, and the vote to remove failed to pass. Samuel Chase was impeached in 1804.

[227] SEGAL & SPAETH, *supra* note 167, at 94-95.

[228] *Id.* at 93.

[229] *Id.* at 95-96.

Although a great deal of empirical research supports the ability of the attitudinal model to predict and explain judicial decisions,[230] the model has numerous weaknesses. First, scholars have suggested that the attitudinal model critiques a legal model that is no longer widely held by anyone: the mechanical jurisprudential model.[231] As noted, although Court decisions are still written in this style, few hold that it is still the model that represents legal thinking. Second, critics have contended that Segal and Spaeth's experimental designs purposefully set up legal model "straw men" that are easy to knock down and do not accurately represent the influence of the law on the Court.[232] For example, while political scientist Gregory Caldeira generally supported the work of Segal and Spaeth, he also argued that the two adopted an extreme version of competing explanations for judicial behavior and did not "set up any realistic competitor to their model of decision making."[233]

Several scholars have argued that in reducing complex observations down to easily measurable variables, the attitudinal model does not accurately capture the complex influence of legal factors on judicial decision making. Prior to his work with Spaeth, Segal's research on search and seizure cases identified several legal and fact pattern variables that influenced the Court's decisions.[234] Similar work has been conducted on First Amendment topics. Political scientist Kevin T. McGuire conducted the same type of research using obscenity

---

[230] *See, e.g., id.* at 279-320; Lawrence Baum, *Measuring Policy Change in the U.S. Supreme Court*, 82 AM. POL. SCI. REV. 905 (1988); Jeffery A. Segal & Albert D. Cover, *Ideological Values and the Votes of U.S. Supreme Court Justices*, 83 AM. POL. SCI. REV. 557 (1989).

[231] *See, e.g.,* Tracey E. George & Lee Epstein, *On the Nature of Supreme Court Decision Making*, 86 AM. POL. SCI. REV. 323, 323-24 (1992); Gillman, *supra* note 220, at 471.

[232] Gerald Rosenberg, *Symposium: The Supreme Court and the Attitudinal Model*, 4 LAW & COURTS 6, 7 (1994). See Gillman, *supra* note 219, at 474-85 for a summary of critiques of Segal and Spaeth's conceptualization of judicial behavior.

[233] Gregory Caldiera, *Review of the Supreme Court and the Attitudinal Model*, 88 AM. POLI. SCI. Q. 485, 485 (1994).

[234] Jeffery A. Segal, *Predicting Supreme Court Cases Probability: The Search and Seizure Cases, 1962-1981*, 78 AM. POLI. SCI. REV. 891 (1984).

cases and measuring individual justices' decisions.[235] McGuire concluded that "case-specific variables," such as the level of governmental participation, the methods of obscenity control, claims made by the parties, and the presence of amici curiae could be used to determine the outcome of cases and the opinions of individual justices.[236] He wrote: "The analysis demonstrates that decision making in obscenity litigation is quite complex. We find variables from across a broad range of predictors contributing to the explanatory capacity of the model."[237] Other research has also shown the influence of amici briefs on the Court,[238] the importance of the solicitor general's role as an amicus curiae or as a litigant,[239] and the influence of oral arguments on decision making.[240]

Still other research has shown that the attitudinal model does not allow for complex goals or strategic voting. It ignores the role of strategic voting to obtain a majority, coalition building, leadership by the chief justice, or other factors related to advancing individual justices' interests.[241] In addition, critics have argued that the attitudinal

---

[235] Kevin T. McGuire, *Obscenity, Libertarian Values, and Decision Making in the Supreme Court*, 18 AM. POLI. Q. 47 (1990).

[236] *Id.* at 48.

[237] *Id.* at 58.

[238] *See, e.g.*, Gregory A. Caldeira & John R. Wright, *Organized Interests and Agenda Setting in the U.S. Supreme Court*, 82 AM. POLI. SCI. REV. 1109 (1988); Gregg Ivers & Karen O'Connor, *Friends or Foes: The Amicus Curiae Participation and Effectiveness of the American Civil Liberties Union and the Americans for Effective Law Enforcement in Criminal Cases, 1969-1982*, 9 LAW AND POL'Y 161 (1987); McGuire, *supra* note 235.

[239] *See, e.g.*, Michael Bailey, Brian Kamoie & Forrest Maltzman, *Signals from the Tenth Justice: The Political Role of the Solicitor General in Supreme Court Decision Making*, 49 AM. J. POLI. SCI. 72 (2005); Caldeira & Wright, *supra* note 238; McGuire, *supra* note 235.

[240] *See, e.g.*, Timothy R. Johnson, Paul J. Wahlbeck & James F. Spriggs II, *The Influence of Oral Arguments on the U.S. Supreme Court*, 100 AM. POLI. SCI. REV. 99 (1998).

[241] *See, e.g.*, Theodore S. Arrington & Saul Brenner, *Strategic Voting for Damage Control on the Supreme Court*, 57 POLI. RES. Q. 565 (2004); Robert Dorf & Saul Brenner, *Conformity Voting on the United States Supreme Court*, 54 J. POLI. 762 (1992); Stacia L. Haynie, *Leadership and Consensus on the U.S. Supreme Court*, 54 J. POLI. 1158 (1992); Forrest Maltzman & Paul J.

model fails to take into account both internal and external judicial restraints and other institutional considerations. Scholars note that the Court as an institution has it own rules and procedures that impact decisions, and the Court is only one part of the government and must consider the behavior, wants, and desires of the other branches of government.[242] Finally, research has documented the influence of public opinion on Court decisions.[243] All of this research suggests that while individual policy preferences are important, even at the Supreme Court level other factors influence decisions as well.

Thus, while both legalism and the attitudinal models have strengths, both fall short of providing a comprehensive model that totally explains and predicts judicial decision making. A third set of models of judicial decision making, strategic models, or models based on rational choice theories, suggests that although judges, like other political actors, seek the implementation of personal policy preferences, they are limited by legal factors as well as the preferences of their fellow judges, the norms and authority of the judicial branch as an institution, and external political and societal factors.[244] This line of reasoning suggests that while judges are constrained by legal

---

Wahlbeck, *May it Please the Chief? Opinion Assignments in the Rehnquist Court*, 40 AM. J. POLI. SCI 421 (1996).

[242] *See, e.g,* LEE EPSTEIN & JACK KNIGHT, THE CHOICES JUSTICES MAKE (1998). Epstein and Knight argued that justices are strategic actors who must consider the preferences of other actors and the institutional context in which they act. They called this the "strategic account" because it is based on the rational choice paradigm advanced by economists and political scientists in fields other than judicial decision making. *Id.* at 10. *See also* Robert Lowry Clinton, *Game Theory, Legal History, and the Origins of Judicial Review: A Revisionist Analysis of* Marbury v. Madison, 38 AM. J. POLI. SCI. 285 (1994); Lori Hausegger & Lawrence Baum, *Inviting Congressional Action: A Study of Supreme Court Motivations in Statutory Interpretation*, 43 AM. J. POLI. SCI. 162 (1999); Jack Knight & Lee Epstein, *On the Struggle for Judicial Supremacy*, 30 LAW & SOC. REV. 87 (1996).

[243] *See, e.g,* Kevin T. McGuire & James A. Stimson, *The Least Dangerous Branch Revisited: New Evidence on Supreme Court Responsiveness to Public Preferences*, 66 J. POLI. 1018 (2004).

[244] *See* EPSTEIN & KNIGHT, *supra* note 242; EPSTEIN & KOBYLKA, *supra* note 168; Kevin T. McGuire & Barbara Palmer, *Issues, Agendas, and Decision Making on the Supreme Court*, 90 AM. POL. SCI. REV. 853 (1996); WALTER F. MURPHY, ELEMENTS OF JUDICIAL STRATEGY (1964).

formalism's reliance on a limited number of legal arguments that can be used to reach — or ex-post facto justify — a decision, there remains a great deal of flexibility in how these arguments can be used. These theorists contend that although the law gives judges a great deal of room to maneuver they must also operate under rules governing their own actions and interactions, protect institutional legitimacy and sway their colleagues with persuasive legal arguments.[245] Thus, while a judge might come to a case with preconceived legal and policy preferences, their opinion must contain legal rationales to sway their colleagues, the other institutions of government and public opinion.[246] For example, strategic theorists who focus on the judicial branch as an institution examine judicial decision-making through the lens of courts' institutional position in relation to the other branches of government.[247]

As early as 1964, Martin Shapiro, a political scientist who is currently a law professor at UC Berkeley, was suggesting that judges make their decisions against a unique backdrop.[248] Shapiro developed the concept of "political jurisprudence," the idea that courts are part of the political structure but that the courts differ from other policy making institutions because their unique relationship with the law affects decision making. Unlike the other branches of government, judges must offer reasons for their decisions, and these decisions must "fit" the law as judges see it. Political scientists Jack Knight and Epstein[249] and legal scholar Howard Gillman[250] have argued that even at the Supreme Court level, freedom from review does not prevent the

---

[245] *See, e.g.,* Forrest Maltzman & Paul J. Wahlbeck, *Strategic Policy Considerations and Voting Fluidity on the Burger Court*, 90 AM. POL. SCI. REV. 581, 581 (1996).

[246] *See generally* FORREST MALTZMAN, JAMES F. SPRIGGS & PAUL J. WAHLBECK, CRAFTING LAW ON THE SUPREME COURT: THE COLLEGIAL GAME (2000).

[247] *See, e.g.,* Frank B. Cross & Blake J. Nelson, *Strategic Institutional Effects on Supreme Court Decisionmaking*, 95 NW. U. L. REV. 1437, 1452 (2001) (contending the even the Supreme Court must consider how Congress might react to decisions).

[248] *See generally* MARTIN SHAPIRO, LAW AND POLITICS IN THE SUPREME COURT (1964).

[249] EPSTEIN & KNIGHT, *supra* note 242.

[250] Gillman, *supra* note 219.

justices from erecting constraints that shape their decision making. Gillman was highly critical of much of the political science literature, writing that behavioralist research has been so internalized by many political scientists that it is considered "common sense" in the discipline that Supreme Court justices are promoters of policy preference and not interpreters of law.[251]

Scholars such as Gillman contend that because law plays a unique role in the judicial system, judicial decisions cannot be understood without addressing this role.[252] Justices must be viewed as lawyers, who were trained to approach problems in a specific way and to find solutions to those problems by thinking about the law. While judges may use aspects of legalism—such as precedent, original intent, and texualism—to justify their policy preferences, these factors may also be a unique influence on the mindset of justices and work as a constraint on policy making. Epstein and Kobylka wrote:

> Interpretation, the giving of meaning to disembodied rules, is clearly colored by the perspective of the interpreter; rules are not self-defining. However, judges are attorneys and attorneys are schooled in the law, therefore—while individual jurists may interpret its commands differently—to the extent that they take it seriously, law shapes their decisions.[253]

According to Gillman, researchers who approach judicial decision making with a focus on the law "do not reject behavioralist descriptions of decision-making patterns, but they insist that behavioralists should not infer that these patterns mean an absence of legal motivations unless they have additional independent evidence that judges are basing decisions on considerations not warranted by law."[254]

Political scientists Mark J. Richards and Herbert M. Kritzer and Epstein and Kobylka conducted research suggesting that while judicial attitudes are important, the law still influences judicial decision making. According to Richards and Kritzer, the law's role in judicial

---

[251] *Id.* at 466.
[252] *Id.* at 486.
[253] EPSTEIN & KOBYLKA, *supra* note 168, at 12.
[254] Gillman, *supra* note 219, at 487.

decision making at the Supreme Court level is best understood as structures created by the justices. They wrote, "[C]ourts, including the Supreme Court, are different [than legislative bodies], and part of this difference is the role of law in decision making."[255] Richards and Kritzer argued that even at the Supreme Court, where justices have a great deal of freedom to enact their policy preferences without restraint, law still mattered.

> [L]aw is created to serve a purpose, and people go along with the institution if they see its purpose as worthwhile or if they are otherwise constrained by the institution. If the adherents of a pure attitudinal model wish to reduce law to nothing more than attitudes formally stated, the attitudinal model becomes tautological; attitudes drive decisions because every decision is made on the basis of attitudes. Our position is that attitudes influence the development of law, but law can also affect the decisions of the Court, and these effects are not purely attitudinal.[256]

Like legal realists, Richards and Kritzer viewed the law as a human construct and used the term "jurisprudential regime" to refer to "a key precedent, or a set of related precedents, that structure the way in which the Supreme Court justices evaluate key elements of cases in arriving at decisions in a particular legal area."[257] For example, Richards and Kritzer cited the First Amendment content neutrality doctrine as an example of a jurisprudential regime that demonstrates "the influence of law." Such regimes govern that area of law until the Court changes regimes. According to Richards and Kritzer, justices engage in a generalized process of reasoning about their decisions and base decisions on their policy preferences, the preferences of the other justices and political actors. Judges then must justify their decisions with arguments that makes sense within the current state of the law and can be justified to others.

---

[255] Mark J. Richards & Herbert M. Kritzer, *Jurisprudential Regimes in Supreme Court Decision Making*, 96 AM. POLI. SCI. REV. 305, 305 (2002).

[256] *Id.* at 306-08.

[257] *Id.* at 315-16.

In their comprehensive study of abortion and death penalty cases, Epstein and Kobylka examined the influence of the law on justices by exploring changes in constitutional interpretation by the Supreme Court.[258] To their surprise, Epstein and Kobylka found that the way legal arguments were framed by litigants had an effect on Supreme Court decision making.[259] While Epstein and Kobylka noted that Supreme Court decisions are most definitely a product of the makeup of the Court and influenced by the political climate, they concluded that "it is the law and legal arguments as framed by legal actors that most clearly influence the content and direction of legal change."[260]

One way judges have the ability to influence case outcomes is by strategically identifying what legal issues are presented by a case or "framing" the case. McGuire and Barbara Palmer noted there is a difference between the cases courts decide and the legal issues they decide. They wrote: "[C]ases simply provide the framework in which issues are addressed. . . . [T]he cases themselves do little more than provide a kind of legal architecture for the principles of law that they represent."[261] Judges have the ability to determine which specific issues to resolve in a case and determine which issues or problems are the salient ones.[262] These authors suggest that because judges have a great deal of flexibility in identifying the key legal issue presented by a case they have a great deal of flexibility to create and interpret law. As McGuire and Palmer noted, because of "the malleability inherent in questions of law," there is often a difference between the issues courts are *asked* to decide and those they ultimately *choose* to decide.[263] According to McGuire and Palmer, courts can expand the issues in a case — termed "issue discovery" — as well as ignore issues raised by either side — known as "issue suppression."[264] Epstein and Kobylka

---

[258] EPSTEIN & KOBYLKA, supra note 168.

[259] *Id.* at xiv.

[260] *Id.* at 8.

[261] McGuire & Palmer, *supra* note 244, at 692.

[262] *See* S. Sidney Ulmer, *Issue Fluidity in the U.S. Supreme Court, in* SUPREME COURT ACTIVISM AND RESTRAINT 691 (Stephen C. Halpern & Charles M. Lambe eds., 1982).

[263] McGuire & Palmer, *supra* note 244, at 691.

[264] *Id.* at 692.

used the term "framing" to describe the process of understanding how the legal arguments judges hear and make shape judicial behavior.[265]

This conceptualization of issue selection and fluidity, which forms the foundation of this book, is similar to the concept of framing in communication research, which focuses on how issues are presented.[266] According to Robert Entman, to frame is to "select some aspects of a perceived reality and make them more salient in a communication context in such a way as to promote a particular problem or issue definition, causal interpretation, moral evaluation, and/or treatment recommendation" for an issue.[267] While applying social science based communication research to legal scholarship might seem novel, as Chemerinsky suggested, a great deal can be learned about law by viewing opinions as communications from courts to specific audiences in an attempt to influence those audiences through reasoned arguments.[268] As noted, he wrote that judicial opinions are written to make results appear to be determinate and value-free, rather than indeterminate and value-based; consistent with precedent, even when they are not; and to make decisions seem restrained, rather than activist. On the other hand, dissents criticize decisions as activist and not restrained.[269] Understood this way, opinions can be examined for internally oriented strategies — those designed to persuade other jurists deciding a case — or externally oriented strategies — those designed to persuade the other branches of government, lower courts, or the public.

Chemerinsky suggested that judicial opinions are best understood as rhetoric, or "reasoned arguments intended to persuade."[270]   He

---

[265] EPSTEIN & KOBYLKA, *supra* note 168, at 302.

[266] *See, e.g.*, TODD GITLIN, THE WHOLE WORLD IS WATCHING: MASS MEDIA IN THE MAKING AND UNMAKING OF THE NEW LEFT (1980); Robert M. Entman, *Framing: Toward a Clarification of a Fractured Paradigm*, 43 J. COMM. 51 (1993); Douglas M. McLeod & Benajmin H. Detenber, *Framing Effects of Television News Coverage of Social Protest*, 49 J. COMM. 3 (1999).

[267] Entman, supra note 266, at 52.

[268] Chemerinsky, *supra* note 170, at 2007-09.

[269] *Id.* at 2010.   Although Chemerinsky wrote about the Supreme Court and focused solely on constitutional law, he also argued that many of the same characteristics that applied to the Supreme Court's constitutional interpretations also applied to lower courts and statutory interpretation.

[270] Chemerinsky, *supra* note 170, at 2008.

argued that Supreme Court decisions are meant to convey important message to fellow justices, the other branches of government, lower courts and the public, and these messages are conveyed in the rhetoric of law.[271] Opinions, Chemerinsky wrote, are the central aspect of American constitutional law and focusing on opinions as rhetoric helps to understand and appraise the Supreme Court's work.[272] Although Chemerinsky wrote about the Supreme Court and focused solely on constitutional law, he also argued that many of the same characteristics that applied to the Supreme Court's constitutional interpretations also applied to lower courts and statutory interpretation.[273]

In sum, this research makes apparent that understanding how courts come to decisions is a complicated affair. The research of political scientists and law professors who attempt to examine the way values, institutions and law structure, inhibit and influence the decisions of judges presents compelling descriptions and explanations of the judicial decision making process. Research indicates that the way issues are identified and framed by the courts and litigants as well as aspects of legalism influence and structure the decisions of individual judges and affect the outcomes of cases. In addition, research suggests that individual cases create patterns and regimes that influence the way similar cases are treated and ultimately create legal structures that define power and controls information. This book applies this research to federal cases that have examined the government's ability to control national security information.

The ability of the government to control information related to national security has been examined by the judiciary in several types of cases. Broadly categorized, these include cases that have addressed the ability of the federal government to keep national security information secret and cases that have addressed the government's ability to punish the unauthorized disclosure of such information.[274] The cases were

---

[271] *Id.* at 2009.

[272] *Id.* at 2010.

[273] *Id.* at 2009-10.

[274] Cases for analysis were identified using Westlaw Key Number and the KeySearch system. Westlaw is an online database of legal documents maintained by the West Publishing Company. KeySearch organizes all legal issues into thirty topics, which are broken down into subtopics. The resulting list of cases was then manually searched to identify cases related to the

divided into three distinct categories: national security and prior restraint cases;[275] national security and post-publication punishment cases;[276] and, finally, national security and access cases.[277] Twenty-one cases involving national security and transparency spanning the years 1959 to 2007 were identified and analyzed.

Individual opinions were examined to determine how judges identified the core legal question(s), principle(s) of law, or issue(s) of a case and which mode of legal analysis or which legal "factors" were used to support a decision.[278] Based on the existing literature on

---

research. In addition, any additional citations in the cases identified through the Westlaw Key Number system were reviewed to determine if they were relevant to the book.

[275] National security information and prior restraint cases were identified by using Key Numbers 92k1525, "Prior Restraints," and 393k41, "Duties of Officers and Agents and Performance Thereof."

[276] National security information and post-publication sanction cases were identified by using Key Number 92k2038 k. "Freedom of Speech, Expression, Press, Civilian Employees," and a KeyCite search on *United States v. Morrison*, 844 F.2d 1057 (4th 1988), a case involving the conviction of government employee Samuel Morrison under sections 793(d) and (e) of the Espionage Act for giving national security information to the British magazine *Jane's Fighting Ships*.

[277] National security and access cases were identified using Key Numbers 402k37, "Powers of the Executive," and 402k48.1, "Access to Secrets or Classified Information; Security Clearances."

[278] This research has several limitations that are important to note. The primary purpose of this book is to identify the frames and legal justifications stated by federal judges when they balance transparency and secrecy in national security cases. While there is reliable data regarding the political ideology of Supreme Court justices, no such database exits for the lower court judges who authored opinions in this study. *See* Segal & Cover, *supra* note 231. Therefore, no attempt was made to compare case outcomes to the political ideologies or ideological preferences of the judges. In addition, research has documented the influence of numerous other factors on judicial decision making such as the identity of the litigants, public opinion, oral arguments, the influence of other judges, or the presence of amicus briefs. However, it is beyond the scope of this book to measure the correlation between such factors and judicial decision making. Finally, because cases were identified using the Westlaw Key Number system, cases identified were only those that Westlaw editors labeled as addressing the appropriate legal issues and cases analyzed were limited to only those that were reported in the Westlaw database.

judicial decision making, the following definitions were used to identify justifications based on the legal model:

- Textualism, according to John B. Gates and Glenn A. Phelps, is "characterized by an appeal to the plain meaning of the words."[279] Therefore, references in opinions to the meaning of words, including the use of legal or regular dictionaries to interpret the meaning of words in the Constitution or statues, were identified as the use of texualism.

- Originalists hold the view that original intent, or original meaning, is authoritative in interpreting the Constitution.[280] Gates and Phelps defined intentionalist arguments as those that relied on some understanding of some authoritative work of an original framer.[281] Based on earlier work by law professor James G. Wilson,[282] Pamela C. Corley, Robert M. Howard and David C. Nixon identified a number of "originalist" citations used by courts. These include the Federalist Papers, Story's *Commentaries*, Hamilton's works, Madison's papers, and Kent's *Commentaries*.[283] In addition, Wilson argued that references to historical events and studies constitute originalist interpretations.[284] Therefore, originalist justifications as they relate to constitutional interpretations were identified by references and citations to the intent of the framers or other important historical documents such as the Federalist Papers. Intentionalist justifications as they relate to statutory interpretation were identified by references to legislative intent or the legislative record.

- While almost every opinion has multiple citations to previous cases, a rationale was categorized as being based on precedent when a court clearly justified its holding by primarily citing to a precedent as controlling or discussed the role of precedent in the

---

[279] Gates & Phelps, *supra* note 198, at 248. *See also* Eskridge, *supra* note 174 for a description of textualist approaches to statutory interpretation.

[280] *See* BOBBITT, *supra* note 173, at 12-13; Phelps & Gates, *supra* note 173, at 581-84.

[281] Gates & Phelps, *supra* note 198, at 248.

[282] James G. Wilson, The *Most Sacred Text: The Supreme Court's Use of the Federalist Papers*, 1985 BYU L. REV. 65, 129-35 (1985).

[283] Corley, Howard & Nixon, *supra* note 182, at 330.

[284] Wilson, *supra* note 282, at 68.

decision making process. In addition, because judges can deviate from precedent by distinguishing a precedent or limiting a precedent in principle or avoid following precedent in the present case by declaring the reasoning as being contained only in dicta,[285] these rationales were also placed in this category.

In addition, because judicial opinions often rely on rhetorical devices to reach or justify decision making two factors were developed based on the use of rhetorical arguments related to First Amendment theory and liberal democratic theory. Arguments and justifications in opinions that discussed the role of the First Amendment in self-government or as a check on government or invoked other values of freedom of expression in a democracy were categorized as "First Amendment theory." Arguments and justifications that discussed the structure or function of government, democracy, the relationships between the people and government, or the duty of the government to provide for national security in a democracy were classified as democratic theory. Finally, other factors used sporadically but specifically addressed in the text of an opinion that did not fit into any of the factors outlined above were described as closely as possible in the language used by the judge.

Chapter two of the book analyzes cases in which the government sought to impose prior restraints on the press or government employees to prevent dissemination of national security information. First, it examines two cases involving the press, followed by six cases involving government employees. Next, it examines three recent cases in which the constitutionality of certain provisions of the USA Patriot Act have been considered. Finally, these cases are compared to five Supreme Court cases that have dealt with prior restraints imposed by the judiciary. Chapter three examines the only three federal cases identified that have dealt with attempts to impose post-publication punishments on the press or government employees for the dissemination of national security information. The conclusion of the chapter compares these cases to the six Supreme Court cases that have dealt with post-publication punishments of information related to judicial proceedings. Chapter four discusses cases that have' dealt with

---

[285] *See* SEGAL & SPAETH, *supra* note 167, at 82-84.

a variety of access issues. First, it examines six federal cases that have dealt with access to national security information. Next, it discusses four cases that have dealt with access to locations dealing with national security. Finally, in the conclusion of the chapter, these cases are compared to six Supreme Court cases that have dealt with access to judicial proceedings and documents. Chapter five summarizes the findings of the research and identifies a number of patterns and trends in the case law analyzed in the four preceding chapters.

CHAPTER 2

Prior Restraints

Not long after the events of September 11, 2001, the United States government enacted sweeping legislation known as the USA PATRIOT Act.[1] In addition to many other things, the Patriot Act amended § 2709 of Title 18 of the U.S. Code. Originally a part of the Electronic Communications Privacy Act of 1986, § 2709 permitted the Federal Bureau of Investigation (FBI) to subpoena records from electronic communication service providers upon *self-certification* that its request complied with statutory requirements. Both prior to and after the Patriot Act amended the section, FBI demands for information under § 2709 were issued in the form of National Security Letters (NSLs). As amended by the Patriot Act, § 2709 authorized the FBI to issue NSLs "to compel communications firms, such as internet service providers (ISPs) or telephone companies, to produce certain customer records whenever the FBI certifies that those records are 'relevant to an authorized investigation to protect against international terrorism or clandestine intelligence activities.'"[2] In addition, § 2709(c)[3] categorically and permanently barred NSL recipients from ever disclosing the existence of an NSL inquiry in every case to any person—including counsel—in perpetuity, with "no vehicle for the ban to ever be lifted from the recipient or other persons affected, under any

---

[1] Pub. L. 107-56. The acronym stands for "Uniting and Strengthening America by Providing Appropriate Tools Required to Intercept and Obstruct Terrorism Act of 2001."

[2] *Doe v. Ashcroft*, 334 F. Supp. 2d 471, 474-75 (S.D.N.Y. 2005) (hereinafter *Doe I*) (quoting 18 U.S.C. § 2709). Previously, the Act required section 2709 inquiries to be relevant to investigations regarding "a foreign power." As amended this standard was replaced "with a broad standard of relevance to investigations of terrorism or clandestine intelligence activities." *Id*. at 479. *Compare*18 U.S.C. § 2709 (2000) *with*18 U.S.C. § 2709 (Supp. 2003).

[3] 18 U.S.C. § 2709(c) (Supp. 2003) ("No wire or electronic communication service provider, or officer, employee, or agent thereof, shall disclose to *any person* that the Federal Bureau of Investigation has sought or obtained access to information or records under this section.") (emphasis added).

circumstances, either by the FBI itself, or pursuant to judicial process."[4] As Judge Victor Marrero of the Southern District of New York noted, NSLs are "a unique form of administrative subpoena cloaked in secrecy and pertaining to national security issues."[5] As Judge Marrero would later note, NSLs are also powerful tools for gathering information, especially when issued to ISPs.[6]

At some point in time prior to April 2004, an ISP, which would become known in court records as "John Doe," received a NSL.[7] In a document printed on FBI letterhead, Doe was "directed" to provide certain information to the government. In the NSL the FBI "certif[ied] that the information sought [was] relevant to an authorized investigation to protect against international terrorism or clandestine intelligence activities."[8] Doe was "'further advised' that § 2709(c) prohibited him, or his officers, agents, or employees, 'from disclosing to *any person* that the FBI ha[d] sought or obtained access to information or records under'" § 2709.[9] Doe was told to deliver the records "'*personally*' to a designated individual, and to not transmit the records by mail or even mention the NSL in *any* telephone conversation."[10] However, rather than comply with the NSL, Doe consulted lawyers with the American Civil Liberties Union and brought suit in federal district court contending § 2709's "broad subpoena power violate[d] the First, Fourth and Fifth Amendments of the United States Constitution, and that the non-disclosure provision violate[d] the First Amendment."[11] Even though thousands of NSLs had been sent in

---

[4] *Doe I*, 334 F. Supp. 2d at 476.

[5] *Id.* at 475.

[6] *Doe v. Gonzales*, 500 F. Supp. 2d 379, 395 (S.D.N.Y. 2007) (hereinafter *Doe III*).

[7] *Doe I*, 334 F. Supp. 2d at 475. The Southern District of New York granted a government motion to seal the record of the proceedings in order to prevent the disclosure of Doe's identity or any other fact relating to Doe's role in the controversy that arose surrounding the NSL that might have identified Doe or otherwise interfered with the underlying FBI activities. Although court records do not indicate when Doe received the NSL, Doe's lawsuit was filed in April 2004.

[8] *Id.* at 478-79.

[9] *Id.* at 479 (quoting NSL received by Doe) (emphasis added by the court).

[10] *Id.* (quoting NSL received by Doe) (emphasis in the original NSL).

[11] *Id.*

the wake of 9/11, Doe's lawsuit was the first time anyone had ever challenged the constitutionality of § 2709 in a court of law.[12]

In deciding the case, District Judge Marrero presented the key legal issue or frame as a need to balance national security with the fundamental rights guaranteed by the U.S. Constitution. He wrote:

> Like most of our constitutional law's hardest cases, this dispute is about two fundamental principles: values and limits. It centers on the interplay of these concepts, testing the limits of values and the values of limits where their ends collide.
>
> National security is a paramount value, unquestionably one of the highest purposes for which any sovereign government is ordained. Equally scaled among human endeavors is personal security, an interest especially prized in our system of justice in the form of the guarantee bestowed upon the individual to be free from imposition by government of unwarranted restraints on protected fundamental rights.[13]

In order to strike that balance, Judge Marrero called upon a wide range of precedents, as well as statutory and constitutional textual analysis and democratic theory. Among the cases Marrero cited and discussed were several that dealt with prior restraints and national security or prior restraints and the judiciary. Marrero used these precedents to guide him as he attempted to correctly weigh national

---

[12] *Id.* at 502. In September 2004, the Southern District of New York estimated that the government issued hundreds of NSLs between October 2001 and January 2003. However, in March 2007, the Department of Justice's Office of the Inspector General (OIG) reported that according to FBI records, there were approximately 39,000 requests for NSLs in 2003, approximately 56,000 in 2004, and approximately 47,000 in 2005. The OIG also noted that the total number of NSL requests were under-reported by the FBI database used to prepare the report. OFFICE OF THE INSPECTOR GENERAL, U.S. DEPARTMENT OF JUSTICE, A REVIEW OF THE FEDERAL BUREAU OF INVESTIGATION'S USE OF NATIONAL SECURITY LETTERS 120 (2007), *available at* http://www.usdoj.gov/oig/special/s0703b/final.pdf. The reported also noted that after the Patriot Act amendments to section 2709 there was a dramatic increase in NSLs. The FBI reported only approximately 8,500 NSL requests in 2000, the year prior to passage of the Patriot Act. *Id.*

[13] *Doe I*, 334 F. Supp. 2d at 476.

security concerns against freedom of expression values. This chapter examines how those cases and others have established the limits of government's ability to impose prior restraints on the press, government employees, or, as in those cases dealing with § 2709, ISPs, librarians and telephone companies.

First it examines two famous cases, *New York Times Co. v. United States*[14] and *United States v. Progressive Magazine*,[15] which dealt with prior restraints aimed at preventing the publication of national security information. Next, it outlines a number of cases in which courts have considered the constitutionality of secrecy agreements signed by employees or contractors of the United States government. Finally, it explores three recent decisions related to the U.S.A. Patriot Act. In addition, it compares the frameworks and legal factors courts used in these cases to those used by the Supreme Court in cases that dealt with prior restraints and judicial proceedings.

These cases demonstrate the important role framing or issue selection plays in judicial decision making in two ways. First, because many of the litigants and jurists were aware of the U.S. Supreme Court's well-established approach to prior restraints, those seeking to uphold government restrictions most frequently identified the key legal issue as something other than the constitutionality of prior restraints. Second, because in some cases litigants recognized a First Amendment frame might not be strong enough to overcome concerns related to national security, they chose to strategically frame their cases in terms of separation of powers. This approach was used in the first case discussed in this chapter, the famous Pentagon Papers case.

Prior Restraints, National Security and the Press

The seminal case dealing with prior restraints and national security, *New York Times v. United States*,[16] or Pentagon Papers, was the first time the Supreme Court considered a case involving prior restraints and national security. In June 1967, acting without then President Lyndon B. Johnson's knowledge, Secretary of Defense Robert S. McNamara commissioned a "massive forty-seven-volume, 7,000-page top-secret

---

[14] 403 U.S. 713 (1971).
[15] 467 F. Supp. 990 (W.D. Wis. 1979).
[16] 403 U.S. 713.

Pentagon study about U.S. involvement in the Vietnam War."[17] The report, officially titled "History of U.S. Decision Making Process on Vietnam Policy," but now known as the "Pentagon Papers," was written by military officers and civilians who worked in the Pentagon, at universities or for the Rand Corporation.[18] Approximately 4,000 pages of the Pentagon Papers consisted of copies of classified documents from sources such as the White House, the State Department, the Defense Department, the Joint Chiefs of Staff, and the CIA. The remainder was a historical analysis of U.S. policy based on those documents.[19]

In early 1970, Daniel Ellsberg, who contributed to the Pentagon Papers as an employee of the Rand Corporation, temporarily removed the Papers from the premises of the Rand Corporation and made copies.[20] Ellsberg subsequently leaked portions of the document to *New York Times* reporter Neil Sheehan in March 1971. On Saturday, June 13, of that year, the *Times* published its first installment in a series of articles about the Papers. On Monday, June 15, the federal government sought to enjoin the *Times* from further publication in federal district court. When Judge Murray Gurfein issued a temporary restraining order against the *Times* and scheduled further arguments for Friday, June 18,[21] Ellsberg contacted the *Washington Post* and subsequently provided that newspaper with a copy of the Papers. The *Post* published its first installment on the Pentagon Papers Friday morning. In response, the government sought an injunction against the *Post*, which Judge Gerhard Gesell denied after a hearing.[22] On June 19, in New York, Gurfein also denied the government's request for an injunction

---

[17] John Anthony Maltese, *National Security v. Freedom of the Press: New York Times v. United States, in* CREATING CONSTITUTIONAL CHANGE: CLASHES OVER POWER AND LIBERTY IN THE SUPREME COURT 233, 234 (Gregg Ivers & Kevin T. McGuire eds., 2004). For a comprehensive review of the case see generally INSIDE THE PENTAGON PAPERS (John Prados & Maragret Pratt Porter eds., 2005).
[18] Melville B. Nimmer, *National Security Secrets v. Free Speech: The Issues Left Undecided in the Ellsberg Case*, 26 STAN. L. REV. 311, 312 (1974).
[19] Maltese, *supra* note 17, at 234.
[20] Nimmer, *supra* note 18, at 312.
[21] U.S. v. New York Times Co., 328 F. Supp. 324, 325 (D.C.N.Y. 1971).
[22] U.S. v. Washington Post Co., 446 F.2d 1327, 1328 (D.C. Cir. 1971).

against the *Times*.[23] The government appealed to both the Court of Appeals for the Second Circuit and the Court of Appeals for the District of Columbia. Both courts rendered judgment on June 23. While the Second Circuit, sitting en banc, remanded the case to Judge Gurfein by a 5-3 vote, instructing the judge to hold further in camera proceedings,[24] the D.C. Circuit, also sitting en banc, refused to grant the government's injunction. On June 24, around 11 a.m., the *Times* filed a petition for certiorari, a motion for accelerated consideration and an application for interim relief with the United States Supreme Court while the government filed its application for interim relief in the *Post* case around 7:15 p.m. the same day.[25] The next day the Supreme Court consolidated the two cases, granted certiorari and scheduled oral arguments for 11 a.m., Saturday, June 26, 1971,[26] only thirteen days after the initial *New York Times* article containing the Pentagon Papers was published.

In a per curiam opinion followed by six concurring and three dissenting opinions, the Court refused to grant the government's request for an injunction to prevent the *Times*, the *Post* or any other newspaper from publishing articles based on the Pentagon Papers. Quoting and citing three previous prior restraint cases, the Court held that any government attempt to prevent publication came to the Court with a heavy presumption of unconstitutionality.[27] Although the per curiam opinion was too short to delve deeply into any legal issues other than the constitutional bar against prior restraints, in their concurring and dissenting opinions the individual justices outlined several different

---

[23] *New York Times Co.*, 328 F. Supp. at 331.

[24] U.S. v. New York Times Co., 444 F. 2d 544 (2nd Cir. 1971).

[25] New York Times Co. v. U.S., 403 U.S. 713, 753 (1971) (Harlan, J., dissenting).

[26] New York Times Co. v. United States, 403 U.S. 702 (1971). Chief Justice Warren Burger and Justices Blackmun, Harlan, White and Stewart voted to grant expedited review. Justices Black, Douglas, Brennan and Marshall voted to vacate the order of the Court of Appeals for the Second Circuit "except insofar as it affirm[ed] the judgment of the District [Court]" to discontinue the restraint imposed upon the *Times* and deny the petition for certiorari. *See also New York Times Co.*, 403 U.S. at 714-15 (Black, J., concurring).

[27] *New York Times Co.*, 403 U.S. at 713 (per curiam).

legal frames and relied on numerous factors to support their conclusions.

It is important to note that the two most prominent legal issues discussed in the case, the First Amendment and separation of powers issues, were purposefully advanced by the *New York Times*.[28] Political scientist John Anthony Maltese described the decision by the *Times'* lawyer, Alexander Bickel, to advance the separation of powers frame in district court:

> Bickel assumed the [case] would get to the Supreme Court, and his decision to rely on the separation of powers argument was a strategic one. He did not worry about getting the votes of Black and Douglas—he was confident they would side with the *Times*, but he did worry about how to get the votes of centrist justices on the Supreme Court. He believed that they would be more responsive to a narrow separation of powers argument than to a broad First Amendment argument. Thus, he pointed out that neither the Constitution nor Congress had explicitly given the executive branch the authorization to sue for the injunctive relief it sought.[29]

When the case went to the Supreme Court "[t]he *Times* continued to emphasize the separation of powers argument, while the *Post* rested its argument on the First Amendment."[30] While Bickel's strategy ultimately proved successful, it is important to note that both concurring and dissenting justices focused on separation of powers issues to support their divergent opinions.

Justice Hugo Black's concurring opinion most prominently framed the case as dealing with the First Amendment and its absolute ban on abridging speech, although he did briefly invoked a separation of powers argument. Although Black's opinion first addressed the text of

---

[28] *See* Brief for Petitioner New York Times Co. at 2, New York Times Co. v. United States, 403 U.S. 713, No. 1873 (1971).

[29] Maltese, *supra* note 17, at 241.

[30] *Id.* at 243. *Compare* Brief for Petitioner New York Times Co., New York Times Co. v. United States, 403 U.S. 713, No. 1873 (1971), *with* Brief of the Respondents Washington Post Company, New York Times Co. v. United States, 403 U.S. 713, No. 1885 (1971).

the First Amendment and is often cited for this reliance on textualism, Black also used framers' intent to support his contention that the government was absolutely barred from prohibiting the newspapers' publication of the Pentagon Papers, regardless of the documents' source or contents. Black wrote:

> Madison and the other Framers of the First Amendment, able men that they were, wrote in language they earnestly believed could never be misunderstood: "Congress shall make no law . . . abridging the freedom . . . of the press . . . ." Both the *history* and *language* of the First Amendment support the view that the press must be left free to publish news, whatever the source, without censorship, injunctions, or prior restraints.[31]

Additionally, Black used textualism, framers' intent and First Amendment and democratic theory to attack the government's argument that the President had the inherent authority to "'protect the nation against publication of information whose disclosure would endanger the national security" based on "'the constitutional power of the President over the conduct of foreign affairs and his authority as Commander-in-Chief.'"[32] Black wrote that the government was not relying on any act of Congress, but rather making a "bold and dangerously far-reaching contention that courts should take it upon themselves to 'make' a law abridging freedom of the press in the name of equity, presidential power and national security."[33] After once again writing about the First Amendment's "emphatic demands," Black focused heavily on James Madison's vision of the Amendment. Black wrote, "No one can read the history of the adoption of the First Amendment without being convinced beyond any doubt that it was injunctions like those sought here that Madison and his collaborators intended to outlaw in this Nation for all time."[34] Finally, Black evoked

---

[31] *Id.* at 716-17 (Black, J., concurring) (emphasis added).
[32] *Id.* at 718 (Black, J. concurring) (quoting Brief for the United States at 13-14, New York Times Co. v. United States, 403 U.S. 713, Nos. 1873, 1885 (1971)).
[33] *Id.*
[34] *Id.* at 719. In addition, in a footnote Black quoted Madison in order to compare the Solicitor General's arguments to the First Amendment author's intention. *Id.* at 718 n.5.

the First Amendment's role in self-government and framers' intent to support his final attack on the government's position that national security justified prior restraints.[35]

As Black had, Justice William O. Douglas framed the case in terms of the First Amendment questions presented by the parties. However, Douglas also discussed separation of powers, specifically the powers of the executive branch under the Constitution. Citing a number of his own and Black's opinions to support his textual analysis, Douglas clearly stated that the wording of the First Amendment left "no room for governmental restraint on the press."[36] Next, after using textual analysis and legislative intent to determine that the Espionage Act did not apply to the case,[37] Douglas turned to the executive branch's argument that the Constitution afforded it the inherent power to prevent publication of the Papers in the name of national security.

First, Douglas determined that although the text of the Constitution granted the executive branch "war powers," because these powers were tied to a state of war and Congress had not declared war, there was no need to discuss the extent of either the executive or legislative branch's war powers.[38] Next, Douglas quoted *Organization for a Better Austin v. Keefe*[39] for the proposition that "'(a)ny prior restraint on expression comes to this Court with a 'heavy presumption' against its constitutional validity'"[40] and cited *Near v. Minnesota*[41] to support his contention that the executive did not have the power to prevent

---

[35] *Id.* at 719.

[36] *Id.* at 720 (Douglas, J., concurring) (citing Beauharnais v. Illinois, 343 U.S. 250, 267 (1952) (Black, J., dissenting); *id.* at 284 (Douglas, J., dissenting); Roth v. United States, 354 U.S. 476, 508 (1957) (Douglas, J., dissenting); Yates v. United States, 354 U.S. 298, 339 (1957) (Black, J., concurring); New York Times Co. v. Sullivan, 376 U.S. 254, 293 (1964) (Black, J., concurring); Garrison v. Louisiana, 379 U.S. 64, 80 (1964) (Douglas, J., concurring)).

[37] *Id.* at 720-21 (Douglas, J., concurring). Douglas' statutory textual analysis focused on the ability of the government to punish the *Times* and the *Post* for publication after the fact under 18 U.S.C. § 793(e).

[38] *Id.* at 721.

[39] 402 U.S. 415 (1971).

[40] *New York Times Co.*, 403 U.S. at 723 (Douglas, J., concurring) (quoting *Organization for a Better Austin*, 402 U.S. at 419).

[41] 283 U.S. 697 (1931).

publication of a newspaper.[42]   Douglas concluded by invoking both framers' intent and democratic theory.

> The dominant purpose of the First Amendment was to prohibit the widespread practice of governmental suppression of embarrassing information. It is common knowledge that the First Amendment was adopted against the widespread use of the common law of seditious libel to punish the dissemination of material that is embarrassing to the powers-that-be. . . .
> Secrecy in government is fundamentally anti-democratic, perpetuating bureaucratic errors. Open debate and discussion of public issues are vital to our national health. On public questions there should be "uninhibited, robust, and wide-open" debate.[43]

Avoiding a discussion of separation of powers issues, Justice William Brennan's short concurrence framed the case solely as a First Amendment issue and relied on precedent to emphasize his belief that "every restraint issued in this case, whatever its form, has violated the First Amendment—and not less so because that restraint was justified as necessary to afford the courts an opportunity to examine the claim more thoroughly."[44]   Citing precedent, Brennan emphatically declared, "[T]he First Amendment tolerates absolutely no prior judicial restraints of the press predicated upon surmise or conjecture that untoward consequences may result"[45] and "'[t]he chief purpose of (the First Amendment's) guaranty (is) to prevent previous restraints upon publication.'"[46]   Additionally, countering the dissenters arguments about the need to restrain free expression rights during times of war, Brennan noted that the country was not technically at war and, even if it were, the government had made no showing that its actions were

---

[42] *New York Times Co.*, 403 U.S. at 723 (Douglas, J., concurring).
[43] *Id.* at 723-24 (quoting New York Times v. Sullivan, 376 U.S. 254, 269-70 (1964)).
[44] *Id.* at 727 (Brennan, J., concurring).
[45] *Id.* at 725-26 (citing Freedman v. Maryland, 380 U.S. 51 (1965) and quoting Roth v. United States, 354 U.S. 476, 481 (1957) in a footnote).
[46] *Id.* at 726 (quoting *Near*, 283 U.S. at 713).

justified under the standard established in previous First Amendment cases.[47]

Justice Potter Stewart's concurring opinion identified two frames or legal issues presented by the case. While his opinion initially discussed the First Amendment and the balance between a free press and national security, ultimately, he too framed the case as dealing with separation of powers issues. First, Stewart discussed presidential power, national security and First Amendment theories related to both self-government and the checking function of the press. He wrote, "In the governmental structure created by our Constitution, the Executive is endowed with enormous power in the two related areas of national defense and international relations."[48] Stewart reasoned that because this power was "largely unchecked by the Legislative and Judicial branches" and had "been pressed to the very hilt since the advent of the nuclear missile age" it was especially important the press be allowed to act as a check on government power.[49]

> In the absence of the governmental checks and balances present in other areas of our national life, the only effective restraint upon executive policy and power in the areas of national defense and international affairs may lie in an enlightened citizenry—in an informed and critical public opinion which alone can here protect the values of democratic government. For this reason, it is perhaps here that a press that is alert, aware, and free most vitally serves the basic purpose of the First Amendment. For without an informed and free press there cannot be an enlightened people.[50]

Next, however, Stewart cautioned that press freedom must be balanced with national security and discussed the power of the executive at length. Stewart wrote that it was "elementary" that the "maintenance of an effective national defense require[s] both

---

[47] *Id.* at 726.
[48] *Id.* at 728 (Stewart, J., concurring).
[49] *Id.*
[50] *Id.*

confidentiality and secrecy."[51] Quoting a lengthy passage from *United States v. Curtiss-Wright Export Corp*[52] about the power and responsibilities of the executive branch,[53] as well as constitutional structure, Stewart concluded "as a matter of sovereign prerogative . . . not of law" the power and responsibility to protect national security information rested solely with the executive branch.[54] Yet despite this seeming endorsement of the executive branch's national security powers, Stewart reasoned that the Court's holding against the government was inevitable because Congress had enacted no law allowing for prior restraints.

> [I]n the cases before us we are asked neither to construe specific regulations nor to apply specific laws. We are asked, instead, to perform a function that the Constitution gave to the Executive, not the Judiciary. . . . I am convinced that the Executive is correct with respect to some of the documents involved. But I cannot say that disclosure of any of them will surely result in direct, immediate, and irreparable damage to our Nation or its people. That being so, there can under the First Amendment be but one judicial resolution of the issues before us. I join the judgments of the Court.[55]

Thus, although Stewart relied on constitutional interpretation while framing the case in terms of the executive's power to advance national security and the role of the judiciary under the Constitution, he did not explicitly use textualism or originalism to support his conclusions. Instead he primarily examined democratic and First Amendment theories.

Justice Byron White's concurring opinion also framed the case as dealing with the separation of power issues presented by the case and

---

[51] *Id.*

[52] 299 U.S. 304 (1936).

[53] *New York Times Co.,* 403 U.S. at 730 n.3 (Stewart, J., concurring) (citing *Curtiss-Wright Exprot Corp.,* 299 U.S. at 320).

[54] *Id.* at 728-30. Stewart did note that Congress had the power to pass legislation that might punish the press for the publication of national security information after the fact and it would be the courts' role to interpret that law.

[55] *Id.* at 730.

advanced by Bickel's brief. Although his opinion began by echoing the per curiam opinion's assessment that the government "ha[d] not satisfied the very heavy burden that it must meet to warrant an injunction against publication" under the First Amendment,[56] the majority of White's opinion focused on textual analysis of congressional legislation. White's main concern in the case was "the absence of express and appropriately limited congressional authorization for prior restraints in circumstances such as these."[57] White noted that without statutory authorization, the government's case rested on an interpretation of the Constitution that gave the executive branch a tremendous amount of power, a proposition with which he could not agree.

> At least in the absence of legislation by Congress, based on its own investigations and findings, I am quite unable to agree that the inherent powers of the Executive and the courts reach so far as to authorize remedies having such sweeping potential for inhibiting publications by the press. . . . To sustain the Government in these cases would start the courts down a long and hazardous road that I am not willing to travel, at least without congressional guidance and direction.[58]

After noting the difference between prior restraints and post-publication punishments,[59] White spent the remainder of his opinion using legislative intent,[60] statutory textual analysis[61] and precedent[62] to determine if post-publication sanctions were appropriate under current statutory schemes. Based on these factors, White concluded that the executive was not authorized to prevent the newspapers from publishing. White wrote:

---

[56] *Id.* at 730-31 (White, J., concurring). Despite his concurrence in the present case, White was clear that he did not think that all prior restraints were unconstitutional. *See id.* at 731 n.1.

[57] *Id.* at 731.

[58] *Id.* at 732.

[59] *Id.* at 733.

[60] *Id.* at 733-34; *id.* at 740 n.9.

[61] *Id.* at 735-40.

[62] *Id.* at 739.

It is thus clear that Congress has addressed itself to the problems of protecting the security of the country and the national defense from unauthorized disclosure of potentially damaging information. It has not, however, authorized the injunctive remedy against threatened publication. It has apparently been satisfied to rely on criminal sanctions and their deterrent effect on the responsible as well as the irresponsible press.[63]

Because he focused so much on legislation, White's opinion was less about whether the First Amendment prohibited prior restraints on the press and more about the question of whether Congress had granted the President the authority to seek an injunction.

The final concurring opinion was written by Justice Thurgood Marshall, who also focused on separation of powers issues. From the outset of his opinion, Marshall wrote that the primary legal question was not whether the First Amendment barred prior restraints but whether the judiciary or the legislative branch had the power to make laws. Marshall wrote: "I believe the ultimate issue in this case is even more basic than the one posed by the Solicitor General. The issue is whether this Court or the Congress has the power to make law."[64]

Citing precedent, Marshall conceded that the President had broad authority under his responsibility to conduct foreign affairs and his role as commander-in-chief[65] and that in some situations there might a basis for the government to invoke the equity jurisdiction of the Supreme Court in order to "prevent the publication of material damaging to 'national security.'"[66] However, Marshall concluded, "It would . . . be utterly inconsistent with the concept of separation of powers for this Court to use its power of contempt to prevent behavior that Congress has specifically declined to prohibit."[67] Citing *Youngstown Sheet and*

---

[63] *Id.* at 740.
[64] *Id.* at 741 (Marshall, J., concurring).
[65] *Id.* at 741-42 (citing Chicago & Southern Air Lines v. Waterman S.S. Corp., 333 U.S. 103 (1948); Kiyoshi Hirabayashi v. United States, 320 U.S. 81, 93 (1943); United States v. Curtiss-Wright Export Corp., 299 U.S. 304 (1936)).
[66] *Id.* at 742.
[67] *Id.*

Tube Co. v. Sawyer,[68] Marshall wrote, "The Constitution provides that Congress shall make laws, the President execute laws, and courts interpret laws."[69] Using statutory textual analysis[70] as well as legislative intent,[71] Marshall determined that Congress had specifically declined to provide the executive branch with the power to stop publication by the newspapers. For this reason, Marshall concluded the Court had no authority to grant the executive branch the injunction it was seeking.[72] Marshall wrote, "It is not for this Court to fling itself into every breach perceived by some Government official nor is it for this Court to take on itself the burden of enacting law, especially a law that Congress has refused to pass."[73]

The three dissenting opinions reached different conclusions about the case than the majority, yet two of the three also framed the case in terms of the First Amendment and separation of powers. In addition, however, the dissenting opinions focused more heavily on balancing the First Amendment rights of the newspapers against national security concerns and used a frame not discussed in any of the concurring opinions. The dissenting opinions raised the issue of proper judicial procedures, discussing the impropriety of deciding a case that had come to the Court with such great speed and the unknown contents of the Pentagon Papers. Chief Justice Burger and Justice Harry Blackmun, both of whom would have remanded the cases,[74] identified two key legal issues. First, they both wrote of the need to balance national security concerns with First Amendment values. Second, each discussed the haste with which the case came to the Court and the lack of facts about the content of the Pentagon Papers.

Although Burger agreed with the majority that the constitutional limitation on prior restraints was so clear the Court rarely had to

---

[68] 343 U.S. 579 (1952).

[69] *New York Times Co.*, 403 U.S. at 742 (Marshall, J., concurring) (citing *Youngstown*, 343 U.S. 579).

[70] *Id.* at 743-46 (discussing the text of 18 U.S.C. § 793).

[71] *Id.* at 745-46 (discussing legislative intent and the difference between prior restraints and post-publication punishments).

[72] *Id.* at 747.

[73] *Id.*

[74] *Id.* at 752 (Burger, C.J., dissenting); *id.* at 761-62 (Blackmun, J., dissenting).

consider a case, he wrote that fact did not make the case simple.[75] According to Burger, cases involving national security and free expression were always difficult because "the imperative of a free and unfettered press comes into collision with another imperative, the effective functioning of a complex modern government and specifically the effective exercise of certain constitutional powers of the Executive."[76] While this alone made these kinds of cases difficult, Burger wrote that the present cases were even more difficult to decide because of their undeveloped nature and the Court's lack of knowledge about the contents of the documents in question. Burger wrote that contrary to the newspapers' claims, the First Amendment was not absolute, and the contents of the Pentagon Papers should determine how much protection the Amendment provided to the newspapers.

> The newspapers make a derivative claim under the First Amendment; they denominate this right as the public "right to know" . . . . The right is asserted as an absolute. Of course, the First Amendment right itself is not an absolute, as Justice Holmes so long ago pointed out in his aphorism concerning the right to shout "fire" in a crowded theater if there was no fire. There are other exceptions, some of which Chief Justice Hughes mentioned by way of example in *Near v. Minnesota*. There are no doubt other exceptions no one has had occasion to describe or discuss. Conceivably such exceptions may be lurking in these cases and would have been flushed had they been properly considered in the trial courts, free from unwarranted deadlines and frenetic pressures.[77]

Quoting Justice Oliver Wendell Holmes admonition that "[g]reat cases make bad laws"[78] because of the sensationalism involved, Blackmun wrote that there would be no harm in letting the cases

---

[75] *Id.* at 748 (Burger, C.J., dissenting).
[76] *Id.*
[77] *Id.* at 749.
[78] *Id.* at 759 (Blackmun, J., dissenting) (quoting Northern Securities Co. v. United States, 193 U.S. 197, 400-01 (1904) (Holmes, J., dissenting).

develop in the lower courts on a regular schedule.[79] Blackmun then turned to the issue of balancing constitutional provisions. "The First Amendment, after all, is only one part of an entire Constitution. Article II of the great document vests in the Executive Branch primary power over the conduct of foreign affairs and places in that branch the responsibility for the Nation's safety," he wrote.[80]

To support his argument that the First Amendment was not absolute, Blackmun relied on precedent. First, he cited *Near* and *Schenck v. United States*[81] for the general proposition that First Amendment absolutism had never commanded a majority of the Court.[82] He then quoted Holmes' opinion from *Schenck*: "When a nation is at war many things that might be said in time of peace are such a hindrance to its effort that their utterance will not be endured so long as men fight and that no Court could regard them as protected by any constitutional right.'"[83] Thus, while Blackmun admitted under different circumstances his vote might change, under the current rushed circumstance of the cases and his view that First Amendment rights needed to be balanced against national security concerns, he dissented.[84]

The third dissenter, Justice John Marshall Harlan II, framed the case as dealing totally with separation of powers. However, Harlan focused solely on presidential and judicial powers without discussing the powers of the legislative branch as the majority opinions had. Although he discussed the timeline of events and the "difficult questions of fact, of law, and of judgment presented by the case," to Harlan, the most important issue was the judiciary's power to review executive decisions based on national security concerns. He wrote:

> It is plain to me that the scope of the judicial function in passing upon the activities of the Executive Branch of the Government in the field of foreign affairs is very narrowly

---

[79] *Id.* at 760-61.
[80] *Id.* at 761 (Blackmun, J., dissenting).
[81] 249 U.S. 47 (1919).
[82] *New York Times Co.*, 403 U.S. at 761(citing Near v. Minnesota, 283 U.S. 697, 708 (1931) and Schenck v. United States, 249 U.S. 47, 52 (1919)).
[83] *Id.* at 761 (quoting *Schenck*, 249 U.S. at 52).
[84] *Id.* at 762.

restricted. This view is, I think, dictated by the concept of separation of powers upon which our constitutional system rests.[85]

To support this conclusion, Harlan relied upon both framers' intent and precedent. First, Harlan quoted a pre-Supreme Court appointment speech of John Marshall as well as statements of George Washington regarding his refusal to hand over documents pertaining to the Jay Treaty to Congress.[86] Next Harlan relied on the rationale of the Supreme Court's decision in *United States v. Reynolds*,[87] the case that created the states secrets doctrine.[88] Harlan wrote that although "Constitutional considerations forbid 'a complete abandonment of judicial control,'"[89] the Court's only roles in matters related to national security information were to determine if the dispute involved national security and that disclosure decisions were made by the proper official.[90] To Harlan, beyond these two functions, the Court had no role. Harlan quoted Supreme Court precedent to reinforce this conclusion:

> "[T]he very nature of executive decisions as to foreign policy is political, not judicial. Such decisions are wholly confided by our Constitution to the political departments of the government, Executive and Legislative. They are delicate, complex, and involve large elements of prophecy. They are and should be undertaken only by those directly responsible to the people whose welfare they advance or imperil. They are decisions of a kind for which the Judiciary has neither aptitude, facilities nor responsibility and have long been held

---

[85] *Id.* at 756.
[86] *Id.* at 756-57.
[87] 345 U.S. 1 (1953).
[88] As noted in chapter one, the states secret doctrine is an evidentiary privilege that belongs to the executive branch. It allows the executive branch to prevent the disclosure in court of any evidence the executive deems detrimental to national security. See *id.* at 7-10 for an explanation of the doctrine.
[89] *New York Times Co.*, 403 U.S. at 757 (quoting *Reynolds*, 345 U.S. at 8).
[90] *Id.*

to belong in the domain of political power not subject to judicial intrusion or inquiry."[91]

Based on the executive branch's constitutional role in matters related to national security, Harlan would have continued the restraints on publication and directed the lower courts to give the proper deference to the executive branch, a "a co-equal branch of the Government operating within the field of its constitutional prerogative."[92]

Thus, although in some ways the Pentagon Papers was a highly fractured decision—Harlan's opinion was the only one to gather more than one other justice—the opinions framed the case in similar ways. Seven of the justices—Black, Douglas, Brennan, Stewart, White, Burger, and Blackmun—framed the case as dealing with the First Amendment. While the concurring opinions and Harlan's dissenting opinion focused on different aspects of separation of powers arguments, a majority of the justices—Black, Douglas, Stewart, White, Marshall, and Harlan—at least addressed the issue, if only in a footnote. This focus on separation of powers and the role of the judiciary in national security would become a theme throughout many later decisions dealing with national security information. While the Supreme Court has never addressed a case quite like the *New York Times v. United States*, a U.S. district court in Wisconsin heard a case with a similar set of facts, but came to a very different conclusion.

In 1979, *The Progressive*, a political magazine founded in 1909 by Wisconsin Senator Robert La Follette, assigned freelance writer Howard Morland to write an article detailing how to build a hydrogen bomb, which would eventually be titled "The H-Bomb Secret: How We Got It-Why We're Telling It."[93] The information in the article was prepared using environmental impact statements, books, articles, personal interviews, and private speculation, rather than classified information.[94] According to court records, *The Progressive*

---

[91] *Id.* at 757-58 (quoting Chicago & Southern Air Lines, Inc. v. Waterman Steamship Corp., 333 U.S. 103, 111 (1948)).

[92] *Id.* at 758.

[93] Ian M. Dumain, *Seminal Issues as Viewed Through the Lens of the Progressive Case: No Secret, No Defense:* United States v. Progressive, 26 CARDOZO L. REV. 1323, 1325-26 (2005).

[94] *Id.* at 1326. The text of the article is available at

commissioned the article to alert people "to the false illusion of security created by the government's futile efforts at secrecy."[95] The magazine argued that the publication would "provide the people with needed information to make informed decisions on an urgent issue of public concern."[96] Upon receiving a copy from a political science professor at the Massachusetts Institute of Technology, the Department of Energy (DOE) offered to rewrite the article in order to prevent the revelation of the process that triggers a hydrogen explosion.[97] When *The Progressive* informed the DOE that it would be publishing the article "as-is," the government sought a temporary restraining order preventing publication of the article. On March 9, 1979, after hearing from both parties, a federal district court judge issued a temporary restraining order enjoining the defendants, their employees, and agents from publishing or otherwise communicating or disclosing in any manner any restricted data contained in the article.[98] On March 26 the court held a temporary injunction hearing and released its opinion that day.[99]

In deciding to uphold his restraining order, District Judge Robert Willis Warren squarely framed the key legal issue of the case as "a basic confrontation between the First Amendment right to freedom of the press and national security,"[100] topics which Warren called "deep and fundamental principles of democratic philosophy."[101] Warren summed up the two sides of the argument:

> The government argues that its national security interest also permits it to impress classification and censorship upon information originating in the public domain, if when drawn together, synthesized and collated, such information acquires

---

http://www.progressive.org/images/pdf/1179.pdf.

[95] United States v. Progressive, Inc., 467 F. Supp. 990, 994 (W.D. Wis. 1979), *reconsideration denied*, 486 F. Supp. 15 (W.D. Wisc. 1979), *dismissed*, 610 F.2d 819 (7th Cir. 1979).

[96] *Id.*

[97] Dumain, *supra* note 93, at 1326.

[98] United States v. Progressive, Inc., 467 F. Supp. 990, 990 (W.D. Wisc. 1979).

[99] *Id.*

[100] *Id.* at 995.

[101] *Id.* at 992.

the character of presenting immediate, direct and irreparable harm to the interests of the United States.

Defendants argue that freedom of expression as embodied in the First Amendment is so central to the heart of liberty that prior restraint in any form becomes anathema. They contend that this is particularly true when a nation is not at war and where the prior restraint is based on surmise or conjecture. While acknowledging that freedom of the press is not absolute, they maintain that the publication of the projected article does not rise to the level of immediate, direct and irreparable harm which could justify incursion into First Amendment freedoms.[102]

To support his conclusion, Warren relied upon First Amendment theory, precedent, textual analysis of the Atomic Energy Act,[103] framers' intent and democratic theory.

Warren's opinion began by laying out support for each side's claim. First, he wrote that one of the most fundamental aspects of a democratic society was its devotion to freedom of the speech and of the press[104] and focused on precedent to establish the limits of First Amendment protection. Citing the *New York Times v. United States*, he wrote that "any prior restraint on publication comes into court under a heavy presumption against its constitutional validity."[105] Next, however, he cited Justice Felix Frankfurter's dissent in *Bridges v. California*[106] and Holmes' opinion in *Schneck v. United States*[107] for the proposition that First Amendment rights were not absolute.[108] Finally, his opinion emphasized the Supreme Court's ruling in *Near v. Minnesota*[109] that there was an "extremely narrow area, involving

---

[102] *Id.* at 991-92.
[103] 42 U.S.C. § 2271-2281.
[104] *Progressive*, 467 F. Supp. at 992.
[105] *Id.*
[106] 314 U.S. 252 (1941).
[107] 249 U.S. 47, 52 (1919).
[108] *Progressive*, 467 F. Supp. at 992 (quoting *Bridges*, 314 U.S. at 282 (Frankfurter, J., dissenting) and *Schneck*, 249 U.S. at 52).
[109] 283 U.S. 697 (1931).

national security in which interference with First Amendment rights might be tolerated."[110]

Next, Warren examined the government's interest in protecting national security that needed to be balanced against the *Progressive's* First Amendment rights. Summing up the government's "right" in the case, as well as the problem with this "right," in just two paragraphs, Warren wrote:

> Juxtaposed against the right to freedom of expression is the government's contention that the national security of this country could be jeopardized by publication of the article.
>
> The Court is convinced that the government has a right to classify certain sensitive documents to protect its national security. The problem is with the scope of the classification system.[111]

The problem Warren faced was that the information contained in the article was not obtained from classified government information and much of it was in the public domain. However, despite these facts, the court ruled that the information was indeed dangerous to national security. The court gave a number of reasons for its decision. First, the court found that although the article was not a "do-it yourself" guide on how to build a hydrogen bomb and much of the information contained in the article was already in the public domain, the article "could accelerate the membership of a candidate nation in the thermonuclear club."[112] Second, the court found "no plausible reason why the public needs to know the technical details about hydrogen bomb construction to carry on an informed debate on this issue."[113]

The court then returned to precedent, noting several reasons why *New York Times Co. v. United States* was not a controlling precedent. Warren reasoned that the Pentagon Papers contained historical data, relating to events that occurred some three to twenty years previously. In addition, he pointed out that the government had advanced no

---

[110] *Progressive*, 467 F. Supp. at 992.
[111] *Id.* at 992-93.
[112] *Id.* at 994.
[113] *Id.*

reasons why the articles affected national security except that publication might cause embarrassment to the United States.[114] Finally, in order to further differentiate the two cases, Warren turned to the Atomic Energy Act itself.

Focusing on textual analysis, Warren held that the terms used in the statute—"communicates, transmits or discloses"—clearly included publishing in a magazine.[115] In addition, he held that the government had shown that *The Progressive* had reason to believe that the data in the article, if published, would injure the United States or give an advantage to a foreign nation. He wrote:

> Extensive reading and studying of the documents on file lead to the conclusion that not all the data is [sic] available in the public realm in the same fashion, if it is available at all. What is involved here is information dealing with the most destructive weapon in the history of mankind, information of sufficient destructive potential to nullify the right to free speech and to endanger the right to life itself.[116]

Finally, the opinion noted that the Atomic Energy Act contained statutory authorization for the attorney general to seek an injunction against publication[117] while in *New York Times Co. v. United States* the Supreme Court took into account the fact that Congress had not specifically authorized an injunction.[118]

Leaving behind precedent and textual analysis, the court turned to originalism and democratic theory. Warren wrote:

> Our Founding Fathers believed, as we do, that one is born with certain inalienable rights which, as the Declaration of Independence intones, include the right to life, liberty and the

---

[114] *Id.*

[115] *Id.* at 995.

[116] *Id.*

[117] 42 U.S.C. § 2280.

[118] *See* New York Times v. United States, 403 U.S. 713, 718 (Black, J., concurring); *id.* at 721-22 (Douglas, J., concurring); *id.* at 730 (Stewart, J., concurring); *id.* at 731 (White, J., concurring); *id.* at 742 (Marshall, J., concurring).

> pursuit of happiness. The Constitution, including the Bill of
> Rights, was enacted to make those rights operable in everyday
> life.[119]

The court used framers' intent to reach a conclusion on how to balance
national security with freedom of the press. Rather than focusing on
the relative values of each, however, Warren focused on the
consequences of his decision, determining that it was safer to error on
the side of national security.

> While it may be true in the long-run, as Patrick Henry
> instructs us, that one would prefer death to life without liberty,
> nonetheless, in the short-run, one cannot enjoy freedom of
> speech, freedom to worship or freedom of the press unless one
> first enjoys the freedom to live.
> . . .
> A mistake in ruling against *The Progressive* will seriously
> infringe cherished First Amendment rights. . . . It will curtail
> defendants' First Amendment rights in a drastic and
> substantial fashion. It will infringe upon our right to know and
> to be informed as well.
> A mistake in ruling against the United States could pave the
> way for thermonuclear annihilation for us all. In that event,
> our right to life is extinguished and the right to publish
> becomes moot.[120]

While the case might have made for an important Supreme Court
precedent, it never made it to the High Court. After the district court's
decision, the U.S. Court of Appeals for the Seventh Circuit scheduled
oral arguments for September 13, 1979.[121]   Before the Seventh
Circuit's opinion was announced, however, *The Madison Press*

---

[119] *Progressive*, 467 F. Supp. at 995-96.
[120] *Id.*
[121] Morland v. Sprecher, 443 U.S. 709, 709 (1979). When *The Progressive*'s
motion for an expedited hearing was denied, the magazine petitioned the
Supreme Court for a *writ of mandamus* ordering the Seventh Circuit to expedite
the appeal. In a per curiam opinion the Court denied the motion. *Id.*

Connection published a letter detailing the contents at issue in *The Progressive* case.[122]   The government, conceding that the secret was out, announced it was abandoning the case.[123]

Prior Restraints, National Security and Government Employees
While only two federal cases have involved prior restraints on the media in the interest of national security, a number of cases have considered national security-based restrictions on government employee speech. In 1972, just one year after the Supreme Court ruled the government could not stop newspapers from publishing national security information in the Pentagon Papers case, the Fourth Circuit heard a case in which the Central Intelligence Agency (CIA) sought to enjoin a former employee from publishing a proposed book in violation of a "secrecy agreement" and "secrecy oath."

United States v. Marchetti[124] began in March 1972 when the United States sought a temporary restraining order against Victor L. Marchetti, a former executive assistant to the deputy director of the CIA.[125] Based on a secrecy agreement signed by Marchetti when he was hired by the CIA and a secrecy oath he took upon his retirement, the U.S. District Court for the Eastern District of Virginia ordered Marchetti to submit to the CIA "any writing, fictional or non-fictional, relating to the Agency or to intelligence" thirty days in advance of release to any person or corporation and ordered him "not to release any writing relating to the Agency or to intelligence without prior authorization from the Director of Central Intelligence or from his designated representative."[126] The government claimed that an article Marchetti submitted to *Esquire* and six other publishers about his experience as a CIA agent contained "classified information concerning intelligence sources, methods and operations."[127]   In addition, Marchetti had submitted a book proposal about his intelligence experiences to a publisher.[128] Citing the Supreme Court's decision in

---

[122] Dumain, *supra* note 93, at 1331-32.
[123] *Id.* at 1332.
[124] 446 F.2d 1309 (4th Cir. 1972).
[125] *Id.* at 1311.
[126] *Id.*
[127] *Id.* at 1313.
[128] *Id.*

New York Times v. United States,[129] Marchetti contended that his First Amendment rights prohibited the government from imposing any prior restraints upon him and appealed the order.[130]

In an opinion by Chief Judge Clement Haynsworth, who later would be nominated to the U.S. Supreme Court by Richard M. Nixon but not confirmed by the Senate,[131] the Fourth Circuit held that the secrecy agreement Marchetti signed was "constitutional and otherwise reasonable and lawful."[132] In his opinion, Haynsworth identified many of the same legal questions that the Supreme Court discussed in *New York Times v. United States*. The court framed the case mainly in terms of balancing freedom of speech and government secrecy, discussing the government's "right to secrecy." However, near the end of his opinion, Haynsworth discussed separation of powers issues as well. To support his conclusion that Marchetti could be prohibited from disclosing information, Haynsworth focused heavily on precedent and, to a lesser extent, on the text of the Constitution and originalism.

Although Haynsworth acknowledged the case implicated Marchetti's First Amendment rights, he began by quoting and citing a number of Supreme Court cases to point out that freedom of speech was not absolute. First, as Judge Warren would later do in *Progressive*, Haynsworth quoted Frankfurter's dissenting opinion in *Bridges v. California*[133] to contend that although freedom of speech was valuable in a democratic society, there were other competing interests that were equally as important.[134] Second, Haynsworth quoted Brennan's opinion for the Court in *Roth v. United States*[135] to establish that, despite its absolute language, the First Amendment was not intended to "protect every utterance" and it was important to consider the intent behind the Amendment.[136] Finally, the opinion cited a number of prior

---

[129] *Id.*

[130] *Id.* at 1311.

[131] *See* Dean J. Kotlowski, *Trial by Error: Nixon, the Senate, and the Haynsworth Nomination*, 1 PRESIDENTIAL STUD. Q. 71 (1996).

[132] *Marchetti,*446 F.2d at 1311.

[133] 314 U.S. 242 (1941).

[134] *Marchetti*, 446 F.2d at 1314. (quoting *Bridges*, 314 U.S. at 293) (Frankfurter, J., dissenting).

[135] 354 U.S. 476 (1957).

[136] *Marchetti,* 446 F.2d at 1314. (quoting *Roth,* 354 U.S. at 483).

restraint cases to show that threats, bribes, extortion, the publication of military information during times of war, speech by prisoners, and the publication of racially discriminatory housing advertisements were not fully protected by the First Amendment.[137]

Haynsworth next used textualism, precedent and originalism to support his argument that the government had a "right to secrecy." First, he cited the text of the Constitution, writing, "Gathering intelligence information and the other activities of the Agency, including clandestine affairs against other nations, are all within the President's constitutional responsibility for the security of the Nation as the Chief Executive and as Commander in Chief of our Armed forces."[138] Next he turned to two precedents cited in *New York Times v. United States* — *United States v. Curtiss-Wright Export Corp.*[139] and *Chicago & Southern Air Lines, Inc. v. Waterman Steamship Corp.*[140] — to demonstrate that the Supreme Court had recognized the government's "need for secrecy,"[141] as well as a third, *E.W. Bliss Co. v. United States*,[142] which had upheld the constitutionality of a government secrecy agreement with "a private contractor who claimed the right to divulge the details of a torpedo to other potential customers."[143] Focusing on constitutional text and original intent to bolster his citation of precedent, Haynsworth concluded, "Although the First Amendment protects criticism of the government, nothing in the Constitution requires the government to divulge information."[144]

Having established both the limits of the First Amendment and the government's "right to secrecy," Haynsworth then appeared ready to

---

[137] *Id.* at 1314-15.
[138] *Id.* at 1315 (citing U.S. Const. art. II, § 2).
[139] 299 U.S. 304 (1936).
[140] 333 U.S. 103 (1948).
[141] *Marchetti,* 446 F.2d at 1315 (quoting *Curtiss-Wright Export Corp.,* 299 U.S. at 320, and *Chicago & Southern Air Lines, Inc.,* 333 U.S. at 111).
[142] 248 U.S. 37 (1918).
[143] *Marchetti,* 446 F.2d at 1315 (quoting *E.W. Bliss Co.,* 248 U.S. at 46).
[144] *Id.* at 1315-16. Haynsworth quoted with approval a lengthy passage from a law review article about the Pentagon Papers case by Columbia University law professor Louis Henkin. *See* Louis Henkin, *The Right to Know and the Duty to Withhold: The Case of the Pentagon Papers,* 120 U. PA. L. REV. 271, 273-74 (1971).

balance Marchetti's First Amendment claim against the government's interest in keeping him quiet. However, Haynsworth determined that because the CIA's secrecy agreement was "entirely appropriate"[145] and "the Government's need for secrecy in this area lends justification to a system of prior restraint against disclosure by employees and former employees,"[146] the secrecy agreement in and of itself was enforceable because by preventing him from divulging only *classified* information the agreement was not a violation of Marchetti's First Amendment rights.[147] Thus, although he discussed the theoretical need to balance freedom of expression and government secrecy, in the end, Haynsworth found no need to actually do so.

However, Haynsworth also concluded that because First Amendment rights were involved, Marchetti was entitled to judicial review.[148] Yet, in another twist, Haynsworth then invoked a separation of powers frame to assert there was "no practical reason" for judicial review. Based on the text of the Constitution,[149] as well as on practical concerns related to the ability of judges to determine what information might harm national security,[150] Haynsworth concluded the only questions fit for a judge to answer were "whether or not the information was classified and, if so, whether or not, by prior disclosure, it had come into the public domain."[151]

Interestingly, it was this final section of Haynsworth's opinion that elicited a response from Judge James B. Craven, Jr. Although Craven concurred in the judgment of the court, in contrast to Haynsworth's assertion that the judiciary had no role to play in the classification of information, Craven was not willing to defer totally to the executive branch. Craven discussed the First Amendment's role in self-governance and the public's "right to know."

> [H]owever difficult the adjudication of the reasonableness of a
> secrecy classification, I cannot subscribe to a flat rule that it

---

[145] *Id.* at 1316.
[146] *Id.* at 1316-17.
[147] *Id.* at 1317.
[148] *Id.*
[149] *Id.*
[150] *Id.*
[151] *Id.* at 1318.

may never be attempted. The "right to know" is in a period of gestation. I think that the people will increasingly insist upon knowing what their government is doing and that, because this knowledge is vital to government by the people, the "right to know" will grow. I am not yet ready to foreclose any inquiry into whether or not secrecy classifications are reasonable. To protect those that are does not require that we also protect the frivolous and the absurd.[152]

Despite Craven's concurrence, Haynsworth's argument that the judiciary was ill-suited to deal with classified information again won a majority of votes four years later when the Fourth Circuit heard arguments in *Alfred A. Knopf, Inc. v. Colby*,[153] the "sequel" to *Marchetti*. In that case, Haynsworth focused heavily on separation of powers issues and the practical problems associated with the judiciary and national security information.

After the Fourth Circuit's decision in *Marchetti*, Marchetti and John Marks, a former employee of the State Department who had also signed a non-disclosure agreement, prepared a manuscript for Alfred A. Knopf, Inc. After reviewing the manuscript, the CIA required the deletion of 339 items said to contain classified information. After reviewing the items with Marchetti and his lawyer, the CIA agreed that all but approximately 168 of the deletions could be published.[154] Alfred A. Knopf, Inc., Marchetti and Marks brought action in the U.S. District Court for the Southern District of New York, seeking an order that would permit the publication of the remaining contested items. On motion of the defendants, William Colby, then Director of the CIA, and Henry Kissinger, then Secretary of State, the case was transferred to the Eastern District of Virginia, "where the *Marchetti* case had been tried

---

[152] *Id.* at 1318-19 (Craven, J., concurring).

[153] 509 F.2d 1362 (4th Cir. 1975).

[154] *Id.* at 1365. The opinion states that initially 339 items contained classified information. However, "after a conference with Marchetti and his lawyer, the CIA agreed to release 114 of the deletions. Later another 29 deletion items were released and still later another 57." Although it would seem from this statement that there were 139 items the CIA still claimed were classified, the court wrote that there were "168 deletion items upon which the CIA stood fast." It is unclear where this apparent discrepancy in numbers comes from.

and where it could come before the same judge who had tried *Marchetti.*"[155]

After being presented at trial with evidence related to the CIA's review of Marchetti's manuscript, the district judge ruled that the CIA was making "ad hoc" decisions about whether the information in the manuscript was classified without any real proof that the information was properly classified.[156] In short, the judge believed that the standards established by the Fourth Circuit in *Marchetti* to protect Marchetti's and Mark's First Amendment rights required the government to show "strict proof" that the material contained classified information.[157] Although the trial judge admitted that much of the information in the manuscript might be sensitive, he ruled that such information was not properly classified until "a classifying officer makes a conscious determination that the governmental interest in secrecy outweighs a general policy of disclosure and applies a label of 'Top Secret' or 'Secret' or 'Confidential' to the information in question."[158]

Shifting its stance slightly from *Marchetti*, the Fourth Circuit held that the judiciary had a somewhat larger role in classification decisions than it had previously indicated. Although Haynsworth claimed the court was adopting a new standard,[159] in reviewing the trial court's decision Haynsworth again framed the case in terms of separation of powers issues and argued for a great deal of deference to the executive branch. He also explicitly refused to reconsider any First Amendment claims.[160] While Haynsworth discussed legislative intent, textual analysis and some precedent, his opinion once again relied upon what he saw as the practical problems associated with the inability of the judicial branch to handle classified information. To Haynsworth, courts were neither capable of keeping information safe nor competent to know what information should be classified.

---

[155] *Id.*
[156] *Id.* at 1366.
[157] *Id.* at 1366-67.
[158] *Id.* at 1366.
[159] The court claimed that in *Marchetti* it was primarily relying on the principle that classification decisions were not reviewable by the judiciary, but that it would now rely upon the FOIA amendments. *Id.* at 1367.
[160] *Id.* at 1370.

Based on textual analysis and the legislative intent behind amendments to the Freedom of Information Act[161] that provided for judicial review of classification decision,[162] the Fourth Circuit concluded that the deletion of items by the CIA from the manuscript "should be suppressed only if they are found both to be *classified* and *classifiable* under the Executive Order."[163] However, Haynsworth wrote that the government only needed to "show no more than that each deleted item disclosed information which was required to be classified in any degree and which was contained in a document bearing a classification stamp."[164] It did not need to show when the information was classified, who classified it, "nor was it necessary for the government to disclose to lawyers, judges, court reporters, expert witnesses and others . . . sensitive but irrelevant information in a classified document in order to prove that a particular item of information within it had been classified."[165] In addition, Haynsworth wrote that it was not even necessary for the government to show the information was actually secret or had been properly classified. Rather the government need only show that the information was *potentially* classifiable.[166]

To support these conclusions, Haynsworth focused once again on the abilities of the judiciary to deal with national security information. Justifying his decision that the government did not have to show the actual documents or potentially sensitive information to the court, Haynsworth wrote:

It is not to slight judges, lawyers or anyone else to suggest that any such disclosure carries with it serious risk that highly sensitive information may be compromised. In our own chambers, we are ill equipped to provide the kind of security highly sensitive information should have. The national interest requires that the government withhold or delete unrelated

---

[161] 5 U.S.C. § 552(b)(1).
[162] *Knopf*, 509 F.2d 1362 at 1367.
[163] *Id.* (emphasis added).
[164] *Id.*
[165] *Id.* at 1369.
[166] *Id.*

items of sensitive information, as it did, in the absence of compelling necessity.[167]

Thus, although Haynsworth initially appeared to change his stance and seemed inclined to rule that a more stringent judicial review of classification decisions was appropriate, the standards he set forth did little to strengthen the role he established for the judiciary in *Marchetti*. Haynsworth still believed that the judiciary's only role was to verify that the executive vouched for the fact that the information was classified or classifiable. In addition, Haynsworth still refused to address any of Marchetti's First Amendment rights or the public's right to know.

In 1980, the Supreme Court heard similar arguments in *Snepp v. United States*,[168] a case involving proceeds from a book published by a former CIA agent, Frank W. Snepp III. In 1968, as an express condition of his employment with the CIA, Snepp signed a non-disclosure agreement similar to the one Marchetti had signed. The agreement stated that Snepp would not "divulge *classified* information and not . . . publish *any* information without prepublication clearance."[169] When Snepp published a book based on his experiences without submitting it to the Agency for review, the government brought suit seeking a declaration that Snepp had breached his contract, an injunction requiring Snepp to submit all future writings to the CIA prior to publication, and an order imposing "a constructive trust for the Government's benefit on all profits that Snepp might earn from publishing his book."[170] Both the District Court for the Eastern District of Virginia and the Fourth Circuit Court of Appeals found that Snepp had breached a valid contract.[171] However, while the district court both enjoined future breaches of Snepp's agreement and imposed a constructive trust on Snepp's profits from his book, the Fourth Circuit held that "the imposition of a constructive trust was improper and that

---

[167] *Id.*
[168] 444 U.S. 507 (1980).
[169] *Id.* at 508.
[170] *Id.* at 509.
[171] U.S. v. Snepp, 456 F. Supp 176, 179 (E.D. Va. 1978), *aff'd in part, rev'd in part*, 595 F.2d 926, 935 (4th Cir. 1979), *rev'd*, 444 U.S. 507 (1980).

the government's sole remedy for breach of the contract should be the recovery of compensatory and punitive damages as the proof may support and as a jury may assess."[172] The Fourth Circuit based its decision on its findings that Snepp had a First Amendment right to publish *unclassified* information and that the government did not claim any classified material was ever published.[173] Thus, the appellate court held that while Snepp had violated his contractual duty[174] and the government could sue for breach of contract in order to win both nominal and punitive damages,[175] a constructive trust was inappropriate because Snepp's fiduciary duty[176] to the government only extended to his agreement not to publish *classified* information.[177]

In a per curiam opinion issued by a six-member majority,[178] the Supreme Court rejected the Fourth Circuit's decision as well as its framing of the case in terms of Snepp's First Amendment right to publish unclassified information.[179] In fact, the majority only mentioned the First Amendment once in its entire opinion. In a footnote, the Court noted that Snepp's contention that his contract was unenforceable as a prior restraint on speech was in conflict with the Court's previous decisions that had made it clear a substantial government interest allowed the government to impose "reasonable restrictions on employee activities that in other contexts might be

---

[172] *Snepp*, 595 F.2d at 935.

[173] *Id.*

[174] "A duty arising under a particular contract" or "[a] duty imposed by the law of contracts." BLACK'S LAW DICTIONARY 543-44 (8th ed. 2004).

[175] Although punitive damages are not normally available in a breach of contract suit, because the court found that Snepp had deliberately misled the government about his intention to submit his manuscript for prepublication review, punitive damages were appropriate. *Snepp*, 595 F.2d at 937.

[176] "A duty of utmost good faith, trust, confidence, and candor owed by a fiduciary (such as a lawyer or corporate officer) to the beneficiary (such as a lawyer's client or a shareholder); a duty to act with the highest degree of honesty and loyalty toward another person and in the best interest of the other person." BLACK'S LAW DICTIONARY 543-44 (8th ed. 2004).

[177] *Snepp*, 595 F.2d at 936.

[178] The majority consisted of Chief Justice Burger and Justices Stewart, White, Blackmun, Powell, and Rehnquist.

[179] Snepp v. United States, 444 U.S. 507 (1980).

protected by the First Amendment."[180]   In Snepp's case this was represented by the government's compelling interest in "protecting both the secrecy of information important to our national security and the appearance of confidentiality so essential to the effective operation of our foreign intelligence service."[181]

After summarily dismissing any First Amendment issues presented by the case, the majority framed the case in terms of breach of trust/contracts law and the need for government secrecy. Citing no cases other than *Marchetti* and *Adolf A. Knopf*, the Court began with a lengthy discussion of the CIA's need for secrecy and the inability of a single agent to determine what information—classified or unclassified—might harm national interests.[182]   Based on this the Court concluded, "Undisputed evidence in this case shows that a CIA agent's violation of his obligation to submit writings about the Agency for prepublication review impairs the CIA's ability to perform its statutory duties."[183]   The Court held that the Fourth Circuit's decision left the government "with no reliable deterrent against similar breaches of security"[184] because a trial would expose the very secrets the Agency was trying to protect. The Court wrote:

> The Government could not pursue the only remedy that the Court of Appeals left it without losing the benefit of the bargain it seeks to enforce. Proof of the tortious conduct necessary to sustain an award of punitive damages might force the Government to disclose some of the very confidences that Snepp promised to protect. The trial of such a suit, before a jury if the defendant so elects, would subject the CIA and its officials to probing discovery into the Agency's highly

---

[180] *Id.* at 766 n.3 (citing CSC v. Letter Carriers, 413 U.S. 548, 565 (1973); Brown v. Glines, 444 U.S. 348 (1980); Buckley v. Valeo, 424 U.S. 1, 25-28 (1976); Greer v. Spock, 424 U.S. 828 (1976); *id.*, at 844-48 (Powell, J., concurring); Cole v. Richardson, 405 U.S. 676 (1972)).

[181] *Id.*

[182] *Id.* at 511-13.

[183] *Id.* at 512.

[184] *Id.* at 514.

confidential affairs. Rarely would the Government run this risk.[185]

Justice Stewart, joined by Justices Brennan and Marshall, issued a strongly worded dissent. Framing the case in terms of the First Amendment and judicial powers, Stewart disagreed with the majority's unwillingness to discuss Snepp's First Amendment claims as well as its focus on trusts and contracts law. He wrote, "The uninhibited character of today's exercise in lawmaking is highlighted by the Court's disregard of two venerable principles that favor a more conservative approach to this case."[186] Stewart began his opinion by attacking the majority's mode of legal analysis. Stewart wrote:

> The Court's *per curiam* opinion seems to suggest that its result is supported by a blend of the law of trusts and the law of contracts. But neither of these branches of the common law supports the imposition of a constructive trust under the circumstances of this case.[187]

Next, Stewart differentiated Snepp's fiduciary duty to protect classified information from his contractual duty not to publish unclassified information without prior approval. Because Stewart found that Snepp had violated his contractual duty, but not his fiduciary duty, he focused on contract law *and* invoked Snepp's First Amendment rights.

Stewart equated Snepp's secrecy agreement with other contracts "designed to ensure in various ways that an employee fully complies with his duty not to disclose or misuse confidential information," such as non-compete covenants.[188] Based on precedent, Stewart wrote that such covenants were only enforceable under the "rule of reason," which required "that the covenant be reasonably necessary to protect a legitimate interest of the employer (such as an interest in confidentiality), that the employer's interest not be outweighed by the public interest, and that the covenant not be of any longer duration or

---

[185] *Id.* at 514-15.
[186] *Id.* at 526 (Stewart, J., dissenting).
[187] *Id.* at 517-18.
[188] *Id.* at 519.

wider geographical scope than necessary to protect the employer's interest."[189] Stewart wrote that although the CIA, like any employer, had an interest in protecting confidential information, this interest had to be balanced with Snepp's First Amendment rights and his interests in securing work as an author, as well as the public's interest in a proper accommodation that would preserve the intelligence mission of the Agency while not abridging the free flow of unclassified information."[190] Based on his analysis of contract law and the "rule of reason," Stewart concluded such a harsh[191] restriction might be found unenforceable by an equity court.[192]

Stewart also found fault with the majority's reliance on precedents because the First Amendment right to publish both classified *and* unclassified national security information was at issue and the Court had never decided such a case.[193] Stewart wrote, "[E]ven if such a wide-ranging prior restraint would be good national security policy, I would have great difficulty reconciling it with the demands of the First Amendment."[194] Stewart invoked the First Amendment's role in self-government and took the majority to task for underestimating the impact of the Court's ruling. He wrote:

> [T]he Court seems unaware of the fact that its drastic new remedy has been fashioned to enforce a species of prior restraint on a citizen's right to criticize his government. Inherent in this prior restraint is the risk that the reviewing agency will misuse its authority to delay the publication of a critical work or to persuade an author to modify the contents of his work beyond the demands of secrecy. The character of the covenant as a prior restraint on free speech surely imposes an especially heavy burden on the censor to justify the remedy

---

[189] *Id.* (citing Mitchel v. Reynolds, 1 P. Wms. 181, 24 Eng.Rep. 347 (Q.B. 1711)).

[190] *Id.* at 520.

[191] Citing a number of cases out of the Fourth Circuit, Stewart concluded that a prior restraint of such wide scope and indefinite duration would make most similar covenants unenforceable. *Id.* at 520 n.9.

[192] *Id.* at 520.

[193] *Id.* at 520 n.10.

[194] *Id.* at 522.

it seeks. It would take more than the Court has written to persuade me that that burden has been met.[195]

In the years following *Snepp*, both the D.C. District Court and D.C. Court of Appeals further refined the judiciary's approach to government confidentiality agreements. In 1983, the D.C. Circuit again reviewed the government's prepublication requirements when Ralph W. McGehee, a former CIA officer, challenged the constitutionality of the CIA's "classification and censorship scheme" and the "propriety, under that scheme," of classifying portions of an article he wrote for *The Nation*.[196] Unlike Snepp, McGehee had submitted his manuscript for review. McGehee, however, challenged the Agency's decision to categorize categorized information in his manuscript as "Secret," the middle level of classification between "Top Secret" and "Confidential."[197] Thus, unlike *Snepp*, *McGehee v. Casey* did not involve an agent who did not abide by his secrecy agreement, but rather was a challenge to "the constitutionality of the CIA's substantive criteria and scheme for deciding how to classify, and thereby censor, writings of former agents."[198]

The D.C. Circuit presented the case as dealing with both the need to balance freedom of speech with national security and separation of powers. Discussing a number of precedents related to the speech rights of government employees,[199] the court articulated two "consistent

---

[195] *Id.* at 526. In a footnote, although Stewart admitted he was not prepared to rule that the contract was unenforceable, he contended that the issue deserved to be decided by the Court after a full briefing. In addition, he cited *Pentagon Papers* and *Nebraska Press Association v. Stuart*, 427 U.S. 539 (1976), a case involving the judiciary and prior restraints, to support his contention that the government's restriction would at the very least be considered unconstitutional in other situations. *Id.* at 526 n.17.

[196] McGehee v. Casey, 718 F.2d 1137, 1140 (D.C. Cir. 1983).

[197] *Id.* at 1140. At the time McGehee submitted his article to the CIA, classification decisions were governed by Exec. Order No. 12,065, 43 Fed. Reg. 28,949 (June 28, 1978).

[198] *Id.* at 1141.

[199] In addition to *Snepp* the court discussed *Brown v. Glines*, 444 U.S. 348 (1980); *CSC v. Letter Carries*, 413 U.S. 548 (1973); *Cole v. Richardson*, 405 U.S. 676 (1972); and *Pickering v. Board of Education, 391 U.S. 563* (1968).

themes" found in the cases. Quoting *Brown v. Glines*,[200] a case involving a First Amendment challenge to an Air Force regulation that prohibited service members from soliciting signatures for petitions, Circuit Judge Patricia Wald wrote, "First, restrictions on the speech of government employees must 'protect a substantial government interest unrelated to the suppression of free speech.'"[201] Next, she said, "[T]he restriction must be narrowly drawn to 'restrict speech no more than is necessary to protect the substantial government interest.'"[202]   In addition, citing precedent and using originalism, Wald concluded that courts should show "sensitivity to the special institutional needs of particular governmental services, such as the military and the foreign intelligence services."[203]   The court thus determine that the government had not just a *substantial* interest but a *compelling* interest in keeping national security information secret and ruled that the CIA's classification scheme was not unconstitutional on its face.[204]

The court next considered what standard of judicial review of CIA decisions was appropriate. Again adopting a balancing frame, Wald began by clarifying just what type of right the court was addressing. Citing precedent, Wald reasoned that because McGehee was disseminating information already in his possession his rights were "stronger" than they would be under a FOIA analysis of an individual's right to *gather* information.[205]   However, although Wald stated McGehee had a "a strong first amendment interest in ensuring that CIA censorship of his article results from a *proper* classification of the censored portions,"[206] she also noted that because no court order in the case "constitute[d] a prior restraint in the traditional sense,"[207] the court would not place as heavy of burden on the government as the Supreme Court did in *New York Times v. United States*.[208]

---

[200] 444 U.S. 348 (1980).
[201] *McGehee*, 718 F.2d at 1142 (quoting *Brown*, 444 U.S. at 349).
[202] *Id.* (quoting *Brown*, 444 U.S. at 355).
[203] *Id.* at 1142 n.11.
[204] *Id.* at 1143.
[205] *Id.* at 1147.
[206] *McGehee*, 718 F.2d at 1147 (emphasis in original).
[207] *Id.*
[208] *Id.* at 1148 n.22.

Having established the strength of McGehee's First Amendment claims, Wald articulated a balancing test based on the need for the court to defer to the expertise of the CIA in matters of national security with the role of the courts in protecting individual rights. Wald wrote that courts must adhere to a standard of review that both "afford[ed] proper respect to the individual rights at stake while recognizing the CIA's technical expertise and practical familiarity with the ramifications of sensitive information."[209] Based on this standard, the court concluded that "reviewing courts should conduct a *de novo* review of the classification decision, while giving deference to reasoned and detailed CIA explanations of that classification decision"[210] and "must . . . satisfy themselves from the record, *in camera* or otherwise, that the CIA in fact had good reason to classify, and therefore censor, the materials at issue."[211] According to the court, this approach would ensure both a proper balance between First Amendment rights and national security as well as a proper balance between the CIA's tasks of protecting national security and maintaining secrecy and the judiciary's task of protecting individual rights. To support this conclusion, the court turned to First Amendment theory, citing the role of free speech in self-government.[212] After applying these standards and examining the affidavits of the parties *in camera*, the court concluded that the CIA had properly classified the information in question.[213]

In addition to Wald's discussion of First Amendment theory in the court's opinion, a "separate statement" by Wald discussed the First Amendment implications of the case. Wald's statement specifically focused on the right to know as supporting the checking function of the First Amendment.[214] Wald emphasized that while the court's decision reflected current law it did not take into account the developing concept

---

[209] *Id.* at 1148.
[210] *Id.*
[211] *Id.*
[212] *Id.* at 1149.
[213] *Id.*
[214] *Id.* at 1150 (Wald, J., special statement). *See also* Weaver v. U.S. Info. Agency, 87 F.3d 1429, 1444-56 (D.C. Cir. 1996) (Wald, J., dissenting).

of the right to know and was not necessarily the best balance between national security and self-government.[215]

Five years later, in 1988, the D.C. District Court used a similar approach when it considered challenges to government non-disclosure agreements brought by two federal employees' unions. In *National Federation of Federal Employees v. United States*[216] the National Federation of Government Employees and the American Federation of Government Employees sought to enjoin the implementation and enforcement of provisions of federal government employment forms that contained agreements that imposed civil sanctions on federal employee for making unauthorized disclosures of "classified" or "classifiable" government information.[217] In addition to other challenges, the labor unions argued that the use of the term "classifiable" was unconstitutional.[218] Again framing the case as dealing with the need to balance freedom of expression with national security, District Judge Oliver Gasch wrote, "At the heart of this case is a constitutionally inherent conflict between the obligation of the Executive to safeguard national security information and the rights of citizens to speak freely and be guided by reasonably clear and narrow statutory proscriptions on the free speech right."[219]

Relying on *Snepp, McGehee,* and a series of other precedents used in *McGehee,* Gasch reached much the same conclusion as Wald. He determined that while executive branch employees had "an obligation to preserve the secrecy of national security information"[220] and the

---

[215] *Id.* In addition to the court's opinion and Wald's special statement, Senior Circuit Judge George MacKinnon wrote a separate concurrence. MacKinnon wrote that while he was in general agreement with the court's opinion, there was "an essential difference between upholding the secrecy agreement . . . and a case where the government might seek a prepublication injunction of the same information." *Id.* (MacKinnon, J., concurring).

[216] 695 F. Supp. 1196 (D.D.C. 1988).

[217] *Id.* at 1197.

[218] *Id.* at 1198. Although the three agreements in question used different language, the term "classifiable" was common to all three. For a full discussion of the language of the agreements and the various changes the agreements underwent prior to the trial, see *id.* at 1197-99.

[219] *Id.* at 1199.

[220] *Id.* at 1199 (citing Dep't. of Navy v. Egan, 484 U.S. 518 (1988); Snepp v. United States, 444 U.S. 507, 510-11 & n.6 (1980)).

executive branch had "broad discretion to ensure" that employees did not disclose national security information,[221] "'restriction[s] on the speech of government employees must 'protect a substantial government interest unrelated to the suppression of free speech'"[222] and be "narrowly drawn to 'restrict speech no more than is necessary to protect the substantial government interest.'"[223] The district court ruled that while the Supreme Court had held that non-disclosure agreements did not violate the First Amendment rights of federal employees,[224] the use of the term "classifiable" information in the agreements was unconstitutional. The court held that "[i]n the absence of any definition, the term is far too broad to comport with the constitutional requirement that restraints on free speech be narrowly drawn to bar no more speech than is necessary."[225]

While these cases might seem to suggest the judiciary had settled on an approach to employee cases by the late 1980s, in a 2007 case, the D.C. District court chose not to completely adopt either of the two major frames seen in the opinions above. Although District Judge Emmet G. Sullivan discussed the need to balance deference to the executive with the judiciary's role in protecting individual rights, he framed his opinion almost solely in terms of national security, focusing on the government's need to keep national security information secret without discussing a need to balance the First Amendment with national security at any length.

That 2007 case, *Stillman v. CIA*, involved a book about China's nuclear weapons program written by Danny Stillman, a former employee of Los Alamos National Laboratory (LANL).[226] In 2000,

---

[221] *Id.* at 1199-1200 (citing *Egan*, 484 U.S. at 824-25; CIA v. Sims, 471 U.S. 159, 170 (1985); Cole v. Young, 351 U.S. 536, 546 (1956); United States v. Curtiss-Wright Corp., 299 U.S. 304, 320 (1936)).

[222] *Id.* at 1200 (quoting McGehee v. Casey, 718 F.2d 1137, 1142-43 (D.C.Cir.1983) (quoting Brown v. Glines, 444 U.S. 348, 354 (1980) and citing *Snepp*, 444 U.S. at 509 n.3).

[223] *Id.* (quoting *McGehee*, 718 F.2d at 1142-43 (quoting *Brown*, 444 U.S. at 355 and citing United States Civil Serv. Comm'n v. Nat' Ass'n of Letter Carriers, 413 U.S. 548, 580 (1973)).

[224] *Id.* at 1202.

[225] *Id.* at 1205.

[226] 517 F. Supp. 2d 32, 33 (D.D.C. 2007).

when Stillman submitted his manuscript, *Inside China's Nuclear Weapons Program*, for prepublication review as required by the non-disclosure agreement he had signed while an employee at LANL, he was informed that the DOE, DOD and CIA did not want any part of his manuscript published. [227] Although the government subsequently released all but twenty-three passages of the manuscript, Stillman brought suit raising two First Amendment claims. First, Stillman argued that the agencies lacked authority to prohibit him from publishing "information he obtained as a private citizen and not as a result of his employment at LANL or his signing of a secrecy agreement."[228] Stillman contended that because six of the nine trips he had made to China to visit nuclear weapons facilities and engage in discussions with Chinese scientists and officials took place after his retirement from LANL, the government had no ability to censor information he had learned as a private citizen. Although Stillman retained his security clearance and admitted he was still "affiliated" with the government, he argued the information he obtained "on the fourth through ninth trips was not obtained within the course of employment nor d[id] it fall within the scope of any secrecy agreement he signed."[229] Second, Stillman challenged the classification decision itself, claiming the CIA had "failed to show that his right to publish [was] outweighed by a substantial government interest."[230] The court agreed with neither argument.

Discussing both of Stillman's claims, Sullivan relied exclusively on precedent. Considering Stillman's first claim, Sullivan simply noted that *McGehee*, *Marchetti* and *Snepp* had already established that "current and former government employees have no First Amendment right to publish properly classified information to which they gain access by virtue of their employment."[231] He then simply extended that to "individuals who maintain a security clearance and contract with the government as either an employee or affiliate."[232]

---

[227] *Id.* at 35.
[228] *Id.* at 36.
[229] *Id.* at 37.
[230] *Id.* at 36.
[231] *Id.* at 38.
[232] *Id.*

Turning to the classification decision, Sullivan wrote the case was about separation of powers issues. Once again focusing on precedent, Sullivan began by writing about the CIA's unique role in protecting national security information. Sullivan wrote that "the government is entitled to substantial deference in its classification decisions"[233] because it was in the best position to know what harm would result from disclosure,[234] and the court was "mindful that due to the "mosaic-like nature of intelligence gathering, . . . what may seem trivial to the uninformed may appear of great moment to one who has a broad view of the scene and may put the questioned information in context."[235] Quoting *McGehee*, however, Sullivan wrote he was not willing to give complete deference to the agency.

> Despite this high level of deference, the Court will not just rubber stamp the government's classification decision. To uphold the government's classification decision, the Court must satisfy itself "from the record, *in camera* or otherwise, that the [government agencies] in fact had good reason to classify, and therefore censor, the materials at issue."[236]

Thus, although Sullivan eventually ruled the government had properly classified all of the passages in question after he conducted an *in camera* review of government affidavits and the manuscript, the court at least appeared to take its role seriously. While it would be impossible to truly know if the court was doing more than simply deferring to the government agencies, Sullivan's opinion at least suggests that it was not.

In these cases then, as was the case with *New York Times v. United States*, there was a consistent focus on separation of power frames as well as First Amendment frames. From *Marchetti* to *Stillman*, the common thread throughout these opinions was the judiciary's struggle with what role it should play in national security issues and how much deference to give to the executive branch. While some opinions have

---

[233] *Id.* at 39; *McGehee*, 718 F.2d at 1149.

[234] *Id.*; Dep't of Navy v. Egan, 484 U.S. 518, 529 (1988).

[235] *Id.* (quoting *McGehee*, 718 F.2d at 1148-49).

[236] *Id.* (quoting *McGehee*, 718 F.2d at 1148).

contained stronger First Amendment frames than others, the separation of powers frame has remained fairly consistent. In addition, while the level of deference the courts give to the executive has fluctuated, the basic question of how much deference has remained. In 2004, over thirty years after the Supreme Court introduced these two frames in the Pentagon Papers, they continued to play an important role when courts began considering prior restraint issues raised by the Patriot Act.

Prior Restraints, National Security and the USA PATRIOT Act
The final three cases involving prior restraint and national security all deal with National Security Letters (NSLs) issued under the Patriot Act. As noted above, as originally amended by the Patriot Act, Title 18, § 2709(c) of the U.S. Code prohibited recipients of NSLs from ever disclosing to anyone that they received NSLs or that the FBI sought access or obtained information or records through the use of NSLs.[237] When the Internet access firm that would become known as "John Doe" in court records received an NSL, it became the first—but not the last—plaintiff to contend that the provisions of the Patriot Act violated the First, Fourth and Fifth Amendments. First, in *Doe v. Ashcroft*,[238] or *Doe I* as it was later called in court records, the Internet service provided challenged § 2709 in the Southern District of New York in 2004. Next, in 2005, four Connecticut librarians, who were initially described in court documents as simply an "entity with library records," challenged the non-disclosure provision in the United States District Court of Connecticut in *Doe v. Gonzales*,[239] or *Doe II*. Finally, in 2007, in *Doe v. Gonzales*,[240] or *Doe III*, the Southern District of New York heard the issue one more time after its decision in *Doe I* was remanded by the Second Circuit for further consideration in light of changes in the provisions made by the USA Patriot Improvement and Reauthorization Act of 2005.

---

[237] 18 U.S.C. § 2709(c) (Supp. 2003).
[238] Doe v. Ashcroft, 334 F. Supp. 2d 471 (S.D.N.Y. 2004) (hereinafter *Doe I*).
[239] Doe v. Gonzales, 386 F. Supp. 2d 66 (D. Conn. 2005) (hereinafter *Doe II*).
[240] Doe v. Gonzales, 500 F. Supp. 2d 379 (S.D.N.Y. 2007) (hereinafter *Doe III*).

As noted above, when Judge Victor Marrero wrote the opinion in *Doe I*, he clearly framed the issue in terms of balancing the First Amendment and national security concerns. He wrote:

> National security is a paramount value, unquestionably one of the highest purposes for which any sovereign government is ordained. Equally scaled among human endeavors is personal security, an interest especially prized in our system of justice in the form of the guarantee bestowed upon the individual to be free from imposition by government of unwarranted restraints on protected fundamental rights.[241]

In addition, he identified a second core legal issue presented by the case as the need for the judiciary to have an active role in balancing national security with personal freedoms. Marrero wrote that during times of war and national crisis it was especially important for the judiciary to remain vigilant of government attempts to curtail personal freedoms.[242] Marrero's opinion discussed legislative history and intent, textual analysis and precedents related to anonymous speech, the right of association and prior restraints. However, at the heart of Marrero's decision that the § 2709(c) was unconstitutional was a reliance on democratic theory.

Marrero began by explaining why he could not focus solely on textual analysis, legislative intent or history. After a discussion of the legislative history of § 2709[243] and a lengthy analysis of the text of § 2709 and other statutes that granted the government information-gathering authority, [244] Marrero concluded these methods were not sufficient to reach a conclusion about the constitutionality of the statute. Marrero wrote that he could not "fairly infer clear congressional intent in the enactment of § 2709 solely by comparing it with other complex, analogous statutes."[245] For example, Marrero pointed out that while some of the statutes specifically allowed a

---

[241] *Doe I*, 334 F. Supp. 2d at 476.
[242] *Id.* at 478.
[243] *Id.* at 480-84.
[244] *Id.* at 484-91.
[245] *Id.* at 491.

recipient to discuss the receipt of an NSL with "persons whose assistance is necessary to comply with the demands of the NSL," others, such as § 2709, appeared through their silence to prevent disclosure to anyone and it was unclear which of the statutes had enforcement mechanisms or allowed for judicial review.[246] After discussing Doe's Fourth Amendment challenges and the anonymous speech rights and association rights of Doe's subscribers, Marrero turned to the issue of prior restraints.[247]

The government argued that the statute's non-disclosure provision was not a traditional prior restraint and, thus, should only be subject to intermediate scrutiny,[248] citing the Supreme Court's decisions in *Ward v. Rock Against Racism*[249] and *Consolidated Edison Co. of New York v. Public Service Commission,*[250] as well as a Second Circuit decision, *Kamasinski v. Judicial Review Council.*[251] The court, however, held that because § 2709 was both a prior restraint on speech and a content-based regulation[252] it was subject to strict scrutiny. Applying this standard, the court held that while the Supreme Court had previously determined that protecting national security information was a compelling state interest,[253] § 2709 was not sufficiently narrow to survive. To support this ruling, the court returned to textual analysis,

---

[246] *Id.* at 492.

[247] Although the court discussed Fourth Amendment issues, as well as issues related to the anonymous speech and association rights of Doe's subscribers, because this chapter focuses on prior restraints, those issues are not examined.

[248] The government argued that the provision was not a prior restraint because it did not create a licensing system, arguing that section 2709(c) did not "authorize any government official to grant a speaker permission to make any particular disclosure. Rather, the statute simply prohibit[ed] certain disclosures." *Id.* at 512. The government argued that the provision was not content based because it did not seek to silence less favored views. The court held that while the provision was *viewpoint*-neutral it was still *content*-based because "the restriction pertain[ed] to an entire category of speech." *Id.* at 513.

[249] 491 U.S. 781 (1989).

[250] 447 U.S. 530 (1980).

[251] 44 F.3d 106 (2d Cir.1994).

[252] *Doe I*, 334 F. Supp. 2d at 512-13.

[253] *Id.* at 513-14.

reasoning that other analogous statutes were less restrictive than § 2709 because they provided for judicial review.[254]

Next, the court considered the government's argument that a less exacting First Amendment standard should apply because Doe had only learned of the information he was being prevented from disclosing because of the government's investigation. Engaging in an extensive exploration of cases in which courts had upheld government secrecy in connection with official investigations, including the Supreme Court's decisions in *Seattle Times Co. v. Rhinehart*[255] and *Butterworth v. Smith*,[256] as well as decisions by the Second,[257] Third[258] and Tenth Circuits,[259] the court concluded, "A basic principle emerging from these cases is that laws which prohibit persons from disclosing information they learn solely by means of participating in confidential government proceedings trigger less First Amendment concerns that laws which prohibit disclosing information a person obtains independently."[260]

The court, however, returned to its focus on balancing competing interests to conclude the doctrine established by these cases had its limits. The court wrote:

> The relevance of this doctrine reaches its limit, however, when the Court considers that the NSL statutes, unlike other legislation cited above, impose a *permanent* bar on disclosure in every case, making no distinction among competing relative public policy values over time, and containing no provision for lifting that bar when the circumstances that justify it may no longer warrant categorical secrecy.
>
> . . .
>
> The Government's claim to perpetual secrecy surrounding the FBI's issuance of NSLs . . . presupposes a category of

---

[254] *Id.* at 514-15.

[255] 467 U.S. 20 (1984).

[256] 494 U.S. 624 (1990).

[257] Kamasinski v. Judicial Review Council, 44 F.3d 106 (2d Cir.1994).

[258] First Amendment Coalition v. Judicial Inquiry & Review Bd., 784 F.2d 467 (3d Cir. 1986) (*en banc*).

[259] Hoffmann Pugh v. Keenan, 338 F.3d 1136 (10th Cir. 2003).

[260] *Doe I*, 334 F. Supp. 2d at 518.

information, and thus a class of speech, that, for reasons not satisfactorily explained, must forever be kept from public view, cloaked by an official seal that will always overshadow the public's right to know. In general, as our sunshine laws and judicial doctrine attest, democracy abhors undue secrecy, in recognition that public knowledge secures freedom. Hence, an unlimited government warrant to conceal, effectively a form of secrecy *per se,* has no place in our open society. Such a claim is especially inimical to democratic values for reasons borne out by painful experience.[261]

Finally, the court addressed the government's argument that the unique nature of its fight against international terrorism called for drastic measures. Marrero focused on the role of the judiciary, writing that although courts traditionally give deference to the political branches in these matters, the judiciary had an important role to play as well. Marrero concluded that unlike what the government was asking the court to do in the present case, in previous cases, even when courts chose to defer to the other branches of government, they still retained some sort of judicial review. "[T]he central flaw in the Government's argument is that it invites the Court to 'assume that [§ 2709] will *always* advance the asserted [Government] interests sufficiently to justify its abridgment of expressive activity,'" he wrote.[262] Based on these arguments, Marrero concluded § 2709 was an unconstitutional restraint on freedom of expression. As noted, however, *Doe I,* was only the beginning.

In 2005, Judge Janet C. Hall of the U.S. District Court of Connecticut considered the constitutionality of § 2709 when the four Connecticut librarians who were initially identified only as "John Doe" brought suit against the FBI in *Doe II.*[263] Like the ISP plaintiff in *Doe*

---

[261] *Id.* at 519-20.

[262] *Id.* at 524 (quoting Members of the City Council v. Taxpayers for Vincent, 466 U.S. 789, 803 n.22 (1984)(emphasis added by the court).

[263] 386 F. Supp. 2d 66 (D. Conn. 2005). As the court had done in *Doe I,* the *Doe II* court sealed information related to the case, including a section of the opinion, and attempted to keep the identity of the plaintiffs and any information related to the NSL confidential. *See, e.g., id.* at 77 n.7 & n.8. In addition, the government requested that the court examine much of the evidence it submitted

I, the plaintiffs in *Doe II* raised a number of challenges to § 2709, including a First Amendment challenge to the non-disclosure provision.[264] They argued that § 2709's "ban on speech prohibit[ed] them from engaging in constitutionally protected speech that [was] relevant and perhaps crucial to an ongoing and time-sensitive national policy debate" about the Patriot Act and moved "for preliminary relief to enjoin enforcement of § 2709(c) as to Doe's identity."[265] Hall identified the primary legal issues in the case as Doe's First Amendment rights and judicial power. The modes of legal analysis Hall used to reach her conclusion were First Amendment theory, specifically the role of freedom of expression in self-governance and as a check on the government, and precedent.

Hall began her discussion of the legal issues presented by noting that the case called for a higher standard of review because allowing Doe to reveal its identity would render a trial on the merits meaningless.[266] Citing Second Circuit precedent, the court ruled that Doe had to show both that the government's prohibition on speech was causing irreparable harm and that there was a clear or substantial likelihood Doe would prevail on the merits.[267] Examining the harm caused by § 2709, Hall cited previous cases that had determined the loss of First Amendment rights unquestionably constituted irreparable harm.[268] In addition, Hall invoked the self-government theory of the First Amendment, writing: "The subject matter of the speech at issue in the pending motion places it at the center of First Amendment protection. Furthermore, in the specific instance at issue in the pending motion, there is a current and lively debate in this country over renewal

---

ex parte. The court granted the request. *See id.* at 70-71. However, on appeal the government agreed to let Doe II reveal its identity because of changes made to the Patriot Act.

[264] See *id.* at 69 for a summary of the challenges.

[265] *Id.* at 70.

[266] *Id.* at 71-72.

[267] *Id.* at 72. According to the court, the normal standard required "'first, irreparable injury, and, second, either (a) likelihood of success on the merits, or (b) sufficiently serious questions going to the merits and a balance of hardships decidedly tipped in the movant's favor.'" *Id.* at 72 n.3 (quoting Green Party of N.Y. State v. N.Y. State Bd. of Elections, 389 F.3d 411, 418 (2d Cir. 2004)).

[268] *Id.*

of the PATRIOT Act."[269] Although Hall agreed with the government's argument that Doe was free to still speak out against the Patriot Act in a "general manner," she wrote that preventing Doe from identifying itself as a recipient of a NSL prevented Doe from commenting fully on the issue.

> Considering the current national interest in and the important issues surrounding the debate on renewal of the PATRIOT Act provisions, it is apparent to this court that the loss of Doe's ability to speak out now on the subject as a NSL recipient is a real and present loss of its First Amendment right to free speech that cannot be remedied. Doe's speech would be made more powerful by its ability to put a "face" on the service of the NSL, and Doe's political expression is restricted without that ability. Doe's right to identify itself is a First Amendment freedom independent from Doe's right to speak generally about its views on NSLs. Doe's statements as a known recipient of a NSL would have a different impact on the public debate than the same statements by a speaker who is not identified as a recipient.[270]

Hall next considered Doe's likelihood of success on the merits, considering what level of scrutiny should be applied to the non-disclosure provision.

First, she considered the government's argument that § 2709 was not a prior restraint because, typically, prior restraints were court orders or licensing schemes.[271] Hall, however, concluded that prior restraints are not limited to these two categories of restrictions, noting that the Supreme Court had "found a prior restraint when a state commission encouraged booksellers not to sell certain books that the commission deemed objectionable."[272] In addition, Hall held that the government incorrectly argued that § 2709 should be subject o intermediate scrutiny because it was analogous to a judicial order that the Supreme Court

---

[269] *Id.*
[270] *Id.* at 72-73.
[271] *Id.* at 74.
[272] *Id.*

subjected to intermediate scrutiny in *Seattle Times Co. v. Rhinehart.*[273] Echoing the reasoning from *Doe I*, Hall wrote that a court order preventing the *Seattle Times* from disclosing information it learned because of forced government disclosure was entirely different from "a law barring disclosure of the use of the government's authority to compel disclosure of information."[274] Finally, Hall determined that § 2709 was a content-based restriction and, therefore, subject to strict scrutiny. Although Hall admitted that the government might intend for the provision to serve some purpose other than the suppression of speech, a situation which would call for intermediate scrutiny, the non-disclosure requirement had the practical effect of silencing those who could best comment on the practical effects of the Patriot Act itself.[275]

Next, Hall considered the government's contention that even if § 2709 was a prior restraint it met strict scrutiny because it was narrowly tailored to meet a compelling government interest. Hall framed this portion of the case in terms of the judiciary's role in national security. Although Hall "recognize[d] the defendants' expertise in the area of counter-terrorism" and was "inclined to afford their judgments in that area deference, those judgments remain[ed] subject to judicial review." To support this, she quoted the Supreme Court's recent decision in *Hamdi v. Rumsfeld* that "'the United States Constitution . . . most assuredly envisions a role for all three branches when individual liberties are at stake'"[276] and a Fourth Circuit case[277] that warned of the historical dangers of deferring too much to national security concerns.[278]

After justifying judicial review of the FBI's determinations, Hall concluded that nothing in the record indicated the government had a compelling interest in preventing the disclosure of Doe's identity.[279] Hall called the government's arguments "speculative" and noted that *New York Times v. United States* required a higher standard than

---

[273] 467 U.S. 20 (1984).

[274] *Doe II*, 386 F. Supp. 2d at 74-75.

[275] *Id.* at 75.

[276] *Id.* at 76 (quoting Hamdi v. Rumsfeld, 542 U.S. 507, 536 (2004)).

[277] *In re* Washington Post, 807 F.2d 383 (4th Cir. 1986).

[278] *Doe II*, 386 F. Supp. 2d at 76 (quoting *In re* Washington Post, 807 F.2d at 391-92.

[279] *Id.* at 76-77.

speculation to support a prior restraint.[280] Finally, the court cited *McGehee* to counter the government's argument that the "mosaic concept," which had been used to prevent disclosures under Freedom of Information Act, should prevent Doe's disclosure. The court concluded that this argument was not persuasive because it was considering a constitutional right to disseminate information already in Doe's possession rather than a statutory right to gather information.[281]

Next, considering if the statute was narrowly tailored, Hall cited the same cases the *Doe I* court had, *Butterworth* and *Kamasinski*, as well as *Doe I* itself, to determine that a permanent ban on speech was inherently not narrowly tailored.[282] Concluding its discussion, the court then invoked the role of free speech plays as a check on government to further supports the conclusion the statute was not narrowly tailored. The court wrote:

> § 2709(c) creates a unique situation in which the only people who possess non-speculative facts about the reach of broad, federal investigatory authority are barred from discussing their experience with the public. This ban is particularly noteworthy given the fact that advocates of the legislation have consistently relied on the public's faith in the government to apply the statute narrowly in order to advocate for passage and reauthorization of various provisions of the Patriot Act. The potential for abuse is written into the statute: the very people who might have information regarding investigative abuses and overreaching are preemptively prevented from sharing that information with the public and with the legislators who empower the executive branch with the tools used to investigate matters of national security.[283]

---

[280] *Id.* at 77.

[281] *Id.* at 77-78.

[282] *Id.* at 79-80.

[283] *Id.* at 81-82 (citing Attorney General John Ashcroft, Protecting Life and Liberty (Sept. 18, 2003) (transcript available at http://www.usdoj.gov/archive/ag/speeches/2003/091803memphisrem arks.htm) (accusing those who fear executive abuse of the increased access to library records under the PATRIOT Act of "hysteria" and stating that "the Department of Justice has neither the staffing, the time nor the inclination to monitor the

However, although Hall ruled in favor of Doe and granted a preliminary injunction, she stayed the injunction, noting that the government could be irreparably harmed should the preliminary injunction be reversed by the court of appeals.

Although the government appealed the case, while appeals in both *Doe I* and *Doe II* were pending, Congress passed the USA Patriot Improvement and Reauthorization Act of 2005,[284] which substantially changed § 2709 and added new provisions to the Act. Based on this action, the Second Circuit remanded *Doe I* to the Southern District of New York[285] to "consider the validity of the revised § 2709(c) and the new procedures codified in § 3511."[286] When the case came before District Judge Marrero the second time, Doe sought to declare §§ 2709 and 3511 unconstitutional "on their face and as applied under the First Amendment and the principle of separation of powers,"[287] as well as to have the demand for records from Doe set aside. However, because the government no longer sought to enforce the underlying NSL and only moved for dismissal of Doe's constitutional challenges,[288] the court did not consider the validity of the NSL.

Noting that the government was contending that the changes made to the Act directly addressed the concerns he raised in *Doe I*,[289] Marrero began by summarizing the changes made in the Reauthorization Act.

> Instead of a categorical, blanket prohibition on disclosure with respect to the issuance of any NSL, § 2709(c) now calls for a case-by-case determination of the need for a nondisclosure

---

reading habits of Americans. No offense to the American Library Association, but we just don't care.")).

[284] Pub. L. No. 109-177, 120 Stat. 192 (Mar. 9, 2006).

[285] Doe v. Gonzales, 449 F.3d 415, 419 (2d Cir. 2006). The appeal was a consolidation of *Doe I* and *Doe II*. However, on appeal the government conceded that the defendants in *Doe II* could identify themselves. Therefore, the Second Circuit dismissed *Doe II* as moot. *Id.* at 421.

[286] *Doe III*, 500 F.Supp. 2d 379, 386 (S.D.N.Y. 2007).

[287] *Id.*

[288] *Id.*

[289] *Id.* at 388-89.

order to accompany an NSL. Specifically, the statute provides that a recipient of an NSL is barred from disclosing that the FBI "has sought or obtained access to information or records" under the NSL statute if the Director of the FBI, or his designee, "certifies" that disclosure "may result" in "a danger to the national security of the United States, interference with a criminal, counterterrorism, or counterintelligence investigation, interference with diplomatic relations, or danger to the life or physical safety of any person" (here collectively referred to as the "Enumerated Harms").[290]

In addition, although the statute now specifically provided for judicial review of NSLs, the amended statute mandated the level of review, stating that courts could only overturn the non-disclosure provision if it found there was "'no reason to believe' disclosure 'may result' in one or more of the Enumerated Harms."[291] Furthermore, as amended the statute provided that if an "authorized senior FBI officials 'certifies that disclosure may endanger the national security of the United States or interfere with diplomatic relations, such certification shall be treated as conclusive unless the court finds that the certification was made in bad faith.'"[292] Doe contended the statute remained an unconstitutional prior restraint and a content-based restriction on speech because it failed "to provide constitutionally mandated procedural safeguards, . . . invest[ed] the FBI with unbridled discretion to suppress speech, . . . foreclose[ed] reviewing courts from applying a constitutionally mandated standard of review, and . . . authorize[d] the issuance of nondisclosure orders that [were] not narrowly tailored."[293]

In its opinion, the court focused on balancing, discussing the need for balance both in terms of the First Amendment[294] and separation of powers.[295] To support the conclusion that the Act was still facially unconstitutional, the court relied upon precedents related to national

---

[290] *Id.* at 389.
[291] *Id.* (citing 18 U.S.C. § 3511(b)(2)).
[292] *Id.* (citing 18 U.S.C. § 3511(b)(2)).
[293] *Id.*
[294] *Id.* at 395.
[295] *Id.* at 395-96.

security and the First Amendment but also discussed democratic theory and originalism.

The court began by discussing Doe's claim that the statute did not provide constitutionally mandated procedural safeguards. The court held that the Act should be subjected to strict scrutiny because the non-disclosure provision was still a prior restraint[296] and allowing the FBI to decide on a case-by-case whether the non-disclosure would be enforced made the non-disclosure provision both a viewpoint *and* content-based restriction.[297] Based on this determination, the court ruled that the non-disclosure provision could survive only if it were "'narrowly tailored to promote a compelling government interest,'"[298] there were no "'less restrictive alternatives [that] would be at least as effective in achieving the legitimate purpose that the statute was enacted to serve,'"[299] and the statute contained sufficient "'procedural safeguards designed to obviate the dangers of a censorship system.'"[300] Applying strict scrutiny to the law, as it had done in *Doe I*, the court cited a number of precedents to determine that national security was a compelling government interest.[301] The court next considered the procedural safeguards required under precedent. Based on *Maryland v. Freeman*,[302] a case involving a statute that made it unlawful to exhibit a motion picture prior to obtaining approval, the court held the law did not provide enough procedural safeguards. The court ruled that in order for the nondisclosure provision to be constitutional, the government had to "bear the burden of going to court to suppress the speech and . . . the

---

[296] *Id.* at 397.

[297] *Id.*

[298] *Id.* at 398 (quoting United States v. Playboy Entm't Group, Inc., 529 U.S. 803, 813 (2000).

[299] *Id.* (quoting Reno v. ACLU, 521 U.S. 844, 874 (1997)).

[300] *Id.* at 399 (quoting Freedman v. Maryland, 380 U.S. 51, 58 (1965)).

[301] *Id.* at 398-99.

[302] 380 U.S. 51 (1965). In *Freedman*, the Court held that licensing schemes that imposed prior restraints on protected speech required three procedural safeguards. First, in advance of judicial review prior restraints could only be imposed for "a specified brief period." Second, further restraints prior to "a final judicial determination on the merits" must be limited to "the shortest fixed period compatible with sound judicial resolution." Third, the government had the burden of going to court to suppress the speech and the burden of proof once in court. *Id.* at 58-59.

burden of proof once in court."[303] The court concluded that while the government need not get judicial approval prior to issuing an NSL, "within a reasonable and brief period of time, it must either notify the NSL recipient that the order is no longer in effect, or justify to a court the need for a continued period of nondisclosure."[304]

Considering the scope of § 2709(c), as it had in *Doe I*, the court focused on the length and totality of the ban on speech. Citing a concurring opinion from *Doe II*, the court invoked democratic theory and the checking function of the First Amendment to criticize the reach of the statute. Marrero wrote: "[A] ban on speech and a shroud of secrecy in perpetuity are antithetical to democratic concepts and do not fit comfortably with the fundamental rights guaranteed American citizens. Unending secrecy of actions taken by government officials may also serve as a cover for possible official misconduct and/or incompetence."[305] Therefore, although the revised Act incorporated provisions for case-by-case review of the nondisclosure requirements, because it "continue[d] to authorize nondisclosure orders that *permanently* restrict an NSL recipient from engaging in *any* discussion related to its receipt of the NSL,"[306] Marrero held it was not narrowly tailored.

Again focusing on balancing the roles of the courts and the executive branch and citing precedent, the court turned to Doe's claim that the nondisclosure provision conferred unbridled discretion on the FBI to censor protected speech. Although the court noted that the Supreme Court had established that any statute that provided government officials with discretion to suppress speech must have narrow, objective and definite standards to govern decisions[307] and "national security" was a vague term, subject to broad interpretations which invited abuse,[308] it remained "'well-settled doctrine that courts grant substantial deference to the political branches in national security

---

[303] *Doe III*, 500 F. Supp. 2d at 406.
[304] *Id.*
[305] *Id.* at 421-22.
[306] *Id.* at 421.
[307] *Id.* at 407.
[308] *Doe III*, 500 F. Supp. 2d at 407.

matters.'"[309] Thus, Marrero was unwilling to rule that the statute's self-certification procedure granted too much discretion to the FBI.

Finally, considering the separation of powers issues presented by the case, Marrero again relied upon precedent but also included a discussion of framers' intent. In a scolding tone, Marrero began by noting that while his discussion might seem "like unnecessary rehashing" or "tedious repetition," "sometimes we are compelled to recite the obvious again because on occasion, counter to even the most constant refrain of the same theme, the message still goes unnoticed, or inadequately considered, perhaps ignored."[310] After discussing framers' intent and citing the *Federalists Papers*,[311] *Marbury v. Madison*[312] and, finally, *Hamdi v. Rumsfeld*,[313] Marrero concluded that the Act was an unconstitutional violation of long established constitutional principles.

> Against this backdrop of history and constitutional premises, § 3511(b) is invalid because it does not reflect full account of these controlling principles and the long-standing national experience from which their force derives. That provision amounts to a significant congressional incursion, one with profound implications, into exclusive jurisdictional ground the Constitution reserves for the judiciary's role in our government.[314]

Marrero went on to admonish Congress for its foray into judicial powers, warning of the consequences of such actions even in the wake of the terrorist attacks of 9/11.

> As *Doe I* noted, the Court recognized the "heavy weight" of September 11, 2001, "a murderous attack of international terrorism, unparalleled in its magnitude, and unprecedented in

---

[309] *Id.*
[310] *Id.* at 409.
[311] *Id.*
[312] 5 U.S. 137 (1803).
[313] 542 U.S. 507 (2004).
[314] *Doe III*, 500 F. Supp. 2d at 411.

America's national security," that looms over this proceeding. Its effect is still felt and acknowledged by this Court, which sits just a few blocks from where the World Trade Center towers fell. . . . However, new methods of protecting and combating threats that result in asserted expansions of executive power underscore the courts' concerns of the dangers in suffering any infringement on their essential role under the Constitution. The Constitution was designed so that the dangers of any given moment would never suffice as justification for discarding fundamental individual liberties or circumscribing the judiciary's unique role under our governmental system in protecting those liberties and upholding the rule of law.[315]

Thus, as the previous national security/prior restraint cases had done, the courts in *Doe I*, *Doe II* and *Doe III* focused on both balancing the First Amendment with national security and examined the proper role of the judiciary in national security decisions. Although the *Doe I* court was primarily concerned with balancing freedom of expression, by the time the same judge considered the reworked Patriot Act in *Doe III*, Congress' attempts to place limits on the judiciary's power caused the court to invoke a strong and deliberate separation of powers frame. The cases outlined above are, therefore, as much, if not more, about the judiciary's attempt to articulate its role in national security vis-à-vis the other branches' roles as they are about the judiciary's attempt to balance national security with freedom of expression. While the judiciary/prior restraint cases share much in common with the national security/prior restraint cases—such as a reliance on *New York Times v. United States*, a focus on balancing the First Amendment with other interest, and statements that prior restraint are the least tolerable abridgement of expression—they lack any discussing of the power of the courts. This is as should be expected, considering the cases do not deal with the other branches of government.

---

[315] *Id.* at 415 (citation and footnotes omitted).

Prior Restraints and the Judiciary

In the 1960s the U.S. Supreme Court overturned four criminal convictions on the grounds that media coverage of the trials had deprived the defendants of their right to a fair trial by an impartial jury.[316] Although the Court recognized that prejudicial publicity and media activities within the courtroom might affect the fair administration of the judicial process, the Court never suggested that trial courts impose prior restraints on the media, instead declaring that trials were public events and the press was "plainly free to report whatever happens in open court."[317] Nonetheless, some trial judges decided to impose prior restraints on the press in an effort to protect the integrity of the judicial process.[318] The first such case reached a Supreme Court Justice in 1974, when Justice Powell, sitting as the circuit justice for the Fifth Circuit, reviewed a gag order directly imposed on the press.[319] In the years following, the Court considered a number of similar cases. As in the national security and prior restraints cases discussed above, the Court often framed the cases in terms of the need to balance freedom of expression with other values and rights, in the court cases the right of criminal defendants to a fair trial and the need for the proper functioning of the judicial system. However, because the Court was discussing the powers of the judiciary, there was no need to frame any of the cases in terms of separation of powers. Thus, the Court never had to consider how much deference to give to other branches of government. Despite this difference, the two types of cases have some remarkable similarities.

Typically, both kinds of cases note that while the First Amendment is not absolute, its primary purpose is to prevent prior restraints and the government will have a difficult time overcoming that burden. Furthermore, the majority of opinions in both categories of cases frame

---

[316] *See, e.g.,* Sheppard v. Maxwell, 384 U.S. 333 (1966); Estes v. Texas, 381 U.S. 532 (1965); Rideau v. State of Louisiana, 373 U.S. 723 (1963); Irvin v. Dowd, 366 U.S. 717 (1961).

[317] Estes, 381 U.S. at 541-42.

[318] *See, e.g.,* Seattle Times v. Rhinehart, 467 U.S. 20 (1984); Oklahoma Pub'g Co. v. Dist. Court, 430 U.S. 308 (1977); Nebraska Press Ass'n v. Stuart, 427 U.S. 539 (1976); Times-Picayune Pub. Corp. v. Schulingkamp, 419 U.S. 1301 (1974).

[319] Times-Picayune Pub. Corp. v. Schulingkamp, 419 U.S. 1301 (1974).

the key legal issue as the need to balance the First Amendment with some other constitutional mandate. In addition, they often cite the same cases as controlling and apply the same tests to determine when a prior restraint is constitutional. In fact, many of the judiciary cases discussed in this section of the chapter were used to reach and justify the decisions discussed above. For example, the Patriot Act cases, frequently discussed cases involving the judiciary.

The first time a prior restraint related to media coverage of a judicial proceeding reached a Supreme Court Justice was in *Times-Picayune Publishing v. Schulingkamp*, a case involving a request for a stay of an order of the Louisiana Criminal District Court for the Parish of Orleans, which had prevented publication of information obtained at pretrial proceedings and the trials of two defendants accused of rape and murder.[320] The court's order imposed "a total ban on reporting of testimony given in hearings on pretrial motions" and "other selective restrictions on reporting" for the duration of the trial.[321] Justice Powell identified the main legal issue in the case as the need to balance the First Amendment rights of the press with the Sixth Amendment rights of the defendant to a fair trial.[322] Although he wrote that "[t]he task of reconciling First Amendment rights with the defendant's right to a fair trial before an impartial jury [was] not an easy one," Powell relied upon precedent to determine the restraint was unconstitutional.[323]

Powell began his opinion by citing a number of previous Supreme Court rulings that had also been relied upon in the prior restraints and national security cases.[324] Powell discussed and cited *New York Times v. United States*,[325] *Organization for a Better Austin v. O'Keefe*,[326] *Bantam Books v. Sullivan*[327] and *Near v. Minnesota*.[328] Turning to precedents related to attending, viewing or reporting on the judicial process, Powell noted that a number of the Court's decisions had

---

[320] *Id.* at 1301.
[321] *Id.* at 1304.
[322] *Id.* at 1305.
[323] *Id.* at 1308.
[324] *Id.* at 1307.
[325] 403 U.S. 713 (1971).
[326] 402 U.S. 415 (1971).
[327] 372 U.S. 58 (1963).
[328] 283 U.S. 697 (1931).

"recognized that trials are public events."[329] Yet, Powell countered this by citing previous Court decisions that had "shown a special solicitude for preserving fairness in a criminal trial,"[330] focusing especially on *Branzburg v. Hayes,*[331] the famous reporter's privilege case. Powell reasoned that while the Court had stated in dictum in *Branzburg* that "newsmen might be prohibited from publishing information about trials if such restrictions were necessary to assure a defendant a fair trial,"[332] nothing in the Court's opinion indicated a prior restraint issued by a court would be subjected to a standard materially different from any other prior restraint.[333] Powell concluded that in the present case, the government had not met the high burden of proof required to sustain a prior restraint, especially one that was "both pervasive and of uncertain duration."[334]

Two years later, the full Court considered the right to report on judicial proceedings in *Nebraska Press Association v. Stuart* and ruled that a gag order was unconstitutional.[335] The landmark case involved the prosecution of Erwin Charles Simants for the murder of six individuals in Sutherland, Nebraska. The preliminary hearing for Simants was held in an open courtroom, but because of the pervasive publicity, the trial judge issued an order barring publication of testimony and evidence, as well as requiring journalists to abide by the Nebraska Bar-Press Guidelines, voluntary standards dealing with the reporting of crimes and criminal trials.[336] When members of the media appealed, District Court Judge Hugh Stuart entered a new order that incorporated the press-bar guidelines and prohibited publication of "the existence or contents of a confession Simants had made to law enforcement officers, which had been introduced in open court," certain aspects of medical testimony from the preliminary hearing, information that indicated that Simants had sexually assaulted some of the victims after murdering them, and the existence of the order itself until after a

---

[329] *Times-Picayune Pub. Corp.*, 419 U.S. at 1307.
[330] *Id.* at 1307.
[331] 408 U.S. 665 (1972).
[332] *Times-Picayune Pub. Corp.*, 419 U.S. at 1307.
[333] *Id.*
[334] *Id.* at 1308.
[335] 427 U.S. 539 (1976).
[336] *Id.* at 542.

jury had been impaneled.[337] Noting that Nebraska law did not allow the trial to be postponed more than six months and allowed a change of venue only to adjoining counties, where there would still be publicity, the Nebraska Supreme Court modified the order, but refused to overturn it.[338] The Nebraska Supreme Court's order removed references to the press-bar guidelines but prohibited the disclosure of "the existence and nature of any confessions or admissions made by the defendant to law enforcement officers, . . . any confessions or admissions made to any third parties, except members of the press, and . . . other facts 'strongly implicative' of the accused."[339] The U.S. Supreme Court granted certiorari eleven days after the Nebraska Supreme Court's decision but denied a motion to expedite review or to stay the gag order.[340]

Although all nine justices agreed the order was unconstitutional, they offered different reasons for their conclusions and framed the case in different terms. Both the majority's opinion, written by Chief Justice Burger, and a concurring opinion by Powell followed Powell's opinion in *Times-Picayune* and focused on the need to balance freedom of expression with the proper functioning of the judicial system.[341] Brennan, joined by Marshall and Stewart, however, only framed the case in terms of the First Amendment, arguing for a complete ban on all prior restraints imposed by courts.[342] Finally, in separate concurrences, White and Stevens indicated they might agree to an absolute ban at a later date but were unwilling to do so in the present case.[343]

Burger relied on originalism and First Amendment and Sixth Amendment precedents to support his conclusion. Noting there was a long history of conflict between freedom of expression and the fair administration of justice[344] and using originalism to support his contention that the rights of the press had to be balanced with other

---

[337] *Id.* at 543-44.
[338] State v. Simants, 194 Neb. 783, 797 (1975).
[339] *Nebraska Press Ass'n*, 427 U.S. at 545.
[340] *Id.* at 546.
[341] *Id.* at 570; *id.* at 571-72 (Powell, J., concurring).
[342] *Id.* at 572 (Brennan, J., concurring).
[343] *Id.* at 570-71 (White, J., concurring); *id.* at 617 (Stevens, J., concurring).
[344] *Id.* at 547-50.

rights,[345] Burger concluded that rather than "write a code" to govern all clashes between the two principles the court should rely on ad hoc balancing and look to the particulars of each individual case.[346]

After reviewing a number of decisions involving the Sixth Amendment rights of defendants to a fair trial,[347] Burger concluded that while "taken together, these cases demonstrate[ed] that pretrial publicity, even pervasive, adverse publicity, does not inevitably lead to an unfair trial,"[348] the trial judge had a major responsibility to make sure media coverage did not unfairly influence a jury.[349] Based on this Burger concluded:

> The state trial judge in the case before us acted responsibly, out of a legitimate concern, in an effort to protect the defendant's right to a fair trial. What we must decide is not simply whether the Nebraska courts erred in seeing the possibility of real danger to the defendant's rights, but whether in the circumstances of this case the means employed were foreclosed by another provision of the Constitution.[350]

To accomplish this, Burger again relied on familiar precedent, discussing *Near v. Minnesota*,[351] *Organization for a Better Austin v. Keefe*,[352] and *New York Times Co. v. United States*.[353] Burger concluded that these cases, taken together, demonstrated "prior restraints on speech and publication are the most serious and the least tolerable infringement on First Amendment rights."[354] Returning to

---

[345] *See id.* at 548 (quoting a letter from Thomas Jefferson to John Jay).

[346] *Id.* at 550-51.

[347] Burger discussed *Duncan v. Louisiana*, 391 U.S. 145 (1968); *Irvin v. Dowd*, 366 U.S. 717 (1966); *Rideau v. Louisiana*, 373 U.S. 723 (1963); *Estes v. Texas*, 381 U.S. 532 (1965); *Sheppard v. Maxwell*, 384 U.S. 333 (1966); and *Stroble v. California*, 343 U.S. 181 (1952).

[348] *Nebraska Press Ass'n*, 427 U.S. at 554.

[349] *Id.* at 555.

[350] *Id.* at 555-56.

[351] 283 U.S. 697 (1931).

[352] 402 U.S. 415 (1971).

[353] 403 U.S. 713 (1972).

[354] *Nebraska Press Ass'n*, 427 U.S. at 559.

originalism, Burger wrote that the problem was balancing these two lines of cases.

> The authors of the Bill of Rights did not undertake to assign priorities as between First Amendment and Sixth Amendment rights, ranking one as superior to the other. In this case, the petitioners would have us declare the right of an accused subordinate to their right to publish in all circumstances. But if the authors of these guarantees, fully aware of the potential conflicts between them, were unwilling or unable to resolve the issue by assigning to one priority over the other, it is not for us to rewrite the Constitution by undertaking what they declined to do.[355]

To solve the problem, Burger adopted the clear and present danger test established in the early 20th century sedition cases, reasoning that the constitutionality of a gag order could be decided by determining if "'the gravity of the "evil," discounted by its improbability, justifies such invasion of free speech as is necessary to avoid the danger.'"[356] To determine this, Burger wrote there were three factors that had to be considered: "the nature and extent of pretrial news coverage, . . . whether other measures would be likely to mitigate the effects of unrestrained pretrial publicity," and, finally, "how effectively a restraining order would operate to prevent the threatened danger."[357] Applying the three factors to the case, Burger wrote that while there was a risk that pretrial coverage would have "some adverse impact" on the jurors,[358] Judge Stuart had failed to consider any alternatives to a prior restraint,[359] and it was doubtful that a gag order would be effective in such a small community.[360] Additionally, Burger noted that precedent had established that the press was free to publish

---

[355] *Id.* at 561.
[356] *Id.* at 562 (quoting United States v. Dennis, 183 F.2d 201, 212 (2d Cir. 1950), *aff'd*, 341 U.S. 494 (1951).
[357] *Id.*
[358] *Id.* at 569.
[359] *Id.* at 565.
[360] *Id.* at 566-67.

information it had gathered in an open courtroom.[361] Thus, while Burger wrote that freedom of expression was "not an absolute prohibition under all circumstances," the "barriers to prior restraint remain[ed] high and the presumption against its use continue[d] intact."[362]

In contrast, Brennan's opinion did not accept that there was a need to balance First and Sixth Amendment concerns in these kinds of cases. Noting that judges had a wide range of options to prevent prejudicial publicity from reaching jurors, Brennan concluded there was no need to resort to restraints on expression.[363] Although he framed the case differently than Burger, to support his conclusion Brennan also relied on Sixth[364] and First Amendment precedents,[365] citing many of the same cases as the Chief Justice. However, Brennan also invoked First Amendment theory, including the role of freedom of expression in self-government and as a check on government abuses,[366] and discussed practical problems with ad hoc balancing.[367]

Brennan wrote that although the Court had stated "the right to a fair trial has been called 'the most fundamental of all freedoms,'"[368] there was no need to balance the Sixth Amendment with the First Amendment.

---

[361] *Id.* at 568.

[362] *Id.* at 570.

[363] *Id.* at 572-73 (Brennan, J., concurring). *See also id.* at 601-04 (discussing the other options available to Judge Stuart in the case).

[364] Like Burger, Brennan cited *Duncan v. Louisiana*, 391 U.S. 145 (1968); *Estes v. Texas*, 381 U.S. 532, 540 (1965); *Rideau v. Lousiana*, 373 U.S. 723 (1963); and *Irvin v. Dowd*, 366 U.S. 717, 722 (1961). In addition, Brennan cited *Reynolds v. United States*, 98 U.S. 145 (1879), and *Ristaino v. Ross*, 424 U.S. 589 (1976).

[365] As Burger had done, Brennan relied on *Cox Broad. Corp. v. Cohn*, 420 U.S. 469 (1975); *New York Times Co. v. United States*, 403 U.S. 713 (1972); *Sheppard v. Maxwell*, 384 U.S. 333 (1966); and *Near v. Minnesota*, 283 U.S. 697 (1931). However, Brennan also cited *Miami Herald Pub'g Co. v. Tornillo*, 418 U.S. 241 (1974); *New York Times Co. v. Sullivan*, 376 U.S. 254 (1964); *Craig v. Harney*, 331 U.S. 367 (1947); and *Bridges v. California*, 314 U.S. 252 (1941).

[366] *Nebraska Press Ass'n*, 427 U.S. at 587 (Brennan, J., concurring).

[367] *Id.* at 604-08.

[368] *Id.* at 586 (quoting *Estes*, 381 U.S. at 540).

[T]he past decade has witnessed substantial debate, colloquially known as the Free Press/Fair Trial controversy, concerning this interface of First and Sixth Amendment rights. In effect, we are now told by respondents that the two rights can no longer coexist . . . . I disagree. Settled case law concerning the impropriety and constitutional invalidity of prior restraints on the press compels the conclusion that there can be no prohibition on the publication by the press of any information pertaining to pending judicial proceedings or the operation of the criminal justice system. . . . This does not imply, however, any subordination of Sixth Amendment rights, for an accused's right to a fair trial may be adequately assured through methods that do not infringe First Amendment values.[369]

Brennan next concluded that while First Amendment protections were not unlimited even when evaluating prior restraints,[370] the Court had previously determined that the First Amendment's primary purpose was to prevent prior restraints[371] and it afforded greater protections against them than it did against subsequent punishment for speech.[372] Thus, Brennan concluded that prior restraints were justified only when the speech was "of a lesser value."[373] Turning specifically to prior restraints of judicial information, Brennan argued they were especially problematic for two reasons. First, there was an absolute right to publish information obtained in open court because it was in the public domain.[374] Second, because a judge would have to speculate on the harmful effects of prejudicial information, Brennan concluded that prior restraints were inappropriate regarding "*any* information pertaining to the criminal justice system, even if derived from nonpublic sources and regardless of the means employed by the press

---

[369] *Id.* at 588.

[370] *Id.* at 590.

[371] *Id.* at 588-89.

[372] *Id.*

[373] *Id.* at 590 (citing Miller v. California, 413 U.S. 15 (1973) (obscenity); Roth v. United States, 354 U.S. 476, 481 (1957) (obscenity); Chaplinsky v. New Hampshire, 315 U.S. 568 (1942) (fighting words)).

[374] *Id.* at 597-98.

in its acquisition."[375] Brennan argued that the farthest the Court had ever gone in support of prior restraints was to suggest in dictum that prior restraints might be acceptable in cases of national security where there was evidence of "certain, direct, and immediate harm."[376] Thus, as opposed to Burger who suggested the relative values of the Sixth and First Amendment's must be weighed against each other on a case-by-case basis, Brennan concluded that prior restraints in these kinds of cases were never appropriate.

A year later, the issue returned to the Court in *Oklahoma Publishing Co. v. District Court*,[377] a case involving an order preventing the publication of the name and picture of an eleven-year-old charged with murder. In a short per curiam opinion, the Court reinforced the right to publish information learned in open court, relying entirely on precedent. The Court simply stated that *Nebraska Press Association* and *Cox Broadcasting Corp. v. Cohn*[378] had clearly established that the First Amendment protected "the publication of widely disseminated information obtained at court proceedings which were in fact open to the public."[379] The Court held that although there was a state statute that clearly provided for the closing of juvenile hearings, because the hearing was not closed, it was unconstitutional to order the media not to report what they learned.[380]

In 1984 the Court engaged in a much lengthier analysis of judicial restraints on the press in a case involving a court order prohibiting a newspaper from publishing information divulged as part of discovery in a civil case against the newspaper. *Seattle Times v. Rhinehart*[381] involved a defamation suit by the leader of the Aquarius Foundation, Keith Milton Rhinehart, and others against the *Seattle Times*. Because the plaintiffs were alleging a loss of members and donations due to the *Times'* stories, the *Seattle Times* filed a motion to compel the disclosure of Rhinehart's and the Foundation's financial records, including a list

---

[375] *Id.* at 599.
[376] *Id.*
[377] 430 U.S. 308 (1977).
[378] 420 U.S. 469 (1975).
[379] *Oklahoma Pub'g*, 430 U.S. at 310.
[380] *Id.* at 311.
[381] 467 U.S. 20 (1984).

of the Foundation's donors and members.[382] After a series of motions by both parties, the court issued an order compelling Rhinehart and the Foundation to identify all donors who had contributed to the Foundation in the last five years and reveal membership information. In addition, the court issued an order preventing the *Seattle Times* from "publishing, disseminating, or using the information in any way except where necessary to prepare for and try the case."[383] When the Washington Supreme Court upheld the order, the U.S. Supreme Court granted certiorari, noting there were conflicts among lower courts regarding the placing of restrictions on the publication of information learned during discovery.[384]

Writing for the majority, Justice Powell framed the case as a clash between the *Seattle Times'* First Amendment rights and "the duty and discretion of a trial court to oversee the discovery process."[385] After again noting that First Amendment rights were not absolute,[386] Powell applied intermediate scrutiny rather than strict scrutiny or a balancing test.[387] Although he never specifically explained why he was applying intermediate scrutiny, Powell put forward a number of reasons related to "the extent of the impairment of First Amendment rights"[388] that suggested intermediate scrutiny was proper. Citing two cases dealing with First Amendment access rights, *Zemel v. Rusk*[389] and *Gannett Co. v. DePasquale*,[390] Powell reasoned that "[a] litigant has no First Amendment right of access to information made available only for

---

[382] *Id.* at 24-25.

[383] *Id.* at 27. The order specified that the newspaper was free to publish any information gained by means other than the discovery process.

[384] *Id.* at 29. The Court noted that the Washington Supreme Court's holding was consistent with the Second Circuit's decision in *Inter'l Prod. Corp. v. Koons*, 325 F.2d 403 (2d 1963), but conflicted with the holdings of the United States Court of Appeals for the District of Columbia in *In re Halkin*, 598 F.2d 176 (1979), and "applied a different standard" than the First Circuit's decision in *In re San Juan Star Co.*, 662 F.2d 108 (1st Cir. 1981).

[385] *Id.* at 31.

[386] *Id.* (quoting Am. Commc'ns Ass'n. v. Douds, 339 U.S. 382, 394-95 (1950)).

[387] *Id.* at 32.

[388] *Id.*

[389] 381 U.S. 1 (1965).

[390] 443 U.S. 368 (1979).

purposes of trying his suit,"[391] discovery hearings were traditionally closed to the public,[392] and the order was "not the kind of classic prior restraint that require[d] exacting First Amendment scrutiny."[393] Furthermore, Powell argued that the restriction was not targeted at the *Seattle Times'* First Amendment rights, but rather that the First Amendment infringement was incidental to the effort to protect the discovery process.[394]

Determining that the trial court's duty to protect a liberal discovery process was a substantial interest and the order was narrowly tailored, Powell upheld the Washington Supreme Court's decision.[395] It is important to note, however, Powell made the distinction between information gathered as part of the discovery process and the exact same information if it was learned outside the discovery process. Powell wrote that the *Seattle Times* could "disseminate the identical information covered by the protective order as long as the information [was] gained through means independent of the court's processes."[396] Although it would appear this situation would be at least somewhat analogous to a CIA agent publishing information he learned outside the scope of his duties but identical to information learned as part of his duties, it is a different standard than that used by courts when considering government employee confidentiality agreements.

Brennan, joined by Marshall, filed a brief concurring opinion. Brennan wrote that the governmental interest advanced by the order was not the discovery process itself, but rather the protection of the Foundation members' right to privacy and religious freedom.[397] Therefore, while Brennan did not change his stance that there was no need to balance First Amendment rights with the effective operation of the judicial system, he did retreat from his statement that the press would be protected when publishing truthful information regardless of how it obtained the information.

---

[391] *Seattle Times*, 467 U.S. at 32.
[392] *Id.* at 33.
[393] *Id.* at 33-34.
[394] *Id.* at 34.
[395] *Id.* at 34-35.
[396] *Id.*
[397] *Id.* at 38 (Brennan, J., concurring).

The final time a case involving a prior restraint imposed on the publication of information related to a judicial proceeding came to the Court was the 1990 case of *Butterworth v. Smith*.[398] *Butterworth* involved a Florida statute that prohibited grand jury witnesses from ever disclosing the testimony they gave before a grand jury.[399] The case began when Michael Smith, a reporter for the *Charlotte Herald-News* in Charlotte County, Florida, was called to testify before a special grand jury about information he had obtained while writing a series of newspaper articles about alleged improprieties committed by the Charlotte County State Attorney's Office and Sheriff's Department.[400] Wishing to publish a story and a book about the subject of the investigation and his testimony and experiences before the grand jury, Smith sued in United States District Court. Smith sought a declaration that the Florida statute barring disclosure was unconstitutional and an injunction preventing his prosecution under the statute. Like the other opinions in this section, Chief Justice William Rehnquist's opinion for the Court framed the case as involving the need to balance First Amendment rights against Florida's interest in "preserving the confidentiality of its grand jury proceedings."[401]

Rehnquist began his opinion by discussing the history of grand jury proceedings and laying out a number of reasons why the state had an interest in keep the proceedings secret. First, he noted that if the proceedings were made public, fewer witnesses would be willing to fully and frankly testify. Second, he reasoned that those under investigation might flee or attempt to influence the testimony of witnesses called before the grand jury. Finally, Rehnquist wrote that the state had an interest in making sure those who were not indicted by the grand jury were not subjected to public ridicule.[402]

Next, however, Rehnquist distinguished the case from *Seattle Times v. Rhinehart*, noting that because the restriction involved the dissemination of information lawfully obtained before Smith's grand jury testimony, it was more akin to the Court's post-publication

---

[398] 494 U.S. 624 (1990).
[399] Fla. Stat. § 905.27 (1985).
[400] *Butterworth*, 494 U.S. at 626.
[401] *Id.* at 630.
[402] *Id.*

punishment decisions in *Landmark Communications v. Virginia*,[403] *Smith v. Daily Mail*,[404] and *Florida Star v. BJF*.[405] Based on these precedents, Rehnquist concluded that because the order involved "core First Amendment speech," the permanent ban did not serve many of the state's asserted interests, and those that it did serve were "not sufficient to sustain the statute,"[406] the statute was an unconstitutional infringement on protected speech. Rehnquist wrote that when the investigation ended there was no reason to keep information from the subject of the investigation. Second, he reasoned that after the investigation, there was no reason to worry about the effect of disclosure on witnesses.[407] Third, the statute did not advance the government's interest in preventing retribution because witnesses were still free *not* to divulge their own testimony, and the Court was not considering the statute's ban on disclosing other witnesses' testimony.[408] Finally, Rehnquist concluded that while the state's interest in protecting individuals who were exonerated by the grand jury was advanced by the statute, that interest was not strong enough to overcome Smith's First Amendment rights under the reasoning of *Landmark Communications, Florida Star, Daily Mail* and *Oklahoma Publishing Co.*[409] Foreshadowing Judge Marrero's decision in the Patriot Act cases, Rehnquist concluded that the scope of the statute made its restrictions especially serious.

> The effect [of the statute] is dramatic: before he is called to testify in front of the grand jury, respondent is possessed of information on matters of admitted public concern about which he was free to speak at will. After giving his testimony, respondent believes he is no longer free to communicate this information since it relates to the "content, gist, or import" of his testimony. The ban extends not merely to the life of the grand jury but into the indefinite future. The potential for

---

[403] 435 U.S. 829 (1978).
[404] 443 U.S. 97 (1989).
[405] 491 U.S. 524 (1989).
[406] *Butterworth*, 494 U.S. at 633.
[407] *Id.* at 632-33.
[408] *Id.*
[409] *Id.* at 634.

abuse of the Florida prohibition, through its employment as a device to silence those who know of unlawful conduct or irregularities on the part of public officials, is apparent.[410]

In addition to Rehnquist's opinion, Justice Scalia wrote a short concurring opinion attempting to frame the Court's decision as a narrow one.[411] The opinion is especially noteworthy because, as discussed above, the government would rely on its argument in the Patriot Act cases.[412] Scalia wrote there was a difference between ruling that a witness could divulge what he knew and ruling he could divulge that he told that information to a grand jury. While Scalia wrote he was doubtful the state could ever prevent a witness from disclosing his own information, even while the grand jury was sitting, he did not believe the Court was considering whether Smith could divulge the existence of the grand jury proceeding itself.[413] In language that would be quoted by the government in the Patriot Act cases, Scalia wrote, "There may be quite good reasons why the State would want the latter information—which is in a way information of the State's own creation—to remain confidential even after the term of the grand jury has expired."[414]

Thus, from 1974 to 1990, the Supreme Court ruled multiple times that the First Amendment protected the right to disseminate information obtained in judicial proceedings. The only time the Court ruled that other concerns limited the reach of the First Amendment was its decision in *Seattle Times* that the First Amendment did not protect information learned solely through discovery, although it was willing to allow the dissemination of that information if it was learned in some other manner.

These cases demonstrate that the Court's consistent admonition that the primary purpose of the First Amendment is to prevent prior restraints is strong enough that it runs across categories of cases. Furthermore, prior restraint doctrine is so strong that those attempting

---

[410] *Id.* at 635-36.
[411] *Id.* at 636 (Scalia, J., concurring).
[412] *See e.g.,Doe I,* 334 F. Supp. 2d 471, 517 (S.D.N.Y. 2004).
[413] *Id.*
[414] *Id.*

to uphold government restrictions must either frame the cases as dealing with some issue other than the First Amendment—as the dissenting justices in the Pentagon Papers did—or attempt to convince the court that the restriction is not a prior restraint at all—as the government attempted to do in the Patriot Act cases. Thus, as noted, the major difference between the national security and judiciary cases has not been determining the strength of a First Amendment right to publish information without prior restraint, but rather what level of deference a court should give the executive when determining if classified information will be harmful. Except for this key difference, the vast majority of opinions in both categories of cases at least partially framed the key legal issue presented by the facts in each case as the need to balance the First Amendment with some other constitutional mandate or governmental interest.

Indeed, it is notable how many of the opinions outlined in this chapter rely on similar precedents or each other to justify their conclusions and how many followed similar patterns. After writing that the First Amendment's protections are not absolute, many of the judges attempted to weigh competing interests to determine how far the Amendment's protections extended. Even Brennan's concurring opinion in *Nebraska Press Association*, one of the strongest defenses of the First Amendment discussed in this chapter, admitted that there were some national security cases in which the First Amendment might not protect against a prior restraint. However, despite this focus on the importance of national security and many of the jurists' apparent deference to the executive branch, with the exception of the government employee cases and *Progressive*, the First Amendment's prohibition against prior restraints and the judiciary's refusal to totally defer to the executive branch seem to be consistent in these cases. Yet, while the government employee opinions certainly stand out as cases in which the judiciary was the least willing to intrude on executive decisions, it is interesting to compare these cases, as well as the government's argument in the Patriot Act cases, to *Seattle Times* and Scalia's dissent in *Butterworth*. As Scalia noted, it appears that the courts are least willing to prevent prior restraints when the information in question was gained through direct interaction with the government or—as Scalia put it—is of the government's own creation. It will be telling to see if this argument is advanced by the government as cases dealing with terrorism investigations continue to work their way through the legal system. If the government continues to advance the argument that prohibiting ISPs and librarians from disseminating information related to NSLs is allowable because the information is "of the government's own creation," it is quite possible that several current members of the Court in addition to Scalia will be persuaded by the argument and have an easy way to justify side-stepping the Court's jurisprudential regime against prior restraints.

CHAPTER 3

Post-publication Punishments

On May 21, 2006, while appearing on ABC's *This Week*, then Attorney General Alberto R. Gonzales raised the possibility that *New York Times* journalists could be prosecuted for publishing classified information about the National Security Agency's surveillance of terrorist-related calls between the United States and abroad.[1] When asked if the prosecution of journalists for publishing classified information was legal, the Attorney General responded, "There are some statutes on the book which, if you read the language carefully, would seem to indicate that that is a possibility."[2] Gonzales went on to say:

> I understand very much the role that the press plays in our society, the protection under the First Amendment we want to promote and respect . . . but it can't be the case that that right trumps over the right that Americans would like to see, the ability of the federal government to go after criminal activity.[3]

Although the justice department never prosecuted the journalists, Gonzales' statement raised a number of questions regarding the ability of the government to prosecute journalists for the possession or publication of national security information.[4] While some authors have suggested the U.S. government is in need of a new statute that grants broad powers to prevent the publication of national security

---

[1] *See* Walter Pincus, *Prosecution of Journalists Possible in NSA Leaks*, WASH. POST, May 22, 2006, at A04.
[2] *Id.*
[3] *Id.*
[4] For a discussion of the government's ability to prosecute the press for the possession and/or publication of national security information, *see* Derigan A. Silver, *National Security and the Press: The Government's Ability to Prosecute Journalists for the Possession or Publication of National Security Information*, 13 COMM. L. & POL'Y 447 (2008).

129

information,[5] in reality there is already a large body of laws that punish the dissemination of national security information. [6] However, as at least one court has noted, these laws have been infrequently used to prosecute individuals who disseminate information, except in "classic espionage cases."[7] The most famous cases involving the publication of national security information by a newspaper, *New York Times v. United States*,[8] never directly addressed the government's ability to prosecute an individual for disseminating the information. Although several of the justices discussed the question of whether the two newspapers could be prosecuted for possession or publication after the fact, and in *dicta* some of the justices indicated that the newspapers could or should be prosecuted,[9] the question was never answered because the government never attempted to prosecute either newspaper. Additionally, although the government attempted to prosecute Daniel Ellsberg for giving the Pentagon Papers to the *New York Times* and *Washington Post*, the case was dismissed for prosecutorial misconduct.[10] Thus, while *New York Times v. United States* suggested it would be very difficult for the government to meet the high burden required to impose a prior restraint preventing the dissemination of national security information, the ability of the government to punish the publication of classified information has been infrequently

---

[5] *See, e.g.,* RICHARD A. POSNER, NOT A SUICIDE PACT: THE CONSTITUTION IN A TIME OF NATIONAL EMERGENCY (2006); Eric E. Ballou & Kyle E. McSlarrow, Note, *Plugging the Leak: The Case For A Legislative Resolution of the Conflict Between the Demands of Secrecy and the Need for an Open Government*, 71 VA. L. REV. 801 (1985).

[6] *See* Jennifer K. Elsea, *Protection of National Security Information: Congressional Research Service Report for Congress, June 30, 2006, available at* http://fpc.state.gov/documents/organization/68797.pdf.

[7] United States v. Morison, 844 F.2d 1057, 1066 (4th Cir. 1988).

[8] 403 U.S. 713 (1971).

[9] *Id.* at 735 (White, J., concurring); *id.* at 743 (Marshall, J., concurring); *id.* at 752 (Burger, J., dissenting); *id.* at 754 (Harlan, J., dissenting); *id.* at 759 (Blackmun, J., dissenting).

[10] United States v. Russo, No. 9373-(WMB)-(1) (filed Dec. 29, 1971), *dismissed* (C.D. Cal. May 11, 1973). For a discussion of the case, see Melville B. Nimmer, *National Security Secrets v. Free Speech: The Issues Left Undecided in the Ellsberg Case*, 26 STAN. L. REV. 311 (1974).

addressed by courts. There are, however, a few cases that illuminate the issue.

This chapter of the book discusses three cases that considered post-publication punishments for disseminating national security information and examines how those courts framed the key legal issues presented by the cases and the legal factors the judges used to reach their decisions. The chapter first examines the 1981 Supreme Court decision in *Haig v. Agee*,[11] which considered whether the revocation of a passport for disseminating information about the Central Intelligence Agency (CIA) violated the First Amendment rights of a former CIA employee. Next, it discusses the Fourth Circuit Court of Appeals decision in *United States v. Morison*,[12] the 1988 appeal of former U.S. Navy analyst Samuel Morison, who was convicted of violating 18 U.S.C. § 641 and two subsections of the Espionage Act, 18 U.S.C. § 7939(d) and (e), for giving national security information to one "not entitled to receive it." It continues with the more recent case of *United States v. Rosen*,[13] part of an ongoing attempt by the U.S. government to prosecute two former lobbyists for the American Israel Public Affairs Committee (AIPAC) for violating the Espionage Act. Finally, the chapter compares the frameworks and legal factors these three courts used to those used by the Supreme Court in the few cases the high court has heard involving attempts to punish publication of information relating to or obtained from the judiciary.

Although there have only been a limited number of cases identified that considered post-publication punishments, the opinions are notably complex, many relying on multiple modes of legal interpretation. In addition, unlike the prior restraint cases, there was very little intersection between the two sets of cases examined in this chapter. The opinions discussed below demonstrate that the Court has yet to articulate an approach to post-publication punishment cases that lower courts can follow across categories. While the judiciary cases consistently relied on the clear and present danger line of cases to reach conclusions, the national security opinions did not, and the two sets of cases rarely, if ever, cited each other.

---

[11] 453 U.S. 280 (1980).
[12] *Morison*, 844 F.2d 1057.
[13] United States v. Rosen, 445 F. Supp. 2d 602 (E.D. Va. 2006).

Post-publication Punishments and National Security

In 1981, the U.S. Supreme Court considered the First Amendment rights of a former CIA employee to disseminate information about the agency in *Haig v. Agee*.[14] In 1974, Philip Agee, a former CIA employee living abroad, announced his campaign to fight the CIA by exposing the identities of CIA officers and agents operating around the world.[15] According to the Court, Agee's identifications violated the same secrecy oath at issue in *Snepp v. United States*,[16] "prejudiced the ability of the United States to obtain intelligence," and resulted in the murder of numerous CIA agents.[17] In response to Agee's activities, the U.S. Department of State revoked Agee's U.S. passport in December 1979, advised Agee of his right to an administrative hearing and offered to hold such a hearing in West Germany, Agee's country of residence, on five days notice.[18] Instead of agreeing to attend the hearing, Agee filed suit alleging that the regulation[19] under which the Secretary of State had revoked his passport had not been authorized by Congress, that the regulation was overbroad, that the revocation prior to a hearing violated his Fifth Amendment right to due process, and the revocation violated his Fifth Amendment liberty interest as well his First Amendment right to criticize the government.[20]

Despite Agee's constitutional claims, the district court, the court of appeals and the U.S. Supreme Court found there was no significant First Amendment issue presented by the case. All three courts primarily focused on the statutory grant of powers to the Secretary of State. Finding for Agee, the district court held that the regulation under which the Secretary revoked Agee's passport exceeded the statutory powers of the Secretary.[21] A divided panel of the D.C. Court of Appeals affirmed. Based on the Supreme Court's decision in *Zemel v. Rusk*,[22] a case involving a U.S. citizens' right to travel to Cuba, the

---

[14] 453 U.S. 280 (1980).
[15] *Id.* at 283.
[16] 444 U.S. 507 (1980).
[17] *Haig*, 453 U.S. at 285-86.
[18] *Id.* at 286-87.
[19] 22 CFR § 51.70(b)(4) (1980).
[20] *Haig*, 453 U.S. at 287.
[21] Agee v. Vance, 483 F. Supp. 729 (D.D.C. 1980).
[22] 381 U.S. 1 (1965).

court of appeals held that the Secretary was required to show either that Congress had expressly authorized the regulation or that there was implied approval of "substantial and consistent" administrative actions. Because the court found neither, it held there was no statutory authority for the revocation.[23] Following the lower courts' lead, in an opinion written by Chief Justice Warren Burger, the Supreme Court presented a narrow frame. Burger wrote, "The principal question before us is whether the statute authorizes the action of the Secretary pursuant to the policy announced by the challenged regulation."[24] To support the conclusion that the Secretary had the power to revoke Agee's passport, Burger's opinion relied upon statutory textual analysis,[25] precedent,[26] and a lengthy discussion of statutory history and legislative intent.[27]

After stating the principal legal question presented by the case, Burger quickly dealt with the separation of powers issue, simply writing in a footnote that the Court had "no occasion" to determine the scope of the President's plenary and exclusive power in the field of international relations.[28] Although he engaged in a somewhat lengthier discussion of the First Amendment issues in the case, Burger did not explicitly concede that Agee had a First Amendment claim, often dancing around the issue. For example, Burger suggested that First Amendment protections did not apply to American citizens aboard[29] and later cited *Zemel* for the idea that the revocation punished actions rather than speech.[30] In addition, although Burger admitted that the government's decision to revoke Agee's passport was a content-based decision, he relied upon *Near v. Minnesota* to hold the government was within its constitutional powers to censor Agee.[31] In the end, however, Burger returned to his contention that Agee's First Amendment rights were not truly abridged by the decision to revoke his passport. "Agee is as free to criticize the United States Government as he was when he

---

[23] Agee v. Muskie, 629 F.2d 80 (D.C. Cir. 1980).
[24] *Haig*, 453 U.S. at 289.
[25] *Id.* at 289-90.
[26] *Id.* at 290.
[27] *Id.* at 292-301.
[28] *Id.* at 289 n.17.
[29] *Id.* at 308.
[30] *Id.* at 309.
[31] *Id.* at 308.

held a passport—always subject, of course, to express limits on certain rights by virtue of his contract with the Government," he wrote.[32]

Both Justice Harry Blackmun's concurring opinion and Justice William Brennan's dissenting opinion criticized the majority's use of precedent. Blackmun simply noted that while he agreed with the outcome of the case, it could not be reconciled with the Court's previous decisions in *Zemel* or *Kent v. Dulles*,[33] a case involving the denial of a passport to a communist sympathizer. In addition to accusing the majority of distorting *Zemel* and *Kent*,[34] Brennan's opinion focused on balancing, discussing the issue in terms of both separation of powers issues and the First Amendment. Addressing balancing and separation of powers, Brennan concluded that the Court's decision handed too much power over to the executive branch.[35] Turning to the First Amendment, although Brennan wrote that he did not need to decide the constitutional questions presented by the case because of his conclusion that the regulation was an invalid exercise of authority, he was highly critical of the majority's reliance on *Near*[36] as well as its logic that Agee remained free to criticize the government. He wrote:

> Under the Court's rationale, I would suppose that a 40-year prison sentence imposed upon a person who criticized the Government's food stamp policy would represent only an 'inhibition of action.' After all, the individual would remain free to criticize the United States Government, albeit from a jail cell.[37]

Thus, while Brennan primarily relied on a separation of powers frame, he also framed the issue as a need to balance national security and freedom of expression.[38]

---

[32] *Id.* at 309.
[33] *Id.* at 310 (Blackmun, J., concurring).
[34] *Id.* at 312-18 (Brennan, J., dissenting).
[35] *Id.* at 319.
[36] *Id.* at 320 n. 10.
[37] *Id.*
[38] *Id.*

The other two cases identified by this research, *Morison* and *Rosen*, dealt with attempts to prosecute individuals under sections of the Espionage Act of 1917,[39] which punish a variety of acts in a specific attempt to protect national security information. Enacted in the midst of World War I, the Espionage Act of 1917 was intended to "enable the United States to carry out its duties as a neutral power, to protect the rights and property of United States citizens, and to punish crimes that endangered the peace, welfare, and honor of the United States."[40] It has been amended twice, once in 1950 in response to the perceived threat to the security of the country by the Communist movement, and again in 1986.[41] The 1950 amendment expanded the Act's scope by making the retention of defense information and the publication of "communications information" a crime.[42] In 1986 it was amended again to provide that any property derived from or used in the commission of an offense would become the property of the United States.[43]

In 1988, the Fourth Circuit Court of Appeals considered Samuel Morison's conviction under 18 U.S.C. § 641, which punishes the theft of government property, and two provisions of the Espionage Act, 18 U.S.C. § 793(d) and (e).[44] Under § 793, actions undertaken "for the purpose of obtaining information respecting the national defense with intent or reason to believe that the information is to be used to the injury of the United States" are punishable. Subsection (d) punishes the communication of "information related to national defense" by

---

[39] 18 U.S.C. § 793 (2005).

[40] Jereen Trudell, Note, *The Constitutionality of Section 793 of the Espionage Act and its Application to Press Leaks*, 33 WAYNE L. REV. 205, 205-06 (1986). See *id.* at 205-06 for an extended discussion of the legislative history of the statute. See Harold Edgar & Benno C. Schmidt Jr., *The Espionage Statutes and Publication of Defense Information*, 73 COLUM. L. REV. 929 (1973), for a discussion of the legislative intent of the Act.

[41] Trudell, *supra* note 40, at 205-06.

[42] *Id.* at 206-07.

[43] Anthony R. Klein, Comment, *National Security Information: Its Proper Role and Scope in a Representative Democracy*, 42 FED. COMM. L.J. 433, 437 (1990).

[44] United States v. Morison, 844 F.2d 1057, 1060 (4th Cir. 1988). For a discussion of Morison's prosecution under §641, *see* Silver, *supra* note 4, at 458-61.

individuals who are authorized to have the information to individuals who are not so authorized.[45] Subsection (e) punishes the communication or retention of such information by an individual not authorized to have it.[46] While an employee at the Naval Intelligence Support Center, Morrison did off-duty work for *Jane's Fighting Ships*, a British annual specializing in reporting on current developments in international naval operations.[47] The arrangement with *Jane's* had been submitted to and approved by the Navy, subject to Morison's agreement that he would not supply any classified information on the U.S. Navy or extract unclassified data on any subject and forward the data to *Jane's*.[48] Morison's troubles began when he sought employment with a new publication, *Jane's Defence Weekly*. In violation of his agreement with the Navy, Morrison provided *Jane's Defence Weekly*'s editor-in-chief with three pages of background material from a classified report about a Soviet base where an explosion had occurred, information about previous explosions at the base, and a classified satellite photograph of a Soviet carrier under construction at the base.[49]

Although Morison raised a number of First Amendment claims, Circuit Judge Donald Russell upheld Morison's conviction focusing on the government's ability to prevent an employee from disseminating information under the Espionage Act. To reach his conclusion Russell relied upon textual analysis, legislative history and precedent. It is important to note, however, that while Russell specifically stated that Morison's prosecution did not raise *any* First Amendment concerns, the two dissenting opinions issued clearly framed the case as at least implicating the First Amendment.[50]

After recounting the facts of the case, Russell's opinion considered Morison's claim that "properly construed and applied" the two subsections of the Espionage Act applied only to "classic spying" and

---

[45] 18 U.S.C. § 793(d) (2005).
[46] 18 U.S.C. § 793(e) (2005).
[47] *Id.* at 1060.
[48] *Id.*
[49] *Id.* at 1061.
[50] *See id.* at 1081 (Wilkinson, J., concurring); *id.* at 1087 (Phillips, J., concurring).

not to leaking information to the press.[51] Relying on textualism and legislative history, Russell concluded that neither analysis supported Morison's contention the Espionage Act did not apply to his conduct. First, Russell wrote that on their face, the sections were clear that they applied to "anyone" and "they declare[d] no exemption in favor of one who leaks to the press."[52] Next, turning to a detailed discussion of the legislative history of the Espionage Act, Russell declared that it was evident the history did not support Morison's contention either. Comparing the sections under which Morison was being prosecuted to §794, a statute designed to prevent "classic spying," Russell concluded that Morison's conduct was being punished under the appropriate statute.[53] Finally, the court ruled that simply because §793 (d) and (e) had never been used to punish the disclosure of information to the press before did not mean they couldn't be used to punish disclosure of information to the press.[54]

Russell next addressed Morison's First Amendment arguments. Relying on precedent Russell clearly and completely rejected Morison's attempt to frame the case in terms of the First Amendment, concluding, "[W]e do not perceive any First Amendment rights to be implicated here."[55] Russell wrote the case was "certainly . . . no prior restraint case" such as *New York Times v. United States*[56] or *United States v. Progressive*[57] but rather a case involving the prosecution of a government employee for "purloining from the intelligence files of the Navy national defense materials clearly marked as 'Intelligence Information' and 'Secret' and for transmitting that material to 'one not entitled to receive it.'"[58] Russell focused on the Supreme Court's decisions in *Branzburg v. Hayes*[59] and *Snepp v. United States*[60] and the

---

[51] *Id.* at 1063.
[52] *Id.*
[53] *Id.* at 1065.
[54] *Id.* at 1066-67.
[55] *Id.* at 1068.
[56] 403 U.S. 713 (1971).
[57] 467 F. Supp. 990 (W.D. Wis. 1979).
[58] *Morison*, 844 F.2d at 1068.
[59] 408 U.S. 665 (1972).
[60] 444 U.S. 507 (1980).

Fourth Circuit's decision in *United States v. Marchetti*[61] to determine that there was no support for the contention that prosecution under the Espionage Act implicated the First Amendment. He wrote:

> If *Branzburg, Marchetti,* and *Snepp* are to be followed, it seems beyond controversy that a recreant intelligence department employee who had abstracted from the government files secret intelligence information and had willfully transmitted or given it to one "not entitled to receive it" as did the defendant in this case, is not entitled to invoke the First Amendment as a shield to immunize his act of thievery. To permit the thief thus to misuse the Amendment would be to prostitute the salutary purposes of the First Amendment.[62]

Finally, Russell addressed Morison's vagueness and overbreadth arguments. Considering the vagueness claims, Russell again relied on precedent to reach his conclusions. Morison claimed that the terms "related to the national defense," "willfully" and "entitled to receive," were unconstitutionally vague. Citing and discussing two previous Fourth Circuit cases, Russell held that the trial judge's instructions to the jury had eliminated any vagueness problems related to either "related to the national defense" or "willfully."[63] Similarly, citing precedent the court held that the term "one entitled to receive" was both limited and clarified by the appropriate classification regulations and was thus not unconstitutionally vague.[64] Returning to his focus on the judge's jury instructions, Russell also found they addressed any overbreadth problems associated with the terms "related to the national defense" or "one not entitled to receive."[65]

The two other opinions in the case were not so willing to find that Morison's case implicated no First Amendment rights. Although he concurred in the court's judgment, Circuit Judge James H. Wilkinson

---

[61] 466 F.2d 1309 (4th Cir. 1972).
[62] *Morison*, 844 F.2d at 1069-70.
[63] *Id.* at 1071-72.
[64] *Id.* at 1074-75.
[65] *Id.* at 1076.

identified the key issues presented by the case as the need to balance national security and freedom of expression and the need to balance relative powers of the executive and judicial branches. Referencing framers' intent,[66] the marketplace of ideas,[67] and the checking function,[68] as well as the need for national security[69] Wilkinson wrote:

> Public security can . . . be compromised in two ways: by attempts to choke off the information needed for democracy to function, and by leaks that imperil the environment of physical security which a functioning democracy requires. The tension between these two interests is not going to abate, and the question is how a responsible balance may be achieved. [70]

Writing that he believed it was necessary to directly address Morison's First Amendment claims rather than as "unspoken aspects of a vagueness or overbreadth analysis," Wilkinson started his concurring opinion by stating that the First Amendment issues at stake were "not insignificant."[71] Turning to separation of powers, Wilkinson also discussed on the Supreme Court's decisions in *United States v. Snepp*[72] and *Chicago & Southern Air Lines, Inc. v. Waterman S.S. Corp.*,[73] noting that while the First Amendment issues in the case were important, the judiciary typically deferred to the executive in areas of national security.[74]

After framing the case in term of both issues, Wilkinson next expanded on his discussion of the First Amendment issues involved in the case. First, Wilkinson pointed out that Morison was not a journalist, writing, "No member of the press is being searched, subpoenaed, or excluded, as in a typical right of access case."[75] In

---

[66] *Id.* at 1081 (Wilkinson, J., concurring).
[67] *Id.*
[68] *Id.* at 1085.
[69] *Id.* at 1081.
[70] *Id.* at 1082.
[71] *Id.* at 1081.
[72] 444 U.S. 507 (1980).
[73] 333 U.S. 103 (1948).
[74] *Morison*, 844 F.2d at 1083 (Wilkinson, J., concurring).
[75] *Id.* at 1081.

addition, Wilkinson made it clear that the case was about stealing information, rather than *receiving* it or *publishing* it. He wrote: "[I]t is important to emphasize what is *not* before us today. This prosecution was not an attempt to apply the espionage statute to the press for either the receipt or publication of classified materials."[76] Thus, because no journalist was involved and Morison was not being punished for receiving or distributing information, Wilkinson found that Morison's particular conduct was not protected by the First Amendment. Wilkinson wrote that because Morison was a trained national intelligence officer who had signed a security clearance and because the district court had given proper limiting instructions, neither Morison's vagueness and overbreadth claims nor his contention that his prosecution would have far reaching implications on newsgathering and reporting were persuasive.[77]

Circuit Judge James Phillips' concurring opinion also discussed the First Amendment implications of the case. Calling the Espionage Act "unwieldy and imprecise," Phillips was concerned the Act made it difficult to differentiate between individuals leaking information to the press for public debate and "government moles" passing along information to other countries.[78] He wrote that the term "relating to the national defense" opened the act to overbreadth challenges and threatened to turn it into an "Official Secrets Act."[79] Revisiting the Fourth Circuit precedents discussed by Russell, Phillips wrote it was only "the limiting instruction which required proof that the information leaked was either 'potentially damaging to the United States or might be useful to an enemy'" that made 793 (e) and (d) constitutional.[80] Phillips even went so far as to suggest the solution to the unwieldy and potentially unconstitutional sections of the Act was for Congress to enact more carefully drawn legislation focusing on limiting prosecutions to situations in which there was a real danger to the United States.[81]

---

[76] *Id.* at 1085.
[77] *Id.* at 1083-84.
[78] *Id.* at 1085 (Phillips, J., concurring).
[79] *Id.* at 1085-86.
[80] *Id.* at 86.
[81] *Id.* at 1086.

More recently, in the AIPAC case, *United States v. Rosen*,[82] Judge T.S. Ellis III of the U.S. District Court for the Eastern District of Virginia also considered whether § 793(d) and (e) could be applied to non-governmental employees even when the facts of a case did not fit a classic espionage situation, but rather involved the "leaking" of information.[83] While employed by AIPAC, Steven Rosen and Keith Weissman obtained information from various government officials and transmitted this information to members of the media, officials of foreign governments, and others.[84] Rosen and Weissman were charged with conspiring to transmit information relating to the national defense to those not entitled to receive it and Rosen was additionally charged with "aiding and abetting the transmission of information relating to the national defense" in violation of § 793.[85]

Although the administration of President Barrack Obama effectively ended the prosecution of the lobbyists on May 1, 2009, when it filed a motion to dismiss the charges, citing concerns over disclosure of classified information, damage to national security from disclosure and the likelihood of the government prevailing, while the case was being prosecuted by the Bush Administration the district court released an opinion worth discussing.[86] When Rosen and Weissman filed a pretrial motion to dismiss the charges, arguing that the government's application of § 793(e) violated their Fifth Amendment Due Process Clause rights under the vagueness doctrine and violated the guarantees of the First Amendment, Judge Ellis released a thoughtful opinion analyzing the issues presented by the case.[87] Although Ellis denied the defendants' motion to dismiss the charges based on Fifth[88] and First Amendment claims, he clearly framed the

---

[82] 445 F. Supp. 2d 602 (E.D. Va. 2006).

[83] See *id.* at 628-29 for a discussion of applying the statutes to "leakers" as opposed to "spies."

[84] *Id.* at 608-10.

[85] *Id.* at 607.

[86] See Motion to Dismiss Superseding Indictment, United States v. Rosen, (No. 1:05CR225) (May 1, 2009), *available at* http://www.fas.org/sgp/jud/aipac/dismiss.pdf.

[87] *Rosen*, 445 F. Supp. 2d at 610.

[88] *Id.* at 617-29. For a discussion of Ellis' analysis of the defendants' Fifth Amendment claims, see *Recent Case: Constitutional Law-Due Process and*

case as dealing with the need to balance the First Amendment and national security. Ellis wrote that Rosen and Weissman's First Amendment challenges "exposed the inherent tension between the government transparency so essential to a democratic society and the government's equally compelling need to protect from disclosure information that could be used by those who wish this nation harm."[89] In addition, the court summarily rejected the government's contention that no prosecutions under the Espionage Act would implicate free expression rights.[90] Ellis wrote:

> In the broadest terms, the conduct at issue—collecting information about the United States' foreign policy and discussing that information with government officials (both United States and foreign), journalists, and other participants in the foreign policy establishment—is at the core of the First Amendment's guarantees.[91]

However, although Ellis clearly framed the case at least partially in terms of freedom of expression, in the end he ruled that the First Amendment did not automatically protect the defendants. To support his decision not to dismiss the case, Rosen relied upon democratic and First Amendment theory, original intent, textual analysis, legislative intent and precedent.

Ellis began by examining the abstract values at conflict in the case. Writing that a democratic society demanded the judiciary balance competing societal interests in cases involving national security and freedom of expression, Ellis noted the role of freedom of expression in self-government,[92] invoked framers' intent[93] and cited Justice Stewart's concurrence in *New York Times v. United States* and *Morison* to establish the importance of freedom of expression to self-government

---

Free Speech-District Court Holds That Recipients of Government Leaks Who Disclose Information "Related to the National Defense" May Be Prosecuted Under the Espionage Act, 120 HARV. L. REV. 821 (2007).
[89] *Rosen*, 445 F. Supp. 2d at 629.
[90] *Id.* at 629-30.
[91] *Id.* at 630.
[92] *Id.* at 633.
[93] *Id.* (quoting the writings of James Madison).

and as a check on government.[94] Quoting *Haig v. Agee*, however, Ellis wrote, "[H]owever vital an informed public may be, it is well established that disclosure of certain information may be restricted in service of the nation's security, for '[i]t is "obvious and unarguable" that no governmental interest is more compelling than the security of the Nation.'"[95]

Moving from an abstract discussion of the issues to a concrete application, Ellis wrote it was necessary to make two determinations: first, whether § 793 was "narrowly drawn to apply only to those instances in which the government's need for secrecy is legitimate, or whether it is too indiscriminate in its sweep, seeking in effect, to excise the cancer of espionage with a chainsaw instead of a scalpel;"[96] second, whether the government was allowed to prosecute individuals "who have no employment or contractual relationship with the government, and therefore have not exploited a relationship of trust to obtain the national defense information they are charged with disclosing, but instead generally obtained the information from one who has violated such a trust."[97]

Focusing on textual analysis, legislative history and precedent, Ellis ruled that while terms in the Espionage Act were vague, so long as a judge properly limited terms such as "related to the national defense" and "one not entitled to receive it" and provided proper instructions regarding the statute's intent requirements, § 793 was narrowly drawn to deal with espionage.[98] Next, Ellis wrote that while *United States v. Marchetti*,[99] *Snepp v. United States*[100] and *Morsion* together stood for

---

[94] *Id.*

[95] *Id.* at 633-34 (quoting Haig v. Agee, 453 U.S. 280, 307 (1981) (quoting Aptheker v. Secretary of State, 378 U.S. 500, 509 (1964))).

[96] *Id.* at 634.

[97] *Id.* at 635.

[98] *Id.* at 634-35. Ellis wrote that § 793 "taken together with its judicial glosses" was narrowly tailored. The "judicial gloss" to which he was referring was the judicial limitations that had been placed on the statutory language in various precedents. Ellis wrote at great length about the "gloss" earlier in his decision when discussing the defendant's Fifth Amendment claims. See *id.* at 614-27 for Ellis' discussion of the terms "relating to the national defense" and "entitled to receive" as used in § 793(d) and (e) as well as a discussion of the scienter or intent requirements of the statutes.

[99] 466 F.2d 1309 (4th Cir.1972).

the proposition that there were no constitutional barriers to prior restraints on and post-publication punishments of government employees who disseminated national security information,[101] the analysis was more difficult when non-governmental employees were involved. Because *Marchetti*, *Snepp* and *Morison* all involved government employees, Ellis instead turned to the various opinions in *New York Times v. United States* for guidance. Ellis' analysis of the opinions concluded that three of the concurring justices—Stewart, White and Marshall—and the three dissenting justices—Burger, Harlan and Blackmun—explicitly acknowledged the possibility of a prosecution of the newspapers under § 793(e).[102] Based on these opinions, Ellis concluded that a majority of the Supreme Court felt the statute did not offend the Constitution.[103] However, Ellis was also clear that the Constitution limited prosecutions to situations in which national security was genuinely at risk, there was proof of intent to harm the United States, and there was reason to believe that disclosure would actually cause that harm.[104]

Finally, Ellis turned his attention to the defendants' overbreadth claim. Ellis wrote that the important First Amendment issues at stake in the case required the statute be narrowly construed. Ellis concluded that the statute was not overbroad only so long as it was construed as punishing "only those people who transmit information related to the national defense, in tangible or intangible form, to one not entitled to receive it."[105]

Going into detail, Ellis wrote that to overcome First Amendment concerns and prove the information was related to national defense the

---

[100] 444 U.S. 507 (1980).

[101] *Id.* at 636.

[102] *Id.* at 638-39.

[103] *Id.* at 639. Although Ellis acknowledged that the Court's discussion took place in dicta, he wrote, "While the Supreme Court's discussion of the application of § 793(e) to the newspapers is clearly *dicta,* lower courts 'are bound by the Supreme Court's considered *dicta* almost as firmly as by the Court's outright holdings, particularly when, as here, a *dictum* is of recent vintage and not enfeebled by any subsequent statement.'" (quoting McCoy v. Massachusetts Institute of Technology, 950 F.2d 13, 19 (1st Cir.1991)).

[104] *Id.* at 639-640.

[105] *Id.* at 643.

government had to show "that the information relate[d] to the nation's military activities, intelligence gathering or foreign policy," was "closely held by the government" and not in the public domain, and that disclosure of the information "could cause injury to the nation's security."[106] Ellis wrote that to prove the information was transmitted to someone not entitled to receive it, the government had to show there was an executive branch regulation or order that restricted the disclosure of information to a certain set of people and the information was disclosed to someone outside that set.[107] In addition, he wrote the government had to prove that anyone alleged to have violated the statute "knew the nature of the information, knew that the person with whom they were communicating was not entitled to the information, and knew that such communication was illegal."[108] Thus, although Ellis put several constraints on the government's case, he did not rule that using the Espionage Act to punish individuals who were not classic "spies" was an inherent violation of the First Amendment.

Although there have been only three cases that have discussed post-publication punishments for the dissemination of national security information, several key points emerge from an analysis of these cases. First, although the majority in *Agee* did not find a serious First Amendment concern associated with the case, Brennan's dissent in *Agee*, two of the three judges in *Morison*, and Ellis' opinion in *Rosen* all clearly expressed serious concerns with the ability of the government to prosecute individuals when they were neither government employees nor "classic spies." Judge Wilkinson's concurring opinion in *Morison* went so far as to state that a member of the press "probably could not" be prosecuted under the Espionage Act based on First Amendment concerns.[109]

Second, the cases all engaged in detailed analysis of the legislative history, intent and text of the statutes involved in the cases. The courts were clearly attempting to determine what Congress wanted to accomplish with the laws in question and the extent to which the laws could be applied to individuals engaged in the discussion of national

---

[106] *Id.*
[107] *Id.*
[108] *Id.*
[109] United States v. Morison, 844 F.2d. 1057, 1081(4th Cir. 1988).

security information. There was unquestionably a focus on legislative power and intent in all the cases. Finally, in both *Morison* and *Rosen*, there was a great deal of focus on the need to narrowly construe the Espionage Act so as not to violate the First Amendment.

Thus, while there is limited case law dealing with the issue, these three cases indicate that while punishing individuals for disseminating national security information raises First Amendment concerns, so long as the trial court properly narrows applicable laws there is no true First Amendment barrier to prosecution.

Post-publication Punishments and the Judiciary
Just as the government has sought to punish individuals for disseminating information harmful to national security, both courts and state legislatures have sought to inflict post-publication punishments for disseminating information about judicial proceedings or commenting on the operation of the judicial system itself. These sanctions have come in the form of contempt citations from courts and state statutes designed to punish the dissemination of certain types of information. While the Supreme Court has not established as high a barrier to post-publication punishments as it has in prior restraint cases, the Court has established clear constitutional limits on the power to punish individuals for disseminating information about or critical of the courts. The first time the Court considered a post-publication case dealing with the judiciary, Justice Hugo Black authored an opinion which discussed the need to balance freedom of expression with the fair administration of justice and invoked the clear and present danger standard. While the Court has continued to use the same frame and the same precedents, it has also consistently taken an *ad hoc* approach, weighing the specific facts of each case to determine if there was a substantial likelihood that the effective operation of justice would be impaired.

In 1941, the Court heard a joinder of two appeals, *Bridges v. California* and *Times Mirror Co. v. Superior Court*.[110] Both cases involved punishments for "publishing . . . views concerning cases not in all respects finally determined."[111] *Times Mirror Co.* concerned

---

[110] 314 U.S. 252 (1941).
[111] *Id.* at 259.

three anti-union editorials published in the *Los Angeles Times*.[112] In *Bridges*, labor leader Harry Bridges was held in contempt for calling a judge's ruling in a labor dispute "outrageous" and stating that attempted enforcement of the order "would tie up the port of Los Angeles and . . . the entire Pacific Coast."[113] As noted, Black framed the case as dealing with the balance between freedom of expression and the effective operation of the judicial system.[114] However, he also invoked a secondary frame dealing with the inherent power of the courts.[115] To support his decision that the contempt power of courts did not grant the courts the ability to silence Bridges or the *Los Angeles Times* in the case, Black relied on originalism, discussing the effect of the ratification of the Constitution on the historical "power of judges to punish by contempt out-of-court publications tending to obstruct the orderly and fair administration of justice in a pending case"[116] and on precedent, citing the clear and present danger cases.[117]

Black concluded there were two separate government interests at stake in the case: "disrespect for the judiciary" and the prevention of the "disorderly and unfair administration of justice."[118] Black summarily dismissed a post-publication restraint as a way to advance the first interest, noting that it was a "prized American privilege" to speak out about every aspect of government and enforced silence "would probably engender resentment, suspicion, and contempt much more than it would enhance respect."[119] In contrast, Black wrote that the government's interest in preventing the disorderly administration of justice would be advanced by the contempt citations.[120] However, when he applied the clear and present danger test to the facts of the two cases, Black concluded that the circumstances did not constitute the

---

[112] *Id.* at 271-72.
[113] *Id.* at 276.
[114] *Id.* at 260.
[115] *Id.* at 259-60.
[116] *Id.* at 263.
[117] *Id.* at 261-63.
[118] *Id.* at 270.
[119] *Id.* at 271.
[120] *Id.*

substantive evil or degree of likelihood necessary under the test to justify punishment.[121]

In addition to Black's opinion, Justice Felix Frankfurter wrote a lengthy and complex dissenting opinion, which was joined by Chief Justice Harlan Stone and Justices Owen Roberts and James Byrnes. Although Frankfurter discussed the role of the press in self-government and as a watchdog on governmental misconduct, unlike Black, Frankfurter argued several times that the First Amendment was not truly or seriously implicated by the case. A noted proponent of judicial restraint, Frankfurter began by discussing the limits of the Supreme Court's power. Frankfurter wrote that it was not clear the First Amendment was implicated because the Court was considering the power of California's courts,[122] and, even if the First Amendment was involved, the Court should practice judicial restraint and defer to the wishes of the people of California.[123] In addition, he argued that the traditional power of courts to inflict post-publication punishment through contempt orders had never been thought to raise First Amendment concerns.[124]

To support his conclusion that the contempt orders were not unconstitutional, Frankfurter relied upon originalism, discussing the long history and importance of protecting the fair administration of justice to argue that the courts were unique in their need to be free from influence. [125] While Frankfurter admitted that the checking function applied to judges and courts, and neither was entitled to "greater immunity from criticism than other persons or institutions,"[126] he wrote that both should be protected from speech designed to intimidate or

---

[121] *Id.* at 272-75; *id.* at 275-78.

[122] *Id.* at 280 (Frankfurter, J., dissenting).

[123] *Id.* at 202-03.

[124] *Id.* at 290.

[125] Frankfurter cited a number of historical sources and frequently referenced the long history of protecting the fair administration of justice to support his contention. *See, e.g., id.* at 282 (discussing the Magna Carta); *id.* at 283-84 (discussing the historical importance of the judicial process to "statesmen and constitution makers" and the history of the power to punish for contempt); *id* at 285-86 (discussing the writings of Blackstone, Kent and Story).

[126] *Id.* at 289.

influence.[127]   Based on this argument, Frankfurter determined that when speech referred to a matter under consideration before a court, constituted a threat to the impartial adjudication of the matter and was purposely calculated to interfere with the court's work, it could be punished even if there was no evidence that the speech would actually interfere with justice.[128]   Therefore, considering the *Los Angeles Times* editorials, Frankfurter concluded that because "[a] powerful newspaper brought its full coercive power to bear in demanding a particular sentence"[129] from a judge who within a year would have to run for reelection, the state court was "[c]learly . . . justified in treating this as a threat to impartial adjudication."[130]   Turning to Bridges' comments, Frankfurter similarly concluded that the state court's judgment should not be overturned because the threat made by the union leader constituted "a definite attempt at coercing a court into a favorable decision."[131]   However, despite Frankfurter's dissent, the Court continued to overturn attempts to punish the publication of information by invoking the clear and present danger standard.

In 1946, in *Pennekamp v. Florida*, the Court considered whether two editorials and a cartoon critical of the Circuit Court of Dade County, Florida, published by the *Miami Herald* constituted a clear and present danger to the fair administration of justice.[132] In an opinion by Justice Stanley Reed, the Court once again framed the case as dealing with the need to balance the fair administration of justice with freedom of the press.[133]   Relying primarily on *Bridges*, Reed determined the editorials did not constitute a clear and present danger. Although Reed did not provide a definition or example of what would constitute "a clear and present danger to the fair administration of justice,"[134] he concluded it was obvious the *Miami Herald's* editorials did not rise to that level. He wrote, "For circumstances to create a clear and present

---

[127] *Id.* at 291.
[128] *Id.*
[129] *Id.* at 300.
[130] *Id.* at 299.
[131] *Id.* at 303.
[132] 328 U.S. 331, 333 (1946).
[133] *Id.* at 346-47.
[134] *Id.* at 348.

danger to judicial administration, a solidity of evidence should be required which it would be difficult to find in this record."[135]

In addition to Reed's opinion, Justices Frankfurter, William Francis Murphy and Wiley Rutledge, Jr. wrote separate concurring opinions. While Frankfurter again discussed the need for respect of the judicial process and the limited nature of First Amendment protection in these situations, citing his own dissenting opinion in *Bridges*, he ultimately concurred with the majority because the case was no longer pending.[136] Murphy and Rutledge, on the other hand, argued that it was necessary to extend the press a great deal of protection when commenting on the judicial process. Murphy wrote that it was necessary to provide the press with protection even when its criticism of the judicial system was "vitriolic, scurrilous or erroneous" unless the criticism made it "impossible in a very real sense for a court to carry on the administration of justice."[137] Otherwise, Murphy warned, the Court risked severely limiting liberty. Similarly, while Rutledge was highly critical of the press's coverage of the judiciary,[138] he wrote that it could not be shown that the *Herald's* editorials in any way even tended to block or impede the fair administration of justice.[139]

Just one year later, in 1947, the Court again considered a contempt citation in *Craig v. Harney*.[140] *Craig* involved the jailing of a publisher, an editorial writer and a reporter from the *Corpus Christi Caller-Times* for contempt. The case arose from an editorial and several news stories that criticized a judge for instructing a jury to return a verdict with which it did not agree.[141] Citing *Bridges*, Justice William O. Douglas wrote that the facts of the case showed there was "no threat or menace to the integrity of the trial."[142] Based on the clear and present danger test, Douglas established a formidable standard for a judge to overcome in order to hold a journalist in contempt:

---

[135] *Id.* at 347.
[136] *Id.* at 369 (Frankfurter, J., concurring).
[137] *Id.* at 370 (Murphy, J., concurring).
[138] *Id.* at 372 (Rutledge, J., concurring).
[139] *Id.*
[140] 331 U.S. 367 (1947).
[141] *Id.* at 369.
[142] *Id.* at 377.

The vehemence of the language used is not alone the measure of the power to punish for contempt. The fires which it kindles must constitute an imminent, not merely a likely, threat to the administration of justice. The danger must not be remote or even probable; it must immediately imperil.[143]

Similarly, in a concurring opinion, Murphy was once again adamant about the protection the Court should afford to the press when commenting on all branches of the government, even when the attacks were unjust.[144]

In contrast to the standards advanced by Douglas and Murphy, however, were dissents by Frankfurter and Justice Robert Jackson. Again framing the case in terms of federalism and judicial restraint[145] and the need to protect the impartial administration of justice, Frankfurter, who was joined by Chief Justice Fred Vinson, once again argued that the editorials were not criticism, but rather attempts to influence the outcome of pending litigation:

The publications now in question did not constitute merely a narrative of a judge's conduct in a particular case nor a general commentary upon his competence or his philosophy. Nor were they a plea for reform of the Texas legal system to the end that county court judges should be learned in the law and that a judgment in a suit of forcible detainer may be appealable. The thrust of the articles was directed to what the judge should do on a matter immediately before him.[146]

Although he agreed with Frankfurter that the contempt citation should be upheld, Jackson focused his opinion on the importance of the judicial process. While Jackson framed the case as a conflict between freedom of the press and the fair administration of justice, he clearly placed his thumb on the side of the fair administration of justice. He wrote:

---

[143] *Id.* at 376.
[144] *Id.* at 383 (Murphy, J., concurring).
[145] *Id.* at 385 (Frankfurter, J., dissenting).
[146] *Id.* at 389.

The right of the people to have a free press is a vital one, but so is the right to have a calm and fair trial free from outside pressures and influences. Every other right, including the right of a free press itself, may depend on the ability to get a judicial hearing as dispassionate and impartial as the weakness inherent in men will permit.[147]

Concluding that the majority's opinion sponsored "the myth that judges are not as other men" and are, therefore, not influenced by caustic attacks because they "do not penetrate the judicial armor,"[148] Jackson dissented and ruled that judges must be insulated from such attacks in order to protect judicial impartiality.

In 1962, under slightly different circumstances, the Court considered a contempt citation issued in connection with a grand jury investigation in *Wood v. Georgia*.[149] In 1960, James Wood, an elected sheriff in Bibb County, Georgia, was cited for two counts of contempt of court for issuing a statement regarding a grand jury investigation of election law violations.[150] Again framing the case as a need to balance freedom of expression with the fair administration of justice and relying on the clear and present danger precedents, the Court found Wood's statements did not constitute an imminent danger to the administration of justice.[151] In addition, Chief Justice Earl Warren's majority opinion emphasized the important role free expression played in self-government, even in the realm of the judicial process.[152] Once again, however, other justices disagreed with the majority's application of the clear and present danger test.

Justice John Harlan II, joined by Justice Thomas Clark, wrote a dissent emphasizing the differences between *Bridges*, *Pennekamp*, and *Craig* and the present case. While Harlan still framed the case in terms of conflicts between free expression and the judicial process, as Frankfurter's previous dissents had done, Harlan emphasized the ability

---

[147] *Id.* at 394-95 (Jackson, J., dissenting).
[148] *Id.* at 396.
[149] 370 U.S. 375 (1960).
[150] *Id.* at 380-81.
[151] *Id.* at 388.
[152] *Id.* at 391-92.

of the statements in question to influence the outcome of the judicial proceeding.[153] To differentiate the case, Harlan focused on the unique nature and history of grand jury proceedings[154] and the fact that in *Wood* it was a group of citizens who might be influenced by the statements in question rather than a judge.[155]

In addition to cases involving contempt citations, the court has heard several cases involving state statutes that penalized the disseminating of information relating to the judicial process[156] and one case involving the state of Nevada's rules governing extrajudicial statements made by an attorney. In the 1978 case *Landmark Communications v. Virginia*, the *Virginia Pilot* was fined $500 for

---

[153] Justice Frankfurter did not participate in the case.

[154] *Id.* at 397-99 (Harlan, J., dissenting).

[155] *Id.* at 401 See *id.* at 402 for Harlan's discussion of additional differences between the cases.

[156] In addition to the case discussed in this chapter involving state laws, two notable Supreme Court cases, *Cox Broadcasting v. Cohn*, 420 U.S. 469 (1975), and *Smith v. Daily Mail*, 443 U.S. 97 (1979), also considered the constitutionality of state laws that imposed criminal penalties for publishing information related to the judicial process. However, in neither case was the asserted government interest the protection of the judicial process. In *Cox Broadcasting* the Court considered a Georgia statute that made it a crime to publish or broadcast the name of a rape victim when the parents of a teenage girl who was raped and murdered sued an Atlanta television station for broadcasting the girl's name. The case is not discussed here because the Court framed the main issues in the case as the conflict between free expression and an individual's right to privacy, rather than between free expression and the effective operation of the judicial system. *Cox Broadcasting*, 420 U.S. at 487 (writing that the Georgia statute in question was an attempt to protect the "zone of privacy surrounding every individual"). *Smith* concerned a law that made it a crime to publish the names of juvenile offenders without the written approval of a juvenile court, even if that information was lawfully obtained. *Smith* is not discussed because the issues the Court was considering were freedom of expression and the protection of juveniles for rehabilitation purposes rather than freedom of expression and the fair administration of the judicial process. *Smith*, 443 U.S. at 104 ("The sole interest advanced by the State to justify its criminal statute is to protect the anonymity of the juvenile offender. It is asserted that confidentiality will further his rehabilitation because publication of the name may encourage further antisocial conduct and also may cause the juvenile to lose future employment or suffer other consequences for this single offense.").

accurately identifying a state judge whose conduct was being investigated in violations of a state statute that made it a crime to publish information about the confidential proceedings of a state judicial review commission which was "authorized to hear complaints about judges' disability or misconduct."[157] In an opinion by Chief Justice Burger, the Court framed the case as a conflict between the First Amendment and the effective operation of the judicial system and relied on the cases discussed above to reach its conclusion. Burger wrote there were a number of government interests related to the effective operation of the judicial system associated with the statute.

> First, confidentiality is thought to encourage the filing of complaints and the willing participation of relevant witnesses by providing protection against possible retaliation or recrimination. Second, at least until the time when the meritorious can be separated from the frivolous complaints, the confidentiality of the proceedings protects judges from the injury which might result from publication of unexamined and unwarranted complaints. And finally, it is argued, confidence in the judiciary as an institution is maintained by avoiding premature announcement of groundless claims of judicial misconduct or disability since it can be assumed that some frivolous complaints will be made against judicial officers who rarely can satisfy all contending litigants.[158]

Burger, however, concluded these interests had to be balanced with the *Pilot's* right to press freedom. Although the Virginia Supreme Court had followed the Supreme Court's clear and present danger cases outlined above,[159] Burger questioned the "relevance of the standard" to the case and rejected the state court's "mechanical application of the test."[160] Instead, Burger used an *ad hoc* approach to balance Virginia's interests in protecting judicial reputations and integrity against the *Pilot's* core First Amendment rights to hold that the *potential* harm

---

[157] 435 U.S. 829, 831 (1978).
[158] *Id.* at 835 (citations omitted).
[159] Landmark Commc'n v. Virginia, 233 S.E.2d 120, 129 (Va. 1977).
[160] *Landmark*, 435 U.S. at 842.

caused by publication could not support criminal sanctions against the press.[161]

Relying upon *Pennekamp*, Justice Louis Brandies' opinion in *Whitney v. California*[162] and the function of the First Amendment as a check on legislative power, Burger concluded that the Virginia court should have determined for itself whether the specific statements in the case constituted a clear and present danger rather than simply cite the Virginia legislature's determination that information regarding the proceeding should not be disclosed because it inherently was a clear and present danger to the administration of jutice.[163] Citing *Bridges*, *Penekamp*, *Craig*, and *Wood*, Burger summarized the standard that had to be met:

> What emerges from these cases is the "working principle that the substantive evil must be extremely serious and the degree of imminence extremely high before utterances can be punished," and that a "solidity of evidence," is necessary to make the requisite showing of imminence. "The danger must not be remote or even probable; it must immediately imperil."[164]

Again referencing those cases, Burger concluded, "If the clear-and-present-danger test could not be satisfied in the more extreme circumstances of those cases, it would seem to follow that the test cannot be met here."[165]

In addition to Burger's opinion, Justice Potter Stewart issued a concurring opinion, which framed the case as dealing specifically with the *press* clause of the First Amendment. Writing that "[t]here could hardly be a higher governmental interest than a State's interest in the quality of its judiciary,"[166] Stewart concluded there was nothing

---

[161] *Id.* at 841-42.
[162] 274 U.S. 357 (1927).
[163] *Landmark*, 435 U.S. at 844.
[164] *Id.* at 845 (quoting Bridges v. California, 314 U.S. 252, 263 (1941); Pennekamp v. Florida, 328 U.S. 331, 347 (1946); and Craig v. Harney, 331 U.S. 367, 376 (1947)).
[165] *Id.*
[166] *Id.* at 848 (Stewart, J., concurring).

unconstitutional about punishing someone for violating the confidentiality of the hearings.[167] Stewart concluded, however, that the constitutional problem arose when Virginia attempting to apply the statute to a newspaper:

> [I]n this case Virginia has extended its law to punish a newspaper, and that it cannot constitutionally do. If the constitutional protection of a free press means anything, it means that government cannot take it upon itself to decide what a newspaper may and may not publish. Though government may deny access to information and punish its theft, government may not prohibit or punish the publication of that information once it falls into the hands of the press, unless the need for secrecy is manifestly overwhelming.[168]

Finally, in 1991—fifty years after it considered the contempt citations of Harry Bridges and the *Los Angeles Times*—the Court decided to what extent an attorney could be disciplined for making extrajudicial statements in *Gentile v. State Bar of Nevada*.[169] In the case, the Court considered the First Amendment rights of a lawyer who was disciplined for making statements to the press regarding the innocence of his client. In a complex decision,[170] the Court relied on precedent and ruled that the "substantial likelihood of material

---

[167] *Id.* at 849.

[168] *Id.*

[169] 501 U.S. 1030 (1991).

[170] Chief Justice William Rehnquist wrote the opinion of the Court with respects to Part I and II, in which Justices Byron White, Sandra Day O'Connor, Antonin Scalia and Steven Souter joined. Justice Anthony Kennedy wrote the opinion of the Court with respects to Parts III and VI, in which Justices Thurgood Marshall, Harry Blackmun, John Paul Stevens, and O'Connor joined. Thus, Justice O'Connor was the deciding vote, joining Rehnquist on Parts I and II, and Kennedy on Parts III and VI. In a concurring opinion, O'Connor wrote that she agreed that speech by a lawyer representing a client in a pending cases could more readily be regulated than speech by the press she also agreed with Kennedy's assertion in Part III that Nevada's rules were unconstitutionally vague. *Gentile*, 501 U.S. at 1082-83 (O'Connor, J., concurring).

prejudice" standard used in Nevada's rules governing attorney extrajudicial speech did not violate the First Amendment.[171]

Although Chief Justice William Rehnquist's opinion framed the case as a need to balance the effective operation of justice with Gentile's First Amendment rights,[172] he differentiated the case from *Pennekamp* and *Craig*, as well as from *Nebraska Press Association v. Stuart*,[173] because none of those cases had involved lawyers who represented parties to pending proceedings in court. Instead, Rehnquist relied on a series of other cases to conclude that the Court should engage in a "balancing process, weighing the State's interest in the regulation of a specialized profession against a lawyer's First Amendment interest in the kind of speech that was at issue."[174] Again citing precedent, Rehnquist concluded that because "the speech of lawyers representing clients in pending cases may be regulated under a less demanding standard than that established for regulation of the press"[175] and the "substantial likelihood of material prejudice" properly balanced lawyers' weaker free expression interests with the state's strong interest in the integrity and fairness of its judicial system, Nevada's rules were constitutional.[176]

Thus, in a series of cases from 1941 to 1991, the U.S. Supreme Court set out the standards under which speech related to the judicial process could be punished after the fact. While some of the justices in the cases came to different conclusions about the particular facts of each case and whether a particular statement constituted a clear and present danger, in every case dealing with contempt citations the justices framed the cases in similar ways and relied upon the clear and present danger precedents to reach their conclusions. In addition, while Rehnquist's opinion in *Gentile* did not find the clear and present danger line of cases to be controlling, he still framed the cases in terms of the

---

[171] *Gentile*, 501 U.S. at 1063.

[172] *Id.* at 1073.

[173] 427 U.S. 539 (1976). As discussed in chapter two, *Nebraska Press Association* involved a gag order preventing dissemination of information related to a murder trial issued by a judge against newspapers in Nebraska.

[174] *Gentile*, 501 U.S. at 1073.

[175] *Id.* at 1074.

[176] *Id.* at 1075.

need to balance the fair administration of justice with freedom of expression.

Examining the two sets of cases, several interesting points emerge. First is the limited number of cases that have involved post-publication punishments and national security or the judiciary, relative to prior restraint and access cases. Only three cases were identified that involved national security, and the Supreme Court has only heard a handful of cases dealing with post-publication punishments and the judiciary. Despite this limited number of cases, it is important to note that with the exception of Burger's opinion in *Agee* and Russell's opinion in *Morison* nearly every opinion issued in these cases framed the legal issues presented by the cases at least somewhat in terms of the First Amendment. While the opinions put different weight on the strength of the free speech principle involved, few were willing to totally write it off in favor of national security or the effective operation of the judicial system.

In contrast, it appears that the two sets of cases relied on very different modes of legal analysis to support their conclusions. While the national security cases tended to focus on textualism, legislative intent and history, the judicial cases relied almost exclusively on the clear and present danger precedents. While this is partly explained by the fact that the national security cases all involved applications of federal statutes, those courts could have relied on the clear and present danger test just as easily as the Supreme Court has done in cases involving statutes punishing the publication of information related to the judiciary.

Next, a common thread that runs throughout both sets of cases is the idea that post-publication punishments are not as constitutionally suspect as prior restraint cases. Indeed, both sets of cases reference *New York Times v. United States* to point out what was *not* at stake. Finally, many of the cases point out the difference between punishing an individual involved in either national security or the judiciary—such as Agee, Morison, or Gentile—and punishing the press for disseminating information. For example, it is interesting to note that Rehnquist's decision in *Gentile* that it was easier for a court to control the speech of lawyer's is similar to Ellis' conclusion in *United States v. Rosen* that the government could more easily control the speech of its employees.

Perhaps because of the limited number of cases that have dealt with post-publication punishments, it is also important to note that there is no clear consensus on when a court can punish the dissemination of lawfully obtained truthful information. Indeed, the Supreme Court has consistently been unwilling to categorically answer the question. Although the Court briefly noted the issue in *Landmark Communications*,[177] it refused to rule on it. Because the newspaper did not break any laws in obtaining the information, the Court specifically stated that the issue before it was the "narrow and limited" question of "whether the First Amendment permits the criminal punishment of third persons who are strangers to the inquiry, including the news media, for divulging or publishing truthful information."[178] The Court refused to rule on "the possible applicability of the statute to one who secures the information by illegal means and thereafter divulges it."[179]

Eleven years later, in 1989, the Court again sidestepped the issue in *Florida Star v. B.J.F.*,[180] a case involving the publication of a rape victim's name that was obtained from an official report in a police pressroom. Citing *Smith v. Daily Mail Publishing Co.*,[181] the Court noted that the publication of lawfully obtained truthful information could not be prohibited absent a need to further a state interest of the highest order.[182] However, the Court was clear that *Daily Mail* did not answer the question of whether the possession or publication of unlawfully obtained information could be punished.[183] The Court wrote:

> The *Daily Mail* principle does not settle the issue whether, in cases where information has been acquired *unlawfully* by a newspaper or by a source, government may ever punish not only the unlawful acquisition, but the ensuing publication as well. This issue was raised in *New York Times v. United*

---

[177] 435 U.S. 829 (1978).
[178] *Id.* at 837.
[179] *Id.*
[180] 491 U.S. 524 (1989).
[181] 443 U.S. 97 (1979).
[182] *Florida Star*, 491 U.S. at 534.
[183] *Id.* at 533-34.

States and reserved in *Landmark Communications.* We have
no occasion to address it here.[184]

Finally, in what has become the seminal case in this area of law, a
2001 civil suit, the Court was again careful not to answer the question.
Bartnicki v. Vopper[185] involved the broadcast of an audiotape recording
of a cell phone conversation between two officials of a teachers' union
in which threats were made against local school board members. The
conversation was illegally taped by unknown persons and then
distributed to the press.[186] In a 6-3 ruling the Court held that there was
no liability in the case for broadcasting the tape. However, the Court
was very careful to note that it was doing so only because the
broadcasters in the case had played no part in intercepting or obtaining
the taped conversation and because of the public significance of the
matter.[187] The Court specifically wrote that it was again intentionally
leaving open "the question 'whether, in cases where information has
been acquired *unlawfully* by a newspaper or by a source, government
may ever punish not only the unlawful acquisition, but the ensuing
publication as well.'"[188] The Court wrote that its narrow holding in
Bartnicki was "consistent with this Court's repeated refusal to answer
categorically whether truthful publication may ever be punished
consistent with the First Amendment."[189] Citing *Florida Star*, the
Court wrote, "Our cases have carefully eschewed reaching this ultimate
question, mindful that the future may bring scenarios which prudence
counsels our not resolving anticipatorily."[190] Thus, in comparison to
the prior restraint cases, the post-publication line of cases provides no
consistent answer on when the publication of information can be
punished.

Perhaps because the Court has yet to definitively provide guidance
to lower courts in post-publication punishment cases, a final point must
be made that unlike the prior restraint and access cases discussed in this

---

[184] *Id.* at 535 n.8 (citations omitted) (emphasis in original).
[185] 532 U.S. 514 (2001).
[186] *Id.* at 518-19.
[187] *Id.* at 525.
[188] *Id.* at 528 (emphasis in the original).
[189] *Id.* at 529.
[190] *Id.*

book, the national security and judiciary cases discussed in this chapter rarely cited each other. The two lines of cases don't seem to intersect, and lower courts are not turning to the Supreme Court judiciary cases to provide guidance to lower court national security cases. However, perhaps because the Court has not provided guidance, both sets of cases do spend a great deal of time examining the specific set of facts relevant to the case. That is, both groups of cases consistently use *ad hoc* approaches that put a great deal of emphasis on the particular facts of each case to determine if punishment is constitutional.

CHAPTER 4

Access

During the Vietnam War, although media access to the battlefield was at the discretion of field commanders, it was rarely denied.[1] This unwritten policy of access to military activity "enabled American audiences to observe events daily, including casualties and deaths in vivid and often painful detail."[2] As one observer noted, perhaps because of the unflattering coverage of the Vietnam War, the military would never again grant unrestricted battlefield access to the media.[3] When the United States invaded Grenada and Panama, the Department of Defense (DOD) significantly restrained media coverage, a move that garnered widespread criticism.[4] Despite this criticism, when the United States sent troops to the Middle East in the fall of 1990, the DOD again issued regulations restricting access.[5] The regulations were in effect during both "Desert Shield" (American military presence in the Persian Gulf) and "Desert Storm" (open hostilities) and did not end until March 4, 1991, the informal cessation of hostilities in the Persian Gulf.[6]

Among other things, the DOD regulations created temporary press pools to provide coverage of the war.[7] During combat activities, the only journalists authorized to enter forward areas were the pool

---

[1] For a full description of the history of media coverage of the Vietnam War, see generally Chairman of the Joint Chiefs of Staff Media-Military Relations Panel, Sidle Report, reprinted in OFFICE OF ASSISTANT SECRETARY OF DEFENSE (PUBLIC AFFAIRS) NEWS RELEASE NO. 450-84 (Aug. 23, 1984).
[2] Nation Magazine v. U.S. Dep't of Defense, 762 F. Supp. 1558, 1563 (S.D.N.Y. 1991).
[3] Barry E. Venable, *The Army and the Media*, MIL. REV. 66, 67 (Jan.-Feb. 2002).
[4] *Id. See also* Fred S. Hoffman, "Review of the Panama Pool Deployment, December 1989," Memorandum for Correspondents, The Pentagon, (Mar. 1990); Steven L. Katz, *Ground Zero: The Information War in the Persian Gulf*, 9 GOV'T INFO. Q. 380 (1992).
[5] According to court records, the regulations were modified a number of times. *Nation Magazine*, 762 F. Supp. at 1564 n.4. For the modified regulations, see *id.* Appendices A-D.
[6] *Id.* at 1560.
[7] *Id.* at 1564.

participants. Membership in the pools did not, however, entitle journalists to observe all military activities. Rather, the military determined where pool members would be able to travel, and journalists had to remain with their escorts at all times. Additionally, according to DOD regulations, news stories by pool participants were subject to review by a DOD public affairs officer. In the event there was a disagreement between the press and the public affairs officer about the "sensitive nature" of a story, the information was sent to the Joint Information Bureau in Dhahran, Saudi Arabia. If consensus could not be reached, the issue was ultimately forwarded to the Office of the Assistant Secretary of Defense for Public Affairs for review.[8]

In 1991 various members of the press[9] challenged the regulations as violations of the First and Fifth Amendments. While the regulations were challenged on several grounds, the plaintiffs' fundamental claim in *Nation Magazine v. U.S. Department of Defense* was that the press had "a First Amendment right to unlimited access to a foreign arena in which American military forces are engaged."[10] In his opinion, Federal District Judge Leonard Sand of the Southern District of New York noted that because there was little precedent to guide his decision he was being asked to chart "new constitutional territory."[11] He wrote: "The issues raised by this challenge present profound and novel questions as to the existence and scope of a First Amendment right of access in the context of military operations and national security concerns. Those few precedents which have discussed First Amendment issues in the context of national security have been 'prior restraint' cases."[12]

---

[8] *Id.* at 1564-65. According to DOD policies, although all stories had to go through this process, the ultimate decision on publication remained with "the originating reporter's news organization." *Id.*

[9] The plaintiffs in the case were *The Nation, Harper's*, Pacific News Service, *In These Times, The Guardian, The Progressive Magazine, Mother Jones Magazine, The L.A. Weekly, The Village Voice, The Texas Observer, Pacifica Radio News*, Sydney H. Schanberg, E.L. Doctorow, William Styron, Michael Klare, and Scott Armstrong.

[10] *Nation Magazine*, 762 F. Supp. at 1561.

[11] *Id.* at 1571.

[12] *Id.* The court cited *Near v. Minnesota*, 283 U.S. 697 (1931); *New York Times v. United States*, 403 U.S. 713 (1971); and *Snepp v. United States*, 444 U.S. 713 (1971). The court concluded that while the Supreme Court "has on a

Although Judge Sand would still be correct today in asserting that the U.S. Supreme Court had never considered the existence of a First Amendment right of access to military operations, over the course of the twentieth century various courts have addressed the legal questions surrounding access to locations and information related to national security. As Judge Sand eventually did in *Nation Magazine*, typically in these cases the courts discussed two issues: first, whether access— or the denial of access—implicated the Constitution; second, whether cases involving access and national security were justiciable—or "capable of being disposed of judicially."[13] Some courts framed such access claims as a First Amendment cases or used frames focused on some other constitutional concern and clearly stated the executive branch shares jurisdiction over some areas of national security with the other two branches of government. Others framed the cases as primarily involving separation of powers questions and held that the constitutional structure left the area of national security solely to the executive branch. Similarly, courts have used a wide variety of legal factors to decide these cases. While in early cases courts used textualism or legislative intent and engaged in detailed discussions of framers' intent and constitutional structure, courts in later cases focused almost exclusively on precedent. This stands in stark contrast to Supreme Court cases that have examined access to the judiciary. With the exception of a few early cases, the Supreme Court has framed access to judicial proceedings as a First Amendment issue and invoked democratic theory. In addition, even after the precedent was established, the Court continued to use a variety of legal factors, for example, engaging in detailed discussions of legal history and framers' intent.

First, this chapter of the book examines cases that have dealt with access to information. Second, it analyzes cases that have dealt with access to locations. Finally, it compares the frameworks and legal

---

number of occasions considered the relationship between the First Amendment and national security" none the cases had directly addressed "the role and limits of news gathering under the First Amendment in a military context abroad." *Id.* (citations omitted).

[13] BLACK'S LAW DICTIONARY 882 (8th ed. 2004).

factors courts used in these cases to those used by the Supreme Court in cases that dealt with access to judicial proceedings and documents.

The most frequently discussed frame in the national security and access cases was separation of powers. While this frame was frequently used in both chapters two and three, the cases analyzed for this chapter discussed the power of courts at great length. The opinions repeatedly discussed the existence of a First Amendment-based right of access or a First Amendment theory that might support a "right to know," but ultimately most of the jurists chose to focus on the justiciability of the cases or the power of courts to intervene in national security information cases. In large part because of this focus on the existence of a right to know, although precedent was once again the legal factor most often used to justify an opinion, many of the jurists relied upon First Amendment theory.

Comparing the national security/access cases and the judiciary/access cases further reinforces the complex nature of the national security/access decisions. While the two categories of opinions used similar frames and factors, the outcome of the two types of cases were very different. While the Supreme Court has established a clear First Amendment-based right of access to the judiciary, courts have been reluctant to articulate more than a qualified or tentative right of access to national security information and locations. While the courts have been unwilling to totally embrace the notion that a right of access exists outside of the judicial context, the opinions certainly used the judiciary precedents to support their arguments that there might be some sort of universal qualified right of access guaranteed by the First Amendment. The chapter concludes with a discussion of cases in which the two issues might finally merge: access to court proceedings dealing with national security threats.

Access to National Security Information
Although there is evidence that military documents were marked secret as early as the Revolutionary War, the official system that controls classified information in the United States traces its origins to an executive order[14] issued by Franklin D. Roosevelt in March 1940.[15]

---

[14] Exec. Order 8,381, 5 Fed. Reg. 1,147 (Mar. 22, 1940).

According to Harold C. Relyea, a congressional researcher and specialist in American government, the executive order was prompted by desires to establish a structure for protecting military information during "growing global hostilities," to clarify the authority of civilian personnel in the national defense community to classify information, and to generally better manage the discretionary power to classify information.[16]

Although the classification system was modified shortly after the conclusion of World War II,[17] the most important changes came in an executive order issued in September 1951.[18] Relyea summarized three "sweeping innovations" introduced in Executive Order 10,290. First, because the order indicated the Chief Executive was relying upon "the authority vested in [him] by the Constitution and statutes, and as President of the United States," it strengthened the President's discretion to make official secrecy policy. Second, information was now classified in the interest of "national security" rather than in the interest of "national defense." [19] This change in semantics was especially important because, according to Relyea, "in the view of some," this "somewhat new, but nebulous, concept . . . conveyed more latitude for the creation of official secrets" than the previous term.[20] Finally, the order extended classification authority to nonmilitary entities throughout the executive branch so long as they had "some role in 'national security' policy."[21] Nineteen years after President Roosevelt created the modern classification system, the Supreme Court first reviewed the executive's ability to classify national security

---

[15] Harold C. Relyea, Security Classified and Controlled Information: History, Status, and Emerging Management Issues, CRS Report for Congress RL 33494, January 2, 2008 2 *available at* http://www.fas.org/sgp/crs/secrecy/RL33494.pdf.

[16] *Id.* Prior to this order, information was designated as secret pursuant to Army and Navy general orders and regulations.

[17] Exec. Order 10,104, 15 Fed. Reg. 597 (Feb. 1, 1950).

[18] Exec. Order 10,290, 16 Fed. Reg. 9,795 (Sept. 24, 1951).

[19] Relyea, *supra* note 15, at 3. A new executive order issued in 1953 revived the term national defense. Exec. Order 10,501, 18 Fed. Reg. 704 (Nov. 5, 1953).

[20] Relyea, *supra* note 15, at 3. For a discussion of the evolution of the ability to classify information from 1953 to 2008, see *id.* at 3-5.

[21] *Id.*

information in a case involving the government's revocation of a civilian contractor's security clearance, *Greene v. McElroy*.[22] Although on the surface the case was not about access to national security information, an important dissent in the case made it the first time a member of the Supreme Court wrote about the power of the executive branch to protect national security information.

In 1951, William L. Greene was vice president and general manager of Engineering and Research Corporation (ERCO), a company that developed and manufactured various mechanical and electronic products for the armed forces.[23] While working on classified projects, Greene was denied a renewal of his security clearance based on information indicating he had associated with Communists, visited officials of the Russian Embassy, and attended a dinner given by an allegedly Communist front organization.[24] When Secretary of the Navy Robert E. Anderson overruled an original recommendation to grant Greene access to classified information and Anderson's decision was upheld by the Eastern Industrial Personnel Security Board,[25] Greene brought suit asking for a declaration that the revocation was unlawful and for an order restraining the government from revoking his security clearance.[26] The District Court for the District of Columbia granted summary judgment for the government, and the D.C. Circuit Court of Appeals affirmed.[27]

The court of appeals decided the main legal issue presented by the case was separation of powers. Although the court recognized that Greene had suffered substantial harm from having his security clearance revoked, it held that Greene's suit presented no justiciable controversy. That is, there was no controversy "which the courts can finally and effectively decide, under tests and standards which they can soundly administer within their special field of competence."[28] The court did not discuss any constitutional or theoretical basis for its decision. Instead, citing only its own precedent, the court held that the

---

[22] 360 U.S. 474 (1959).
[23] *Id.* at 475.
[24] *Id.* at 478.
[25] For a detailed procedural history of the case and hearings, see *id.* at 475-91.
[26] *Id.* at 490-91.
[27] Greene v. McElroy, 254 F.2d 944, 952 (D.C. Cir. 1958).
[28] *Id.* at 953.

case involved an issue outside of judicial "experience and competence," and that the executive branch alone was responsible for the classification of national security information.[29]

When Greene appealed, however, the U.S. Supreme Court framed the case in far narrower terms. Instead of addressing the larger issue of classifying and accessing national security information, the Court wrote the principle question of law in the case was whether Greene had been denied due process. In an opinion by Chief Justice Earl Warren, the Court validated Greene's claim that the DOD had "denied him 'liberty' and 'property' without 'due process of law' in contravention of the Fifth Amendment."[30] According to the Court, Greene's property was his employment, and his liberty was his freedom to practice his chosen profession.[31] The Court held that without explicit authorization from either the President or Congress, the DOD was not empowered to create a security clearance program "under which affected persons may lose their jobs and may be restrained in following their chosen professions on the basis of fact determinations concerning their fitness for clearance made in proceedings in which they are denied the traditional procedural safeguards of confrontation and cross-examination."[32] Thus, the majority was very clear that it was steering away from legal questions regarding the inherent powers of the President or Congress.[33]

Relying on statutory textualism and precedent to support its decision, the Court closely analyzed the language of the executive orders and federal legislation that controlled access to national security information. Focusing on the exact wording of Executive Orders 10,290 and 10,501, the Court concluded that neither had authorized the creation of a process that did not allow for cross-examination.

> Clearly, neither of these orders empowers any executive agency to fashion security programs whereby persons are deprived of their present civilian employment and of the

---

[29] *Id.*

[30] Greene v. McElroy, 360 U.S. 474, 492 (1959).

[31] *Id.*

[32] *Id.* at 493.

[33] *Id.* at 496.

opportunity of continued activity in their chosen professions without being accorded the chance to challenge effectively the evidence and testimony upon which an adverse security determination might rest.[34]

Turning to the legislative enactments that "might be deemed as delegating authority to the Department of Defense"[35] to create programs to control access to national security information, the Court again found no explicit text to suggest a person could be deprived of due process rights.[36]

Although the majority did not frame the case as involving access to information and declared it was deciding a very narrow question, Justice Tom C. Clark wrote an important dissenting opinion, which argued the case presented a "clear and simple" legal question: Was there a constitutional right of access to government information?[37] Taking this frame directly from the Solicitor General's brief,[38] Clark was critical of the majority's framing of the issue as well as its reasoning. He argued that the Court was ignoring "the basic consideration in the case. . . that no person, save the President, has a constitutional right to access to governmental secrets."[39]

Clark first attacked the majority's opinion for misrepresenting precedent to reach its conclusion. He wrote:

> [The majority opinion] cites four cases in support of this proposition and says compare four others. As I read those cases not one is on point. In fact, I cannot find a single case in

---

[34] *Id.* at 502.

[35] The Court analyzed the National Security Act of 1947, 50 U.S.C. § 401, the Armed Services Procurement Act of 1947, 41 U.S.C. § 255, and two sections of the Espionage Act, 18 U.S.C. § 798 and 50 U.S.C. § 783(b).

[36] *Greene*, 360 U.S. at 504.

[37] *Id.* at 510-11 (Clark, J., dissenting).

[38] *Id.* at 511 n.1 ("My brother Harlan very kindly credits me with 'colorful characterization' in stating this as the issue. While I take great pride in authorship, I must say that in this instance I merely agreed with the statement of the issue by the Solicitor General and his co-counsel in five different places in the Brief for the United States.").

[39] *Id.* at 513.

support of the Court's position. Even a suit for damages on the ground of interference with private contracts does not lie against the Government.[40]

Next, Clark turned to the "constitutional question." Clark wrote that although the majority's opinion claimed to avoid answering the constitutional question of the executive branch's ability to classify information, its decision was actually establishing a dangerous precedent during a dangerous time. Alluding to the Cold War, Clark wrote that the Court's decision to strike down the program "for lack of specific authorization" was "indeed strange, and hard for me to understand at this critical time of national emergency."[41] Finally, although the majority opinion never mentioned a "right of access" and Clark's dissent did not specifically mention a First Amendment right of access to government information, Clark concluded that the majority opinion would be read to guarantee some sort of broad right of access in the future. He wrote:

> While the Court disclaims deciding this constitutional question, no one reading the opinion will doubt that the explicit language of its broad sweep speaks in prophecy. Let us hope that the winds may change. If they do not the present temporary debacle will turn into a rout of our internal security.[42]

Thus Clark's dissenting opinion in *Greene* was the first time a member of the Court framed a case as involving a constitutional right of access to government information. While the majority supported Greene's claims through texualism, it did so without framing the case in terms of access to information. Although Clark's dissent in *Greene* spoke of broad constitutional interpretations and impending doom, a Supreme Court majority did not frame a case as involving the issue of access to national security information until 1988. In 1965, however, the Court addressed a different access issue, whether a U.S. citizen had

---

[40] *Id.* at 512-13.
[41] *Id.* at 515.
[42] *Id.* at 524.

a First Amendment right to gather information in Cuba despite a government prohibition on traveling to the country.

In 1962, roughly one year after the United States broke diplomatic ties with Cuba and declared U.S. passports invalid for travel to Cuba "unless specifically endorsed for such travel under the authority of the Secretary of State,"[43] Louis Zemel filed a suit in federal court seeking a judgment declaring that he was "entitled under the Constitution and laws of the United States to travel to Cuba and to have his passport validated for that purpose."[44] In *Zemel v. Rusk*, the Court was asked to determine if Zemel had a First Amendment right to travel to Cuba in order to "satisfy [his] curiosity about the state of affairs in Cuba and make [himself] a better informed citizen."[45]

The Court framed three separate legal questions presented by the case. First, the Court framed the case as a separation of powers issue, seeking to determine if Congress had properly conferred upon the Secretary of State authority to grant and validate passports. Using both statutory textual analysis and legislative intent, the Court concluded the Secretary's power to refuse to validate Zemel's passport was supported by the authority granted by Congress in the Passport Act of 1926.[46]

Turning to the constitutional questions presented by the case, the Court first considered if the Secretary's refusal to validate Zemel's passport violated Zemel's due process rights. Relying on a public policy analysis, the Court concluded that the Secretary of State had sufficient reason to restrict Zemel's travel. Focusing on the dangers of the communist Cuban government, the Court held that "the Secretary has justifiably concluded that travel to Cuba by American citizens might involve the Nation in dangerous international incidents, and that the Constitution does not require him to validate passports for such travel."[47] Although the Court cited precedent to support the existence of a constitutional right to travel both inside and outside the country, that right was outweighed by the obvious national security concerns

---

[43] Zemel v. Rusk, 318 U.S. 1, 3 (1965).
[44] *Id.* at 4.
[45] *Id.*
[46] *Id.* at 7-13.
[47] *Id.* at 15.

related to traveling to Cuba, concerns highlighted by the recent Cuban missile crisis.[48]

Finally, the Court considered Zemel's First Amendment claims. In Zemel's petition, he asserted that the refusal to validate his passport was "a direct interference with the First Amendment rights of citizens to travel abroad so that they might acquaint themselves at first hand with the effects abroad of our Government's policies, foreign and domestic, and with conditions abroad which might affect such policies."[49] Although the Court acknowledged that banning travel to Cuba interfered with the free flow of information, it refused to acknowledge the existence of a First Amendment issue.

> We must agree that the Secretary's refusal to validate passports for Cuba renders less than wholly free the flow of information concerning that country. While we further agree that this is a factor to be considered in determining whether appellant has been denied due process of law, we cannot accept the contention of appellant that it is a First Amendment right which is involved. For to the extent that the Secretary's refusal to validate passports for Cuba acts as an inhibition (and it would be unrealistic to assume that it does not), it is an inhibition of action. There are few restrictions on action which could not be clothed by ingenious argument in the garb of decreased data flow.[50]

Relying on a First Amendment theory that did not embrace newsgathering, the Court concluded, "The right to speak and publish does not carry with it the unrestrained right to gather information."[51] Thus, the Court primarily framed the case only in terms of separation of powers and due process issues.

Although the majority did not frame the case as directly implicating the First Amendment, a dissent authored by Justice William O. Douglas and joined by Justice Arthur Goldberg framed a

---

[48] *Id.* at 15-16.
[49] *Id.* at 16.
[50] *Id.* at 16-17.
[51] *Id.* at 17.

"peripheral" First Amendment right as the main legal issue in the case. Relying on the Court's decision in *Kent v. Dulles*,[52] Douglas concluded the Court had already established that the right to travel both at home and overseas was protected by the Constitution.[53] Delving deeper into First Amendment theory, Douglas used a classic marketplace of ideas approach to support his contention that although the Secretary could prevent travel to dangerous locations, Cuba did not qualify as such a location.

> [T]he only so-called danger present here is the Communist regime in Cuba. The world, however, is filled with Communist thought; and Communist regimes are on more than one continent. They are part of the world spectrum; and if we are to know them and understand them, we must mingle with them . . . .
>
> The First Amendment presupposes a mature people, not afraid of ideas. The First Amendment leaves no room for the official, whether truculent or benign, to say nay or yea because the ideas offend or please him or because he believes some political objective is served by keeping the citizen at home or letting him go.[54]

Douglas concluded his opinion writing, "Restrictions on the right to travel in times of peace should be so particularized that a First Amendment right is not precluded unless some clear countervailing national interest stands in the way of its assertion."[55]

In the years following *Greene* and *Zemel*, a number of lower courts applied First Amendment frames in a variety of access cases.[56] In

---

[52] 357 U.S. 116 (1958).

[53] *Zemel*, 381 U.S. at 23-24.

[54] *Id.* at 25-26.

[55] *Id.* at 26.

[56] In addition to the cases discussed here, a number of cases involving the state secrets privilege exist. As noted in chapter one, the state secrets privilege, a judicial creation, is most often used by executive branch officials in civil court cases to protect against subpoenas, discovery motions and other judicial requests for information. For a summary of the state secrets privilege and cases dealing with concept, see William G. Weaver & Robert M. Pallito, *State*

1973, for example, in *Brunnenkant v. Laird*,[57] a relatively obscure and rarely cited case,[58] the D.C. District Court ruled that the First Amendment prevented the government from removing Siegfried Brunnenkant's security clearance solely for voicing his social and political opinions.[59] In a two-page opinion the court clearly framed the case in terms of the First Amendment.[60] Although the court noted that in most cases involving national security the key legal issue was to balance competing interests, it wrote there was no need to engage in balancing here because the evidence overwhelming showed that Brunnenkant, a resident alien in the employ of a private contractor working for the U.S. government, lost his security clearance solely for voicing "heterodox political, social and economic views."[61] Relying upon the Supreme Court's ruling in *Bridges v. California*[62] and "other opinions to numerous to cite,"[63] District Judge John H. Pratt granted Brunnenkant's request for declaratory and injunctive relief. Although Pratt mentioned "balancing" competing interests in his opinion, he did not address any separation of powers issues. At no point did he mention deferring to the executive in matters of national security, hint that the court might be exercising its power in an area in was not meant to, or even cite *Greene*.[64]

Four years later, in 1977 the D.C. Circuit Court of Appeals heard two important cases addressing some of the legal issues that were raised, but not settled, by *Greene*. The first, *United States v. AT&T*,[65] addressed national security information and the inherent power of both the executive and legislative branches of government. The case

---

Secrets and Executive Power, 120 POLI. SCI. Q. 85 (2005). See *United States v. Reynolds*, 345 U.S. 1 (1953), for the genesis of the privilege.

[57] 360 F.Supp. 1330 (D.D.C. 1973).

[58] Westlaw.com's "Citing References" function reported only a single, unreported case that cited *Brunnenkant*, Pamella M. Doviak v. Dep't of the Navy, 1987 WL 908627 (E.E.O.C. 1987).

[59] *Brunnenkant*, 360 F.Supp. at 1332.

[60] *Id.*

[61] *Id.*

[62] 314 U.S. 252 (1942).

[63] *Brunnenkant*, 360 F.Supp. at 1332.

[64] The entire opinion only cites one case other than *Bridges*, United States v. Robel, 389 U.S. 258 (1967).

[65] 567 F.2d 121 (D.C. Cir. 1977).

concerned the issue of congressional access to national security information. The second, discussed later in this chapter, *Sherrill v. Knight*,[66] addressed a First Amendment right of access and the inherent power of the executive branch. That case involved a claim of constitutional right of access by the press.

United States. v. AT&T arose out of a congressional investigation into "the nature and extent of warrantless wiretapping" being conducted by the federal government.[67] In the course of an investigation into the Justice Department's wiretapping program, the Subcommittee on Oversight and Investigations of the House Committee on Interstate and Foreign Commerce issued a subpoena for all national security request letters in the possession of the American Telephone & Telegraph Co. The Justice Department sued to enjoin AT&T from complying with the subpoena on the grounds "that compliance might lead to public disclosure of the documents, with adverse effect on national security."[68] The district court granted the injunction and the chairman of the subcommittee, John D. Moss, appealed. Rather than attempt to resolve the dispute at that time, the D.C. Circuit Court of Appeals remanded the case to the district court with the suggestion that the parties attempt to negotiate a settlement.[69] When the negotiations between the Justice Department and the subcommittee failed, the D.C. Circuit heard the case again.[70]

In an opinion by Circuit Judge Harold Levevnthal, the court squarely framed the case as dealing with separation of powers. First, the court addressed what it considered the "primary issue"[71] of the case, the political question doctrine. Similar to justiciability, the political question doctrine deals with the appropriateness of having a case decided by a court. A political question is one "that a court will not consider because it involves the exercise of discretionary power by the

---

[66] 569 F.2d 124 (D.C. Cir. 1977).

[67] *AT&T*, 567 F.2d at 123.

[68] *Id.* at 123-24.

[69] *See* United States v. AT&T, 551 F.2d 384 (D.C. Cir. 1976).

[70] For a complete description of the proposal made by the Justice Department and the subcommittee's reasons for rejecting the proposal, see *AT&T*, 567 F.2d at 125.

[71] *Id.* at 125-26.

executive or legislative branch."[72] Both the legislative branch and the executive branch claimed in their briefs that the court did not have the authority to make a "determination of the propriety of [their] acts."[73] While Congress based its claim of "absolute discretion" on the Speech or Debate Clause,[74] the executive relied "on its obligation to safeguard the national security."[75]

The court disagreed with both parties, holding "neither the traditional political question doctrine nor any close adaptation thereof is appropriate where neither of the conflicting political branches has a clear and unequivocal constitutional title, and it is or may be possible to establish an effective judicial settlement."[76] Citing the U.S. Supreme Court's 1962 decision in *Baker v. Carr*,[77] the court of appeals noted that simply because a political controversy or conflict existed between the other two branches of government did not inherently mean the issue was beyond the competency of the judiciary to decide.[78] Instead, the court wrote, the political question doctrine applied when only one branch had the "constitutional authority" to make a decision that would settle the dispute.[79]

The court then discussed at length which branch had the constitutional authority to control information classified for national security purposes. Leventhal relied on framers' intent and the text of the Constitution, in combination with the Supreme Court's decision in *Youngstown Sheet & Tube Co. v. Sawyer*,[80] to reach his conclusion. First, the opinion concluded that the framers did not intend for absolute authority over any area of governance to rest with any of the three branches. According to the court's opinion, the framers expected that when "conflicts in scope of authority arose between the coordinate

---

[72] BLACK'S LAW DICTIONARY 1197 (8th ed. 2004).

[73] *AT&T*, 567 F.2d at 127.

[74] U.S. CONST. art. I, § 6, cl. 1.

[75] *AT&T*, 567 F.2d at 127 n.17.

[76] *Id.* at 127.

[77] 369 U.S. 186, 217 (1962).

[78] *AT&T*, 567 F.2d at 126.

[79] *Id.* In addition, in a footnote the court cited a number of cases to support its conclusion that "disputes concerning the allocation of power between the branches have often been judicially resolved." *Id.* at n.13.

[80] 343 U.S. 579 (1952).

branches, a spirit of dynamic compromise would promote resolution of the dispute in the manner most likely to result in efficient and effective functioning of our governmental system."[81] The court wrote that "each branch should take cognizance of an implicit constitutional mandate to seek optimal accommodation through a realistic evaluation of the needs of the conflicting branches in the particular fact situation" in order to avoid "the mischief of polarization."[82]

Next, moving from framers' intent to textualism, Leventhal addressed the executive branch's claim that the Constitution conferred upon it absolute power in the arena of national security. He wrote that such a claim was not supported through textual analysis.

> The executive would have it that the Constitution confers on the executive absolute discretion in the area of national security. This does not stand up. While the Constitution assigns to the President a number of powers relating to national security, including the function of commander in chief and the power to make treaties and appoint Ambassadors, it confers upon Congress other powers equally inseparable from the national security, such as the powers to declare war, raise and support armed forces and, in the case of the Senate, consent to treaties and the appointment of ambassadors.[83]

However, "most significant" to Leventhal was "the fact that the Constitution is largely silent on the question of allocation of powers associated with foreign affairs and national security."[84] The opinion then invoked Justice Robert H. Jackson's much quoted passage from *Youngstown* that such powers are "within a 'zone of twilight' in which the President and Congress share authority or in which its distribution is uncertain."[85]

---

[81] *AT&T*, 567 F.2d at 127.
[82] *Id.*
[83] *Id.* at 128.
[84] *Id.*
[85] *Id.* (quoting *Youngstown Sheet & Tube Co.*, 343 U.S. at 637 (Jackson, J., concurring)).

Thus, after also determining that it did not "accept the concept that Congress' investigatory power is absolute,"[86] the court attempted to balance the executive's interest in national security and Congress' interest in investigating the warrantless wiretapping program by using a "gradual approach."[87] The court reasoned that such an approach was "consistent with our view that the present dispute should be regarded as a concerted search for accommodation between the two branches."[88] While the court's balancing approach was somewhat analogous to the majority's opinion in *Greene*, it framed the case much closer to Clark's dissent, focusing on control of national security information. Using this approach allowed the court to acknowledge that the executive's duty to protect national security information was important while also recognizing competing values.

In 1988, almost thirty years after *Greene*, the Supreme Court decided a case using both Clark's frame of a constitutional right of access to government information and his emphasis on the power of the executive branch to control information and deny access. In *Department of Navy v. Egan*[89] the Court adopted a position put forward by the Solicitor General,[90] ruling that it was solely the executive's role to classify and protect information and make decisions about access to national security information. In 1983, Thomas M. Egan lost his year-

---

[86] *Id.* at 130. For the court's complete discussion of the issue, see *id.* at 128-30.
[87] *Id.* at 131. The court repeatedly referred to "gradualism" throughout the opinion.
[88] *Id.* The court proposed a detailed compromise between the two branches that focused on how large a random sample of documents the Subcommittee would be allowed to review, whether note taking would be allowed, and whether the executive branch would be allowed to substitute documents if the randomly selected documents were found to contain "extraordinarily sensitive" national security information. See *id.* at 131-33 for details of the court's compromise.
[89] 484 U.S. 518 (1988).
[90] *Compare* Reply Brief for the Petitioner Charles Fried, Solicitor General, at 1, Dep't of the Navy v. Egan, 484 U.S. 518 (1988) (No. 86-1552) 1987 WL 880379 (arguing the "narrow" issue in the case was the Merit Systems Protection Board's power to review the Navy's decision to deny Egan security clearance), *with Egan*, 484 U.S. at 520 ("The narrow question presented by this case is whether the Merit Systems Protection Board (Board) has authority . . . to review the substance of an underlying decision to deny or revoke a security clearance in the course of reviewing an adverse action.").

old position as a laborer leader at the Trident Naval Refit Facility in Bremerton, Washington, when he was denied a required security clearance.[91] Because the mission of the Refit Facility was to provide "quick-turn-around repair, replenishment, and systems check-out" of the Trident nuclear submarine, "the most sophisticated and sensitive weapon in the Navy's arsenal," all positions at the Refit Facility were classified as "sensitive."[92] Because Egan could not qualify for any job at the Refit Facility without a security clearance, he was removed from his position. Egan appealed the decision to the Merit Systems Protection Board as provided by the section of the U.S. Code under which he was dismissed.[93] Although Egan initially won his appeal to the head of the Board, after he lost before the full Board he appealed to the Court of Appeals for the Federal Circuit.[94]

The court of appeals, by a divided vote, reversed the full Board's decision that the Board had no authority to review the merits of a security-clearance decision.[95] Like the *Greene* majority, the court of appeals framed the issue as procedural. The court focused on the text and legislative history of the two possible sections of the U.S. Code under which Egan could have been removed, sections 7513 and 7532, to support its ruling. The court wrote:

> The statute provides in 5 U.S.C. § 7532 for the exclusion from Board review of agency actions against employees in national security matters, and establishes a procedure for such

---

[91] *Egan*, 484 U.S. at 520.
[92] *Id.*
[93] 5 U.S.C. § 7513 (1985).
[94] At the initial hearing, the head of the Board reversed the decision not to grant Egan security clearance. Although the government argued that the Board "did not have the authority to judge the merits of the underlying security-clearance determination" and could only determine whether the required removal procedures had been followed, the head of the Board ruled that the Board did have the authority to review security clearance decisions. Additionally, she held that the government had to "specify the precise criteria used in its security-clearance decision" and show that those criteria were "rationally related to national security." After the rehearing, the full Board reversed, holding that the Board did not have the power to review security clearance decisions. *Egan*, 484 U.S. at 523-35.
[95] Egan v. Dep't of Navy, 802 F.2d 1563 (Fed. Cir. 1986).

actions. Mr. Egan's removal was not taken under that provision. The statute provides no exclusion from Board review of removals under 5 U.S.C. § 7513(a), the provision under which Mr. Egan was removed on the ground of failure to receive a job-required security clearance. We have found no indication in the legislative history of the Civil Service Reform Act that such a removal action if taken under § 7513(a) was intended to be exempt from Board review, and the government has not asserted that Congress so intended.[96]

The court remanded the case to the Board for a new review, stating that the Board must rule on the propriety of denying the security clearance, and until it did, the question of an appropriate judicial remedy was not ripe.[97] Noting "the importance of the issue in its relation to national security concerns,"[98] the Supreme Court granted certiorari.

Identifying the core legal issue as a right of access to information, in a 5-3 decision, the Court used a number of legal factors to reach and justify its conclusion. The Court relied on constitutional textualism, precedent, and the text of the statutes as well as "the structure of the statutory scheme, its objectives, its legislative history, and the nature of the administrative action involved"[99] to support its decision to reverse. First, in a nod to the power of the executive to protect national security information, Justice Harry Blackmun's majority opinion began the analysis by noting, "It should be obvious that no one has a 'right' to a security clearance."[100] Using textualism to interpret the Constitution, Blackmun wrote that although the statutory language of section 7513 was important, the statute did not fundamentally alter the power of the executive under the Constitution to control national security information.

The President, after all, is the "Commander in Chief of the Army and Navy of the United States." His authority to classify

---

[96] *Id.* at 1567.
[97] *Id.* at 1573-75.
[98] *Egan*, 484 U.S. at 520.
[99] *Id.* at 530.
[100] *Id.* at 528.

and control access to information bearing on national security and to determine whether an individual is sufficiently trustworthy to occupy a position in the Executive Branch that will give that person access to such information flows primarily from this constitutional investment of power in the President and exists quite apart from any explicit congressional grant.[101]

Next, using precedents to support his arguments, Blackmun noted both the compelling need to keep information secret and the executive's unique ability to decide what should be kept secret. Citing a number of cases, he concluded the Court had long "recognized the Government's 'compelling interest' in withholding national security information from unauthorized persons in the course of executive business."[102]   In addition, the Court relied on precedent for the proposition that "'for reasons . . . too obvious to call for enlarged discussion' the protection of classified information must be committed to the broad discretion of the agency responsible"[103] and the assertion that it was "the generally accepted view that foreign policy was the province and responsibility of the Executive."[104]   In conclusion the Court stated, "Thus, unless Congress specifically has provided otherwise, courts traditionally have been reluctant to intrude upon the authority of the Executive in military and national security affairs."[105]

Justice Byron White, joined by Justices William Brennan and Thurgood Marshall, wrote a dissenting opinion. Although White also framed his argument in terms of the control of national security information, he wrote an opinion that attempted to balance multiple interests, much as the *AT&T* court had done. While White deviated from Blackmun by not focusing on textual analysis, like Blackmun, he focused much of his opinion on legislative intent and precedent. Although White's opinion acknowledged the "compelling interest" of national security, he contended that it was already accounted for in

---

[101] *Id.* at 527.
[102] *Id.*
[103] *Egan*, 484 U.S. at 527 (quoting CIA v. Sims, 471 U.S. 159, 170 (1985)).
[104] *Id.* (quoting Haig v. Agee, 453 U.S. 280, 293-94 (1981)).
[105] *Id.* at 530.

statutes dealing with government employee dismissals and accused the majority of trying to "rewrite" the statutes in the name of national security.[106] White reasoned that Congress *intended* for there to be two statutes to deal with dismissals "to guarantee every discharged employee a hearing into the 'cause' for his removal."[107] The majority's opinion, according to White, "frustrate[d] this congressional intent by denying any meaningful hearing to employees such as respondent who are discharged on national security grounds under provisions other than § 7532."[108]

Next, White turned his attention to precedent, or more specifically, to the lack of reference to *Greene* in the majority's opinion. Taking the majority to task for the omission, White wrote it was "difficult to reconcile today's decision with the Court's discussion in *Greene v. McElroy* of the procedural protections available" to a government contractor who had been denied a security clearance.[109]

Finally, focusing on the practical ability of the government to keep information classified, White concluded the majority's result was "not necessary to protect the Nation's secrets"[110] Although he did not invoke democratic theory, an analysis of constitutional text or structure, or the framers' intent, in a footnote White suggested the executive did not have the sole ability or power to evaluate national security concerns and cited precedent to demonstrate that courts had previously "adjudicated cases involving denials of security clearances without any documented harm to national security."[111] Thus, although the majority's opinion suggested that the Court had traditionally deferred to the executive in the area of access to national security information and the executive was uniquely suited to deal with such concerns, the precedents cited in White's dissent, including *Greene*, cast doubts on those notions.

Despite White's dissent, in the years following *Egan* a number of the U.S. Circuit Courts have cited the case for the idea that courts

---

[106] *Id.* at 534 (White, J., dissenting).
[107] *Id.* at 535.
[108] *Id.*
[109] *Id.* at 536.
[110] *Id.* at 537.
[111] *Id.* at 537 n.1.

should show considerable deference to the executive branch in the area of national security, especially in terms of protecting national security information.[112] In the area of access to classified information, a 1995 case, *Stehney v. Perry*,[113] is a good example of this trend.

The plaintiff, Dr. Ann K. Stehney, was a former employee of a nonprofit agency who refused to take a polygraph examination in order to obtain a security clearance to work on a National Security Agency (NSA) project. Although a failed polygraph was not grounds for automatic denial of security clearance, all individuals with access to "Sensitive Compartmented Information" were required to take the examination. Instead of the taking the examination Stehney asked that she be treated as if she had taken the polygraph examination and failed. Eleven months after Stehney's security clearance was terminated, she filed suit in federal district court seeking mandamus relief to force NSA officials to allow her not to take the polygraph test.[114]

In considering Stehney's claim, the district court framed the case in terms of separation of powers issues and quickly and decisively held that the case was non-justiciable based on the political question doctrine. The court relied on familiar precedents and constitutional text to reach its conclusion. First, the court cited *Baker v. Carr*[115] for the proposition that courts should not decide questions that are "textually committed" to another branch of government.[116] Next the court focused on the President's powers as commander-in-chief and cited a number of cases, including *Egan*, to support its conclusions that "it has long been the 'generally accepted view . . . that foreign policy [is] the province of and responsibility of the Executive,'"[117] and "[t]he same

---

[112] *See, e.g.*, Natural Resources Defense Council, Inc. v. Winter, 502 F.3d 859, 862 (9th Cir. 2007); El-Masri v. United States, 479 F.3d 296, 304 (4th Cir. 2007); Padilla v. Rumsfeld, 352 F.3d 695, 712 (2d Cir. 2003); Doe v. Tenet, 329 F.3d 1135, 1156 (9th Cir. 2003); North Jersey Media Group, Inc. v. Ashcroft, 308 F.3d 198, 219 (3rd Cir. 2002); United States v. McKevee, 131 F.3d 1, 14 (1st Cir. 1997).

[113] 907 F. Supp. 806 (D.N.J. 1995).

[114] *Id.*

[115] 369 U.S. 186, 217 (1962).

[116] *Stehney*, 907 F. Supp. at 816.

[117] *Id.* (quoting Haig v. Agee, 453 U.S. 280, 293-94 (1981)).

principle logically applies to the protection of national-security secrets."[118] Turning to textual analysis, the court wrote:

> [T]he text of the Constitution expressly confers on the President exclusive authority to take action as "Commander in Chief of the Army and Navy of the United States." The authority to classify and control access to information bearing on national security and to determine whether an individual is sufficiently trustworthy to occupy a position . . . that will give that person access to such information flows primarily from this constitutional investment of power and exists quite apart from any explicit congressional grant. . . .
>
> . . . .
>
> Thus, unless Congress specifically has provided otherwise, courts have traditionally been reluctant to intrude upon the authority of the Executive in military and national security affairs.[119]

The district court went on to conclude that because *Egan* gave the President the "final say" in deciding what information to classify, "such plenary authority cannot, by definition, be exercised unconstitutionally."[120]

In addition to showing great deference to the executive branch, the district court dismissed *Greene*. Although the court admitted that the Supreme Court reviewed an executive branch decision in *Greene*, it held that Stehney's reliance on that precedent was misplaced because "no justiciability issue was raised or addressed."[121] Although the Supreme Court never said so, the district court concluded that *Greene* was left inapplicable in the wake of *Egan*.

In summary, although a few opinions have voiced concerns or put restraints on the executive branch's ability to control national security

---

[118] *Stehney*, 907 F. Supp. at 816.
[119] *Id.* at 817.
[120] *Id.* at 818.
[121] *Id.*

information,[122] the general trend has been for courts to rule they are not qualified to consider such cases. In the years following *Egan*, most courts framed cases involving classification and access as justiciability or separation of powers issues. For example, in addition to the District Court of New Jersey's decision in *Stehney*, a number of federal courts, including four U.S. Circuit Courts of Appeals, have held that the executive branch's power to classify and control information is not judicially reviewable.[123] These cases are often excellent examples of issue fluidity, demonstrating the ability of courts to focus on one issue while ignoring others. In addition, they also demonstrate the ability of courts to focus on certain factors that justify or support their conclusion while ignoring others that may not. Since *Egan*, courts have moved away from lengthy analytical discussions of framers' intent, shared powers, legislative history or access to information. Perhaps not surprisingly, a similar trend has emerged in cases that have considered access to locations. Although in many of these cases courts at least framed the issue in terms of access or the First Amendment, they continued to defer to the executive branch or relied on justiciability frames to avoid answering the difficult question of how to balance national security and transparency.

Access to National Security Locations

Just a few months after its decision in *AT&T*, the D.C. Circuit was called upon in *Sherrill v. Knight*[124] to determine if the First Amendment rights of a journalist were violated by the White House's refusal to grant a press pass. While the case did not directly implicate national security information per se, it was framed as an access case, dealt with

---

[122] *See* Dep't of Navy v. Egan, 484 U.S. 518, 534 (1988) (White, J., dissenting); Greene v. McElroy, 360 U.S. 474 (1959); United States v. AT&T, 567 F.2d 121 (D.C. Cir. 1977).
[123] *See* Hall v. U.S. Dep't of Labor, Admin. Rev. Board, 476 F. 3d. 847 (10th Cir. 2007); Bennett v. Chertoff, 425 F.3d 999 (D.C. Cir. 2005); Hill v. White, 321 F.3d 1334 (11th Cir. 2003); Reinbold v. Evers, 187 F.3d 348 (4th Cir. 1999); Makky v. Chertoff, 489 F. Supp. 2d 421 (D.N.J. 2007); Nickelson v. United States, 284 F. Supp. 2d 387 (E.D. Va. 2003); Cobb v. Danzig, 190 F.R.D. 564 (S.D. Cal. 1999); Edwards v. Widnall, 17 F. Supp. 2d 1038 (D.Minn.1998). *But see* Ranger v. Tenet, 274 F. Supp. 2d 1 (D.D.C. 2003).
[124] 569 F.2d 124 (D.C. Cir. 1977).

the ability of the executive branch of the government to curtail newsgathering based on concerns related to the safety of the President, and contained a detailed discussion of a constitutionally based right to know.

In 1966, Robert Sherrill, the White House correspondent for *The Nation*, was denied a press pass based on the results of an investigation by the Secret Service. Although at the time there existed no published or internal regulations on which decisions to grant or deny press passes were based, during discovery it was determined that there was a routine process. First, a journalist would submit a request for a pass to the White House Press Office. Next, the Press Office would determine if the applicant had already obtained a pass for the House and Senate press galleries, resided in the Washington, D.C., area, and needed to report from the White House on a regular basis.[125] If all of these requirements were met, the Press Office would then forward the application to the Secret Service for a security check, including a background FBI investigation.[126] If an application for a pass was denied, the journalist was informed only that the denial was "for reasons relating to the security of the President and/or the members of his immediate family."[127] Sherrill's application had been denied based on his having been arrested and fined for physical assault in the State of Florida.[128]

Sherrill filed for relief in federal district court, alleging that the denial of a press pass violated the First and Fifth Amendments to the Constitution.[129] Although Sherrill's suit asked the district court to

---

[125] According to court records, this was usually verified by an editor of the publication for which the applicant was a correspondent. *Id.* at 126.

[126] *Id.*

[127] *Id.* at 127.

[128] *Id.* Sherrill learned the reasons for the denial when Assistant Secretary of the Treasury Eugene Rossides sent a letter to the American Civil Liberties Union about a Freedom of Information Act request regarding documents pertaining to the issue. Sherrill was never officially informed why he was denied a press pass by the Secret Service.

[129] *See* Forcade v. Knight, 416 F. Supp. 1025 (D.C.D.C. 1975). Thomas Forcade, a correspondent for the Alternate Press Syndicate who was also denied a White House press pass, was a second party to the complaint in the district court case. Although the judgment of the district court pertained to both Forcade and Sherrill, Forcade disclaimed further interest in the case after the

declare the refusal to grant him a press pass unlawful and to enjoin the Press Office from doing so,[130] the court instead crafted a set of specific standards by which the Secret Service should operate. On cross-motions for summary judgment, the district court remanded the case to the Secret Service with an order to: (1) "devise and publicize narrow and specific standards" for press pass denials; (2) in the case of a denial, institute procedures whereby an applicant would be "given notice of the evidence" upon which the Secret Service was to base its denial; (3) grant the journalist an opportunity to rebut or explain the evidence; and (4) issue "a final written decision specifying the reasons for its refusal to grant a press pass."[131] Sherrill appealed the decision to the D.C. Circuit Court of Appeals.

Like the district court, the circuit court found the case implicated the First and Fifth Amendments and framed the dispute as an access issue.[132] First, however, as it did in *AT&T*, the court dealt with the issue of justiciability and the executive's constitutional power. Circuit Judge Carl E. McGowan's opinion soundly rejected the government's attempt to frame the case in terms of separation of powers and its argument that the Constitution prohibited the judiciary from ruling on the case because access to the White House and the safety of the President were outside the power of the judiciary. The court wrote:

> We reject at the outset the contention of appellants that this case is nonjusticiable either because protection of the President is vested within the sole discretion of the Executive or because there are no judicially manageable standards for presidential protection. The former argument is wholly without force. Nothing in the Constitution suggests that courts are not to be the final arbiters of the legality of the actions of those protecting the President. . . .
>
> . . . .
>
> [W]e cannot agree with the Government's argument that

---

parties appealed, but before the court of appeals ruled. *Sherrill*, 569 F.2d at 126 n.1.
[130] *Forcade*, 416 F. Supp. at 1027.
[131] *Id.* at 1039.
[132] *Sherrill*, 569 F. 2d at 128.

mere mention of the President's safety must be allowed to trump any First Amendment issue.[133]

After summarily dismissing that legal question, the court turned its attention to the First Amendment, engaging in a detailed discussion of previous cases involving constitutional protections for newsgathering.

Citing the Supreme Court decision in *Pell v. Procunier*[134] and dicta from *Zemel v. Rusk*[135] for the respective propositions that the press had no greater First Amendment right of access than the general public and the general public had no First Amendment right of access to the White House, the government argued that denial of a White House press pass would violate the First Amendment "only if it is based upon the content of the journalist's speech or otherwise discriminates against a class of protected speech."[136] While McGowan wrote that denying a press pass on content-based criteria would be problematic, he also concluded that there were additional First Amendment arguments to consider. Chief among these was "the protection afforded newsgathering under the first amendment guarantee of freedom of the press."[137] Citing a host of Supreme Court decisions, McGowan concluded:

> [T]he protection afforded newsgathering under the first amendment guarantee of freedom of the press, requires that this access not be denied arbitrarily or for less than compelling reasons. Not only newsmen and the publications for which they write, but also the public at large have an interest protected by the first amendment in assuring that restrictions on newsgathering be no more arduous than necessary, and that individual newsmen not be arbitrarily excluded from sources of information.[138]

---

[133] *Id.* at 128 n.14.
[134] 417 U.S. 817, 833-34 (1974).
[135] 381 U.S. 1, 16-17 (1965).
[136] *Sherrill*, 569 F.2d at 129.
[137] *Id.*
[138] *Id.* at 129-30.

Although the court agreed with the government that protection of the President was a "compelling, even overwhelming interest," the practice of "[m]erely informing individual rejected applicants that rejection was for 'reasons of security' does not inform the public or other potential applicants of the basis for exclusion of journalists from White House press facilities."[139]

However, while the court clearly identified the First Amendment issue in the case, its focus on the specific pragmatic concerns of the case led it to a different conclusion than the district court. Although the court of appeals agreed with the district court that denial of a White House press pass to a bona fide journalist could violate the First and Fifth Amendments, the D.C. Circuit held that neither amendment justified requiring "the articulation of detailed criteria upon which the granting or denial of White House press passes is to be based."[140] The court wrote that protecting the President and his immediate family did not "lend itself to detailed articulation of narrow and specific standards or precise identification of all the factors which may be taken into account" by the Secret Service.[141] Instead, the court ordered the Secret Service to "publish or otherwise make publicly known the actual standard employed in determining whether an otherwise eligible journalist will obtain a White House press pass."[142] In case of a denial, the court required that a final statement of denial be sent to the applicant containing the reason for the denial "in order to assure that the agency has neither taken additional, undisclosed information into account, nor responded irrationally to matters put forward by way of rebuttal or explanation."[143] The court wrote:

> This standard is sufficiently circumspect so as to allow the Secret Service, exercising expert judgment which frequently must be subjective in nature, considerable leeway in denying press passes for security reasons. At the same time, the standard does specify in a meaningful way the basis upon

---

[139] *Id.* at 130.
[140] *Id.* at 129.
[141] *Id.* at 130.
[142] *Id.*
[143] *Id.* at 131.

which persons will be deemed security risks, and therefore will allow meaningful judicial review of decisions to deny press passes.[144]

Additionally, the court wrote that it expected courts to "be appropriately deferential to the Secret Service's determination of what justifies the inference that an individual constitutes a potential risk to the physical security of the President or his family."[145]

Thus, in one year the D.C. Circuit held that the judiciary had a role in determining who had access to information in two cases—*United States v. AT&T.* and *Sherrill*—and that the First Amendment protected at least some newsgathering activity in *Sherrill*, although it limited its ruling based on practical considerations and cautioned courts to defer to the executive branch. While a First Amendment right of access case would not come back before the D.C. Circuit for a number of years, in 1988 the Southern District of New York was called upon to determine if the First Amendment provided unlimited access to a foreign arena in which American military forces were engaged.

As noted above, *Nation Magazine v. Department of Defense*[146] involved a challenge to the Department of Defense (DOD) regulations governing press coverage of American military activities during periods of open hostilities. While the plaintiffs framed the case as a First Amendment right of access case, the government put forth a variety of arguments involving justiciability and separation of powers. Therefore, when considering the media organizations' requests for injunctive and declaratory relief, the Southern District of New York's opinion first addressed issues of justiciability raised by the DOD's brief, including standing, the political question doctrine and mootness.[147] In addition, the court stated that even in "the event the Court determines that at least some of the issues are not moot and that there is jurisdiction to hear the claims, a question remains whether the Court *should* exercise its power to address the controversy."[148]

---

[144] *Id.* at 130.
[145] *Id.*
[146] 762 F. Supp. 1558 (S.D.N.Y. 1991).
[147] *Id.* at 1565.
[148] *Nation Magazine*, 762 F. Supp. at 1565 (emphasis added).

First, the court briefly discussed standing and held that because the charges were "brought before the Court by parties who have allegedly suffered immediate injury resulting from the challenged regulations," the plaintiffs had standing to raise First and Fifth Amendment claims.[149] Next, the court turned its focus to the political question doctrine. Focusing on precedents, the court determined that a "long line of cases addressing the role of the judiciary in reviewing military decisions" had left the clear message that "[c]ivilian courts should 'hesitate long before entertaining a suit which asks the court to tamper with the . . . necessarily unique structure of the Military Establishment.'"[150] Yet, despite this strong language that seemed to favor the government's position that the case was outside judicial power, the court was unwilling to go so far as to accept the government's claim that *all* cases involving the military were outside the power of Article III courts.[151] Instead, the court found the cases cited by the government differed from the case at hand in that they had involved "direct challenges to the institutional functioning of the military in such areas as the relationship between personnel, discipline, and training."[152] Unlike that line of cases, the court ruled that the present case did not impact the executive's foreign relations powers or require the court to move beyond its traditional area of expertise and, therefore, was justiciable.[153]

Finally, the court addressed the mootness doctrine, what it termed the "most difficult of the justiciability questions" raised by the case, and used its discussion to contemplate the existence of a constitutional right of access.[154] Considering the plaintiff's request for injunctive

---

[149] *Id.* Standing is defined as "[a] party's right to make a legal claim or seek judicial enforcement of a duty or a right. To have standing in federal court, a plaintiff must show (1) that the challenged conduct has caused the plaintiff actual injury, and (2) that the interest sought to be protected is within the zone of interests meant to be regulated by the statutory or constitutional guarantee in question." BLACK'S LAW DICTIONARY 1442 (8th ed. 2004).

[150] *Nation Magazine*, 762 F. Supp. at 1566-67 (quoting Chappell v. Wallace, 462 U.S. 296, 300 (1983)).

[151] *Id.* at 1568.

[152] *Id.* at 1567.

[153] *Id.*

[154] *Id.* at 1568-69. The mootness doctrine is "[t]he principle that American courts will not decide . . . cases in which there is no longer any actual

relief, the court wrote, "Since the regulations have been lifted and the press is no longer constrained from traveling throughout the Middle East, there is no longer any presently operative practice for this Court to enjoin." [155] However, on the issue of declaratory relief the court ruled that because the plaintiffs asserted that the existence of the DOD restrictions violated the First Amendment generally, and not simply as applied to operations in the Middle East, the court could hear the challenge. Unfortunately for the media plaintiffs, that did not end the court's discussion. The court then wrote: "The question of the court's power to hear a case is, however, only the beginning of the inquiry. A separate and more difficult inquiry is whether it is appropriate for a Court to exercise that power."[156]

More than in any other case discussed in this chapter, the issue was clearly framed by the court as a conflict between transparency and national security. The court also stated that it needed to consider what branch of government should strike the balance between these two competing interests.

At issue in this action are important First Amendment principles and the countervailing national security interests of this country. This case presents a novel question since the right of the American public to be informed about the functioning of government and the need to limit information availability for reasons of national security both have a secure place in this country's constitutional history. In short, this case

---

controversy." BLACK'S LAW DICTIONARY 1030 (8th ed. 2004). The court addressed mootness because by the time it heard the case, although the DOD regulations still existed, they had been "lifted" in regards to the Persian Gulf conflict. Considering its ability to hear the overall case, the court found that the issue was capable of repetition yet likely to continue to evade judicial review. Because of the short duration of modern military action, the court wrote, "the judicial process often will not be able to resolve legal controversies such as this before hostilities have ceased." In addition, the court wrote that it was "not unreasonable to suppose that in future military activities DOD will behave in a manner that is susceptible to the same challenges as those raised in this complaint." *Nation Magazine*, 762 F. Supp. at 1569.

[155] *Nation Magazine*, 762 F. Supp. at 1570.

[156] *Id.* at 1570.

involves the adjudication of important constitutional principles. The question, however, is not only which principles apply and the weighing of the principles, but also when and in what circumstances it is best to consider the questions.[157]

To determine if it should exercise its power, the court turned to a detailed discussion of First Amendment theory, specifically whether theories related to self-governance and the checking function of the press supported the establishment of a right of access. After framing the case in terms of the First Amendment, the court relied upon precedents to flesh out this discussion of a constitutional right to access.

Although the media organizations argued that they were not asking the court to establish a new constitutional right of access that required "affirmative assistance" from the government to provide information,[158] the court reasoned that the case involved charting "new constitutional territory." The court wrote that while the Supreme Court had considered cases involving the First Amendment and national security, none of those cases had directly addressed "the role and limits of news gathering under the First Amendment in a military context abroad," and therefore there was no direct precedent to rely upon. [159] Instead, the court turned to "case law on questions involving the access rights of the press and public" to answer the novel constitutional questions of a right to access to military endeavors and whether press pools violated that right.[160]

The court began by citing the Supreme Court precedents that had previously established "there is no right of access of the press to fora which have traditionally been characterized as private or closed to the public, such as meetings involving the internal discussions of government officials,"[161] and limitations may be "placed on access to government controlled institutions."[162] Continuing to focus on precedent, the opinion next cited a number of cases that supported a

---

[157] *Id.* at 1571.
[158] *Id.*
[159] *Id.*
[160] *Nation Magazine*, 762 F. Supp. at 1571.
[161] *Id.*
[162] *Id.*

First Amendment "right to know." First, it discussed two cases dealing with a First Amendment access to judicial proceedings—*Richmond Newspapers, Inc. v. Virginia*[163] and *Globe Newspaper Co. v. Superior Court*[164]—as examples of the Supreme Court's support for a "right to know" and the checking function of the press.[165]

> A fundamental theme in *Richmond* and *Globe* was the importance of an informed American citizenry. As the Court wrote, guaranteed access of the public to occurrences in a courtroom during a criminal trial assures "freedom of communication on matters relating to the functioning of government." Learning about, criticizing and evaluating government, the Supreme Court has reasoned, requires some "right to receive" information and ideas.[166]

In addition, the court suggested that in *Globe Newspaper Co.* the Court implied access to other situations might also be included in the Amendment[167] and pointed out that the Supreme Court held the right to be informed about government operations was important "even when the government has suggested that national security concerns were implicated."[168] The court summarized:

> Given the broad grounds invoked in these holdings, the affirmative right to gather news, ideas and information is certainly strengthened by these cases. By protecting the press, the flow of information to the public is preserved. As the Supreme Court has observed, "the First Amendment goes beyond protection of the press and the self-expression of individuals to prohibit government from limiting the stock of information from which members of the public may draw."

---

[163] 448 U.S. 555 (1980).
[164] 457 U.S. 596 (1982).
[165] *Nation Magazine*, 762 F. Supp. at 1572.
[166] *Id.*
[167] *Id.*
[168] *Id.*

Viewing these cases collectively, it is arguable that generally there is at least some minimal constitutional right to access.[169]

Having established a number of precedents that supported a right of access, the court speculated about how this line of cases would apply to the military. Although the court concluded that at least some right of access to the military might exist, it was uncertain because "military operations are not closely akin to a building such as a prison, nor to a park or a courtroom."[170] Ultimately, based on this uncertainty, the hypothetical nature of its discussion, and the lack of concrete facts on which to apply precedent, the court refused to decide if there was a right of access. "Pursuant to long-settled policy in the disposition of constitutional questions, courts should refrain from deciding issues presented in a highly abstract form, especially in instances where the Supreme Court has not articulated guiding standards,"[171] the court wrote.

The court next considered whether the DOD's use of press pools gave preferential treatment to some members of the press. Again the court turned to Supreme Court precedent to support its discussion, this time focusing on the Court's public forum doctrine. First, the court discussed precedent that supported the plaintiffs' case, finding that because the government had decided to "open the door" to press coverage it had created an "expressive area."[172] "Regardless of whether the government is constitutionally required to open the battlefield to the press as representatives of the public, a question that this Court has declined to decide, once the government does so it is bound to do so in a non-discriminatory manner," the court said.[173] Citing *Sherrill v. Knight*, the court ruled that government could not arbitrarily exclude some members of the press once it allowed others to cover the conflict.[174]

The court, however, then noted that the right to be free from discriminatory treatment was "not synonymous with a guaranteed right

---

[169] *Id.* (quoting First National Bank v. Bellotti, 435 U.S. 765, 783 (1978).
[170] *Id.*
[171] *Id.*
[172] *Id.* at 1573
[173] *Id.*
[174] *Id.*

to gather news at all times and places or in any manner that may be desired" and the press could be subjected to reasonable time, place and manner restrictions.[175] Thus, the court concluded that some restrictions might be appropriate at some point. After reaching this conclusion, the court once again declined to decide the issue. Instead, it concluded it was not faced with concrete enough facts to rule on the limitations on access. The court wrote:

> [S]urely a court ruling on the possible appropriateness of such a restriction for some future military conflict must consider the possibility that at times such circumstances may be present. Who can say that during the next American overseas military operation some restriction on the number of journalists granted access at a particular time to a particular battlefield may not be a reasonable time, place, and manner restriction? Who today can even predict the manner in which the next war may be fought?[176]

Faced with two "significant and novel constitutional doctrines"[177] and without clear direction from the Supreme Court or concrete facts to rule on, the court concluded that "based on all the circumstances of the case," the controversy was not "sufficiently concrete and focused to permit adjudication on the merits."[178] Thus, although the court clearly considered a First Amendment right of access to be the main principle of law presented by the case, the court could duck the issue, citing a lack of direction from the Supreme Court and pragmatic concerns related to the hypothetical nature of the situation it was contemplating. While the Supreme Court has yet to provide any clear direction, the U.S. District Court for D.C. has twice decided cases very similar to *Nation Magazine* with nearly identical results. In these cases, *Getty Images v. Department of Defense*[179] and *Flynt v. Rumsfeld*,[180] the court

---

[175] *Id.*
[176] *Id.* at 1574.
[177] *Id.* at 1575.
[178] *Id.* at 1568.
[179] 193 F. Supp. 2d 112 (D.D.C. 2002).
[180] 245 F. Supp. 2d 94 (D.D.C. 2003).

engaged in similar First Amendment discussions as the *Nation Magazine* court, relied on almost identical precedents and again focused on the lack of a concrete controversy.

In *Getty Images*, a case involving access to the U.S. government's detention center at Guantanamo Bay Naval Base in Cuba, the D.C. District Court used similar frames and precedents as *Nation Magazine*. Although the court discussed First Amendment issues as well as an equality frame involving the likelihood that there was at least some sort of constitutional right of equal access to Guantanamo Bay, it ultimately determined that Getty had failed to demonstrate that injunctive relief was needed. In the case, Getty Images News Services Corp., "a reputable press organization that produces over 100,000 photographs annually for subscribers such as *Time* and *Newsweek*,"[181] sought a preliminary injunction to enjoin the DOD to provide Getty with equal access to the detention facilities at Guantanamo Bay, to require the DOD to "promulgate standards and procedures ensuring equal access," and to compel the DOD to create a press pool for access to Guantanamo.[182] According to the court, Getty's claim "framed several constitutional challenges to its alleged treatment by DOD."[183] Getty alleged that the DOD's actions violated the company's First Amendment right to equal access to Guantanamo and Fifth Amendment right to equal protection, and that the company's First and Fifth Amendment rights had been violated "because adequate regulatory standards had not been developed and applied."[184]

In considering Getty's claim, District Judge John D. Bates primarily relied upon *Sherrill* and *Nation Magazine* to reach his conclusions. Comingling First Amendment and non-discrimination issues, the court used these two cases to support Getty's argument that

---

[181] *Getty*, 193 F. Supp. 2d at 113.

[182] *Id.* at 113-14. In addition, Getty also sought to enjoin the DOD from excluding it from participation in the National Media Pool or any ad hoc or regional pools created during Operation Enduring Freedom. However, by the time the case reached the district court, Getty was granted membership in the National Media Pool and the Afghanistan regional pool no longer existed. Therefore, the court dismissed these claims after a short discussion of standing and mootness.

[183] *Id.* at 114.

[184] *Id.*

once the DOD "opened Guantanamo Bay to certain members of the press, all members of the press became constitutionally entitled to equal access to the detention facilities there."[185]   In addition, after a discussion of *Sherrill*, the court concluded that although it was "reluctant to interfere" with military conduct, [186] the First and Fifth Amendments required, "at a minimum, that before determining which media organizations receive the limited access available" there must be some reasonable criteria to guide the DOD decisions.[187] Quoting the *Sherrill* court's discussion of First Amendment protection for newsgathering without truly devolving into First Amendment theory,[188] Bates determined that the First Amendment required the government to have solid reasoning behind its decisions and refrain from arbitrary or capricious decision making.

Ultimately, however, as in *Nation Magazine*, the district court ruled that it was not the appropriate time to grant Getty's motion for an injunction. Although the court wrote that it was persuaded that Getty had raised "a serious question" relating to its request for equal access and that the DOD "at some point in time" would have to establish and publish non-arbitrary criteria and a process to govern media access, the court would not grant Getty's injunction. To support this ruling, the court used both precedent and a pragmatic public policy argument, balancing Getty's interests and likelihood of success against the public interest.[189] The court weighed the potential harm to the public interest that a disruption at Guantanamo Bay would cause against Getty's "speculative" First Amendment claims.   The court reasoned that

---

[185] *Id.* at 118.

[186] The court noted that it agreed with the government's arguments that "that the Guantanamo Bay Naval Base [was] not a public forum and that consideration of Getty's First and Fifth Amendment claims must be undertaken through the prism of the heightened deference due to military regulations and decision-making." *Id.* at 119.

[187] *Id.* at 121.

[188] *Id.* at 119 (quoting *Sherrill v. Knight*, 569 F.2d 124, 129-30 (D.C.Cir. 1977)).

[189] Citing precedent, the court determined that in order to be granted an injunction Getty needed to demonstrate "(1) a substantial likelihood of success on the merits; (2) that it will suffer irreparable harm absent the relief requested; (3) that other parties will not be harmed if the relief is granted; and (4) that the public interest supports granting the requested relief." *Id.* at 118.

"absent some concrete and irreparable diminution of First Amendment rights," it was "not possible to conclude that the public interest favors the injunctive relief Getty seeks."[190] In its conclusion, the district court focused on the speculative nature of both a First Amendment right of access and Getty's claims that it was being harmed to support the decision not to grant an injunction.[191] One year later, the court adopted a similar stance in *Flynt v. Rumsfeld.*[192]

Like *Nation Magazine, Flynt* involved a magazine's claim that DOD regulations violated the "qualified First Amendment right" of media access to the battlefield.[193] While the court discussed the First Amendment implications of access, the court again focused instead on the hypothetical nature of the claim and the need to practice judicial restraint in such situations. In 2001, *Hustler Magazine* requested one of its correspondents be allowed "to accompany and cover American ground forces in Afghanistan and wherever else such forces may be utilized in this campaign against terrorism."[194] While the *Hustler* correspondent was placed on a waiting list of journalists seeking to embed with conventional combat troops, because all of the ground forces in Afghanistan at the time were special operations forces, the correspondent was not allowed to accompany any soldiers on actual missions. In what would become a central argument to the case, the DOD claimed that it was "awaiting approval to allow reporters to accompany special forces on missions."[195]

In challenging the DOD's regulations, *Hustler* made two distinct claims. First, the magazine challenged the DOD regulations as applied,[196] charging that the DOD violated *Hustler's* First Amendment

---

[190] *Id.* at 124. While the court found in favor of Getty on parts one and two of the test, it found that the public interest outweighed the speculative nature of Getty's claims.

[191] *Id.*

[192] 245 F. Supp. 2d 94 (D.D.C. 2003).

[193] *Id.* at 99.

[194] *Id.* at 97.

[195] *Id.* at 99.

[196] "A claim that a law or government policy, though constitutional on its face, is unconstitutional as applied, usually because of a discriminatory effect; a claim that a statute is unconstitutional on the facts of a particular case or in its application to a particular party." BLACK'S LAW DICTIONARY 244 (8th ed. 2004).

rights by "improperly denying a *Hustler* correspondent the right to accompany combat forces on the ground in Afghanistan."[197] Second, the magazine brought a facial challenge,[198] asserting that the DOD regulations were "facially unconstitutional under the First and Fifth Amendments."[199]

The opinion, authored by District Judge Paul L. Friedman, first considered *Hustler's* as-applied challenge. The court held that it had no jurisdiction to address the issue because the controversy was not ripe for review nor did *Hustler* have standing. Although *Hustler* attempted to insert the First Amendment into the argument by contending that a ripe controversy existed because the parties disagreed as to whether there was "a First Amendment right of media access to the battlefield,"[200] the court ruled that this was not enough to make the controversy ripe. The court wrote that the "mere existence of a legal disagreement about the scope of the First Amendment [did] not make that disagreement fit for judicial review."[201] Instead, because the DOD was still technically "awaiting permission" to allow journalists to travel with the only troops on the ground, the court held the issue had not been settled and was, therefore, not ripe for review. It wrote *Hustler's* as-applied claims were "not fit for judicial decision at this juncture because defendants have not made a final decision with respect to plaintiffs' request for access to combat ground forces in battle."[202] In addition, the court concluded that because *Hustler* could not show it had been denied access, it could not demonstrate it had suffered any injury.[203]

Next, considering *Hustler's* facial challenge, although the court admitted "there may be a limited or qualified right of media access to the battlefield"[204] based on the First Amendment, it declined to definitively decide the issue. Instead, the court shifted frames and

---

[197] *Id.* at 99.
[198] "A claim that a statute is unconstitutional on its face—that is, that it always operates unconstitutionally." BLACK'S LAW DICTIONARY 244 (8th ed. 2004).
[199] *Flynt*, 245 F. Supp. 2d at 99.
[200] *Id.* at 102.
[201] *Id.*
[202] *Id.* at 101.
[203] *Id.* at 103.
[204] *Id.* at 109.

turned to the legal issue of judicial power, adopting the frame that the case was more about the role of the courts in making decisions than it was about the First Amendment. Like the *Nation Magazine* court, although the *Flynt* court discussed access, ultimately it did not rely on First Amendment theories related to self-governance or the checking function to decide the case. Instead, the court focused on precedent, the proper role of the judiciary and pragmatic factors to decide not to definitive rule on the First Amendment issue. Not surprisingly, in its discussion the court cited *Nation Magazine* and *Getty Images*, relying multiple times on the reasoning of those cases.

As Judge Sand of the Southern District of New York had done in *Nation Magazine*, the D.C. District Court held it could decide the case under the political question doctrine because *Hustler* was not making a claim that went to "the heart of the military's 'goals, directives and tactics" by challenging the DOD's regulations.[205] The court wrote:

> In their facial challenge claims plaintiffs do not ask the Court to delve into tactical decisions made by defendants. They ask the Court only to consider whether a First Amendment right of media access to the battlefield exists—a right they themselves characterize as a 'qualified right of access' subject to reasonable Executive Branch regulations—and, if so, to direct defendants to enact guidelines that comport with such First Amendment protections.[206]

However, as noted, the court never truly addressed the existence of a First Amendment "qualified right of access." Instead the court ruled that just because it had jurisdiction to hear the facial challenge, that conclusion did "not necessarily result . . . in adjudication of plaintiffs' claims on the merits at this time."[207] After quoting both Judge Bates admonition in *Getty Images* that "the absence of a concrete controversy is of particular concern in light of the important constitutional issues at

---

[205] *Id.* at 106-07.
[206] *Id.* at 107.
[207] *Id.*

stake and the national defense interests that might be implicated,"[208] as well as a lengthy passage from *Nation Magazine*,[209] the court concluded the "prudent course" was to "delay resolution of these constitutional issues until and unless plaintiffs are denied access after having pursued their request through normal military channels."[210] The court therefore "declined to exercise its discretion" to consider the facial challenge.[211] Thus, although the *Nation Magazine* court engaged in a discussion of First Amendment values and the *Flynt* court at least cited the *Nation Magazine* discussion in its decision, ultimately neither court relied on self-governance or the checking function to support a First Amendment based right of access. While both courts agreed there might be at least a qualified First Amendment right of access,[212] both turned away from First Amendment issues and instead framed the cases in terms of judicial powers, relied heavily on precedents and clearly deferred to pragmatic factors related to not deciding undeveloped or hypothetical cases. Neither court was willing to advance a right of access based on abstract issues and hypothetical situations.

From *Greene* to *Flynt*, a pattern emerged in cases considering access and national security. Although many of the courts engaged in detailed discussions of a First Amendment right of access, ultimately most of the courts focused on the justiciability of the cases. Furthermore, many of the courts considering national security and transparency were reluctant to inject themselves into disputes about access. In addition, later cases involving national security clearances abandoned detailed discussion of frameworks and legal factors and instead simply cited *Egan* as holding that the executive branch has authority in matters of national security. As noted, in *Nation Magazine* the court discussed how the judiciary's approach to national security access cases compared with cases involving access to the judiciary itself.[213] As the *Nation Magazine* court noted, in cases that have

---

[208] *Id.* at 109. (quoting *Getty Images News Services, Corp. v. Dep't of Defense*, 193 F.Supp.2d 112, 113, 118 (D.D.C. 2002)).
[209] *Id.*
[210] *Id.* at 110.
[211] *Id.* at 110.
[212] *Id.* at 108; *Nation Magazine*, 762 F. Supp. at 1572. *See also* Flynt v. Rumsfeld, 180 F. Supp. 2d 174, 175 (D.D.C. 2002).
[213] *Nation Magazine*, 762 F. Supp. at 1572.

considered a right of access to the judiciary, the Supreme Court has consistently framed access in terms of the First Amendment and articulated a broad right of access. In addition, many of the justices in these cases have written thoughtful opinions, providing in-depth discussions of a number of legal factors to support their conclusions. These cases also provide an excellent example of how the justices frame issues and cite factors to support their differing conclusions.

Access to Judicial Proceedings and Documents
As opposed to cases involving access and national security, over the last thirty-eight years the U.S. Supreme Court has found that the First Amendment guarantees a broad right of access to criminal judicial proceedings. In addition, although the Court has never specifically said there is a constitutional right of access to court documents, at least two decisions imply there is a First Amendment right of access to records of open proceedings or proceedings that should have been open.[214] It is important to note however, that the Court did not initially frame access to the judiciary as a First Amendment issue. Although the Court addressed judicial secrecy in a number of cases between 1947 and 1966,[215] the Court discussed access in terms of the Sixth Amendment, not the First, and said the Sixth Amendment right to a public trial belonged to the accused, rather than the public or the press.[216] For example, in *Gannett Co., Inc. v. DePasquale*,[217] a 1979 case involving a pretrial evidence suppression hearing, the Court wrote, "The Constitution nowhere mentions any right of access to a criminal trial on the part of the public; its guarantee, like the others enumerated, is

---

[214] *See, e.g.,* Press Enter. v. Riverside County Superior Court, 478 U.S. 1 (1986); Press Enter. v. Riverside County Superior Court, 464 U.S. 501 (1984). In addition, some lower courts have ruled that there is at least a qualified First Amendment right to some types of judicial records. *See, e.g.,* United States v. Schlette, 842 F.2d 1574 (9th Cir. 1988); CBS v. United States District Court, 765 F.2d 823 (9th Cir. 1983); Associated Press v. United States District Court, 705 F.2d 1143, 1145 (9th Cir. 1983). *But see, In re* Providence Journal Co., 293 F.3d 1 (1st Cir. 2002).
[215] *See, e.g.,* Sheppard v. Maxwell, 384 U.S. 333, 349-50 (1966); Estes v. Texas, 381 U.S. 532, 538-39 (1965); *In re* Oliver, 333 U.S. 257, 268-69 (1948); Craig v. Harney, 331 U.S. 367, 374 (1947).
[216] *See, e.g., In re* Oliver, 333 U.S. at 266-68.
[217] 443 U.S. 368 (1979).

personal to the accused."[218] In addition, in 1978, when the Court considered a right of access to documents in the possession of a court, it followed a path similar to some of the national security cases, focusing on textual analysis of congressional legislation, refusing to frame the case as dealing with the First Amendment.

In *Nixon v. Warner Communications, Inc.,*[219] television networks appealed an order of the U.S. District Court for the District of Columbia that held that the networks could not make copies of tape recordings made by the Nixon administration and introduced into evidence at the Watergate criminal trials. The networks framed the case as involving two access issues, a common law and First Amendment right of access to judicial records. Although the Court acknowledge a common law right of access to documents in the possession of the judiciary,[220] instead of framing the question in terms of access and deciding the case by weighing the pros and cons of access under a common law right as it normally would have, the Court engaged in issue discovery, taking a position that was not argued by either side or contained in any brief.[221] The Court ruled that release of the records would ultimately be controlled by the Presidential Recordings Act.[222] Writing for the Court, Justice Lewis Powell justified this rationale by relying on textual analysis of the Act without a great deal of explanation[223] and very briefly stating that the courts were not as well equipped to handle the details of access to presidential records as the other two branches of government.[224] The Court failed to address any of the major legal issues raised by either side in a

---

[218] *Id.* at 379-80.

[219] 435 U.S. 589 (1978).

[220] *Id.* at 597.

[221] *Id.* at 602-03.

[222] *Id.* at 603.

[223] *Id.* at 603 n.15.

[224] *Id.* at 606. The Court spent so little time framing the case, it is difficult to say it identified the major legal principle as a separation of powers issue. The only time the majority addressed the issue was in response to the network's claims that immediate release by the Court would advance the intent of the Act. The Court did not agree, writing, "The Executive and Legislative Branches . . . possess superior resources for assessing the proper implementation of public access and the competing rights, if any, of the persons whose voices are recorded on the tapes." *Id.*

meaningful way. In addition, the Court refused to frame the issue as involving either a First Amendment freedom of the press claim or a Sixth Amendment guarantee of a public trial claim, dismissing these arguments in one short section by citing precedents that found the press had no greater rights of access than the public.[225]

In *Gannett Co., Inc. v. DePasquale*,[226] the Court once again dismissed the First Amendment claims of the press, focusing on the Sixth Amendment instead. *Gannett* involved the closure of a courtroom during a pretrial hearing to suppress evidence in a murder case.[227] Although the trial judge indicated there was a constitutional right of access to judicial proceedings, he concluded that such a right had to be balanced with the accused's right to a fair trial. As noted, the Supreme Court focused on the Sixth Amendment, not the First, as the core legal issue. Relying upon *In re Oliver*[228] and *Estes v. Texas*[229] to support its argument, the Court ruled that the "constitutional guarantee of a public trial is for the benefit of the accused."[230] Although Justice Potter Stewart's opinion invoked democratic theory[231] as well as framers' intent[232] when discussing the public benefits of the Sixth Amendment, ultimately Stewart concluded, "Recognition of an independent public interest in the enforcement of Sixth Amendment guarantees is a far cry, however, from the creation of a constitutional right on the part of the public."[233] Stewart avoided discussing Gannett's claim that the order violated the First Amendment by noting even if there was such a right,[234] the trial judge had already dealt with the issue by weighing the competing societal interests involved.[235]

---

[225] *Id.* at 608-10.
[226] 443 U.S. 368 (1979).
[227] *Id.* at 375.
[228] 333 U.S. 257 (1948).
[229] 381 U.S. 532 (1965).
[230] *Gannett*, 443 U.S. at 381.
[231] *Id.* at 383.
[232] *Id.* at 385-86.
[233] *Id.* at 383. Furthermore, the Court noted that even if there had been a common law right to attend trials that was intended to be incorporated by the Sixth Amendment, there was certainly no evidence there had ever been a common law right to attend pretrial hearings. *Id.* at 389.
[234] *Id.* at 392.
[235] *Id.* at 392-93.

Despite these rulings, in 1980—just one year after *Gannett*—the Court limited the ability of judges to bar the public from attending trials based on the First Amendment in *Richmond Newspapers v. Virginia*.[236] It is important to note from the outset that the Court has never discussed access to a court based on the First Amendment without acknowledging that the right is not absolute. However, what sets these discussions apart from their national security/transparency counterparts is that since *Richmond Newspapers* there has been little effort to frame these cases as anything other than First Amendment right of access cases and the justices have typically carefully weighed competing interests instead of merely deferring to the executive branch or debating how much deference to give. In many of the cases, as the trial judge had done in *Gannett*, the justices weigh how a right of access might affect other important societal concerns and equate the rights of the press with the rights of the general public. Indeed, as will be discussed below, some justices have ruled both for and against courtroom closures based on their interpretation of the strength of the government's arguments or their use of divergent legal justifications, all the while acknowledging a First Amendment-based right of access. Therefore, the cases serve as a contrast to the national security cases, as well as examples of how selective use of key factors can be used to justify different conclusions, even when justices agree on the core legal issues or basic legal frames presented by the cases.

Richmond Newspapers v. Virginia began when the attorney for John Paul Stevenson moved to have the courtroom closed for Stevenson's fourth trial on the same murder charge.[237] When the prosecution did not object to the closure, the trial judge ordered "that the Courtroom be kept clear of all parties except the witnesses when they testify."[238] After the judge ordered the courtroom closed, Richmond Newspapers asked for a hearing on a motion to vacate the order. At the conclusion of the hearing, the trial court denied the motion to vacate and ordered the trial to continue the following morning "with the press and public excluded."[239] The next day, after

---

[236] Richmond Newspapers v. Virginia, 448 U.S. 555 (1980).
[237] *Id.* at 559.
[238] *Id.* at 560.
[239] *Id.* at 561.

dismissing the jury, the trial judge declared Stevenson not guilty in a two-sentence order. Although the trial was now over, Richmond Newspapers appealed the closure order to the Virginia Supreme Court. When the state court denied the appeal, finding no reversible error, Richmond Newspapers appealed again. In a 7-1 decision that produced seven different opinions,[240] the U.S. Supreme Court reversed the order for closure, holding that the First Amendment prohibited closing a criminal trial to the public "[a]bsent an overriding interest articulated in findings."[241]

The various opinions in *Richmond Newspapers* differed from the national security/transparency cases both in terms of how the justices framed the issues and the variety of legal factors used. Most of the opinions in the case focused on some combination of historical analysis, First Amendment theory and democratic theory, specifically the role of transparency in an open society. In part, this is explained by *Gannett*. Because the Court had just ruled the previous term there was no constitutional right of access to trials under the Sixth Amendment, the justices had to distinguish *Richmond Newspapers* by framing their argument in terms of the First Amendment. For example, after concluding the issue was "'capable of repetition, yet evading review,'"[242] and, therefore, not moot, Chief Justice Warren Burger, writing for the Court, clearly framed the issue as dealing with a right to attend trials based on the First Amendment.[243] Although Burger also distinguished *Richmond Newspapers* from *Gannett* as dealing with *trials* as opposed to *pretrial hearings*,[244] as Justice Harry Blackmun pointed out in his concurring opinion, the *Gannett* majority wrote

---

[240] No opinion was joined by more than three justices. Chief Justice Burger, joined by Justices White and Stevens, wrote the opinion of the Court. Justices White and Stevens filed concurring opinions. Justice Brennan filed an opinion concurring in judgment in which Justice Marshall joined, and Justices Stewart and Blackmun also filed opinions concurring in the judgment. Justice Rehnquist filed a dissenting opinion. Justice Powell did not participate.

[241] *Richmond Newspapers*, 448 U.S. at 581.

[242] *Id.* at 563 (quoting Southern Pacific Terminal Co. v. ICC, 219 U.S. 498 (1911)).

[243] *Id.* at 564. *See also id.* at 583-84 (Stevens, J., concurring); *Id.* at 585 n.1 (Brennan, J., concurring); *Id.* at 599 (Stewart, J., concurring).

[244] *Id.* at 564.

twelve separate times that its opinion applied "to the *trial* itself."[245] Thus, although Burger did not acknowledge it, as Justice White noted in his concurring opinion, because of *Gannett* the Court was "required" to make *Richmond Newspapers* a First Amendment case.[246] Of the seven opinions written, only Justice William Rehnquist's dissent did not frame the issue as a First Amendment right of access case. Instead, Rehnquist framed the case as involving core legal questions of federalism, the power of the Supreme Court and constitutional interpretation.[247]

The case also stands out for the variety of legal factors used and the depth of discussion of those factors. A number of the opinions included long and detailed historical accounts of courtroom openness and discussion of democratic theory, focusing on the benefits of transparency. Burger's opinion, for example, focused on history, analysis of the framers' understanding of access and democratic theory. Burger spent ten pages discussing "the history of criminal trials being presumptively open" and the benefits openness brings to society.[248] Considering the benefits of transparency, Burger wrote, "People in an open society do not demand infallibility from their institutions, but it is difficult for them to accept what they are prohibited from observing."[249] Brennan's concurring opinion also delved deeply into historical analysis, examining the "legacy of open justice" to conclude, "As a matter of law and virtually immemorial custom, public trials have been the essentially unwavering rule in ancestral England and in our own Nation."[250]

In addition to history and democratic theory, many of the opinions discussed textual analysis of the Constitution, framers' intent and orginalism, as well as First Amendment theory. Rejecting textualism in favor of a more flexible interpretation of the Constitution, the justices found a right of access in the First Amendment. Because the text of the First Amendment does not explicitly discuss access or criminal trials,

---

[245] *Id.* at 601-02 (Blackmun, J., concurring) (emphasis in original).
[246] *Id.* at 582 (White, J., concurring).
[247] *Id.* at 606 (Rehnquist, J., dissenting).
[248] *Id.* at 565-75.
[249] *Id.* at 572.
[250] *Id.* at 593.

the justices spent a great deal of time explaining why the Amendment should be read to include a right to attend trials. Burger discussed multiple sources of the right to attend trials, including the "right of access," the "right to gather information," and the "right to receive information and ideas," all rights he found in the First Amendment.[251] Burger went on to examine "constitutional structure" and the framers' intent, reasoning that even though the Constitution contained no provision that explicitly guaranteed the right to attend criminal trials, the Court had recognized that some unenumerated fundamental rights were "indispensable to the enjoyment of enumerated rights."[252]

Both Brennan's and Justice John Paul Stevens' concurring opinions discussed a First Amendment right of access as well. Brennan's opinion included both a section discussing democratic theory and the structural benefits of openness to society[253] and a section focused on a discussion of the extent of a First Amendment theory, namely how different First Amendment theories or values might support a right of access and the "countervailing interests" that might justify restricting access.[254]   While Stevens also discussed how to balance access and other interests,[255] perhaps more so than any other justice, he avoided a straight balancing frame and instead framed the case as a landmark First Amendment decision that newsgathering was protected. Stevens wrote: "This is a watershed case. Until today the Court has accorded virtually absolute protection to the dissemination of information or ideas, but never before has it squarely held that the acquisition of newsworthy matter is entitled to any constitutional protection whatsoever."[256]   In fact, Stevens' opinion suggested the case was about a broad right of access that included—but might not be limited to—access to the judiciary. "I agree that the First Amendment protects the public and the press from abridgment of their rights of

---

[251] *Id.* at 576. Ultimately, Burger concluded it was not crucial how the right was described.
[252] *Id.* at 580.
[253] *Id.* at 593-97.
[254] *Id.* at 597-600 (Brennan, J., concurring).
[255] *Id.* at 583 (Stevens, J., concurring).
[256] *Id.* at 582.

access to information about the operation of their government, including the Judicial Branch," Stevens wrote.[257]

Two years after *Richmond Newspapers*, the Court continued to expand access to the judiciary based on the First Amendment. In *Globe Newspaper Co. v. Superior Court*[258] the Court held unconstitutional a Massachusetts statute[259] that had been construed as *requiring* trial judges to exclude the press and public from trials for sexual offenses involving a victim under the age of 18 during the testimony of the victim. Writing for the 6-3 majority, Brennan held that a court could only deny the constitutional right of access to trials on a case-by-case basis when the denial was necessary to advance a compelling governmental interest and "was narrowly tailored to serve that interest."[260] Although Brennan's opinion was similar to Burger's opinion in *Richmond Newspapers*, it diverged in some important ways.

Similar to *Nation Magazine* and Burger's *Richmond Newspapers* opinion, Brennan's opinion quickly dealt with mootness, holding that because the conflict was "capable of repetition, yet evading review" the issue was a live controversy.[261] Brennan then elaborated on the structural benefits transparency brings. Brennan was quick to acknowledge that the right of access to the judiciary was not explicitly mentioned in the First Amendment, but he relied on the framers' intent as well as precedent, citing *Richmond Newspapers*, to support his claim that there was a broad constitutional right of access. He wrote:

[T]he Framers were concerned with broad principles, and wrote against a background of shared values and practices. The First Amendment is thus broad enough to encompass those rights that, while not unambiguously enumerated in the very terms of the Amendment, are nonetheless necessary to the enjoyment of other First Amendment rights.[262]

---

[257] *Id.* at 584.
[258] 457 U.S. 596 (1982).
[259] Massachusetts Gen.Laws Ann., ch. 278, § 16A (1981).
[260] *Globe Newspaper Co.*, 457 U.S. at 607.
[261] *Id.* at 603.
[262] *Id.* at 604.

Brennan went on to explain that a right of access was protected by the First Amendment because access was necessary to ensure the proper functioning of a democratic society. Turning to First Amendment theory and the role transparency plays in self-government, Brennan wrote that access was necessary to ensure the free flow of information about governmental affairs.

> Underlying the First Amendment right of access to criminal trials is the common understanding that "a major purpose of that Amendment was to protect the free discussion of governmental affairs." By offering such protection, the First Amendment serves to ensure that the individual citizen can effectively participate in and contribute to our republican system of self-government. . . . Thus to the extent that the First Amendment embraces a right of access to criminal trials, it is to ensure that this constitutionally protected "discussion of governmental affairs" is an informed one.[263]

Concluding his discussion of First Amendment theory, Brennan emphasized democratic theory, writing that it was "particularly proper" a right of access to the judiciary was afforded protection by the First Amendment.[264] Brennan wrote that the right was protected by the Amendment both because of the history of open judicial proceedings and the "particularly significant role" a right of access to the judiciary "play[ed] in the functioning of the judicial process and the government as a whole."[265] Thus, like Stevens' concurring opinion in *Richmond Newspapers*, Brennan's language suggested that access to the judiciary was just one part of a broader constitutional right of access.

While the Court's opinion in *Globe Newspaper Co.* was very different from the opinions in the national security cases in terms of framing, legal factors and outcome, it is important to note that it would have been easy for the Court to follow a path similar to the national

---

[263] *Id.* at 604-05 (quoting Mills v. Alabama, 384 U.S. 214, 218 (1966), and citing Thornhill v. Alabama, 310 U.S. 88, 95 (1940); *Richmond Newspapers, Inc.*, 448 U.S. at 587-88 (Brennan, J., concurring); *id.* at 575 (plurality opinion)).

[264] *Id.* at 605.

[265] *Id.* at 606.

security cases. Two dissenting opinions in *Globe Newspaper Co.* illustrate this point. The first, authored by Burger and joined by Rehnquist, demonstrated the ease with which the Court could have used historical analysis and/or balancing to deny access. Although Burger's opinion identified a First Amendment right of access as the key legal issue involved in the case, by relying on different factors than Brennan to reach a conclusion, Burger's opinion demonstrated how judges can reach vastly different conclusions even while using the same frame. In his dissent, Burger emphasized that the key legal factor that justified the Court's decision in *Richmond Newspapers* was its focus on the historical tradition of open criminal trials.[266] Such an emphasis could not support access here as there was a strong history of no access at all to sex trials.

Although Brennan's majority opinion in *Globe Newspaper Co.* was similar to Burger's plurality opinion in *Richmond Newspapers* in some ways, the differences between the two opinions provide an excellent illustration of how the use of certain factors can justify a decision. Brennan's opinion included structural arguments that focused on democratic and First Amendment theory, yet strayed from the Chief Justice's extensive focus on historical analysis. The Chief Justice, dissenting because he didn't think access should be granted in the case, eschewed a broad First Amendment-based right of access, arguing that because there was a long history of excluding the public from trials involving sexual assault, particularly those involving minors, there was no support for the majority's decision that such trials could not be presumptively closed.[267] In addition, Burger argued that because a transcript of the trial was available, the Massachusetts law had "a relatively minor incidental impact on First Amendment rights" while giving "effect to the overriding state interest in protecting child rape victims."[268] Although both Burger and Brennan agreed that the main legal question was whether the First Amendment right of access to trials applied, they were able to support different conclusions by simply focusing on different factors. Thus, the case demonstrates that both the

---

[266] *Globe Newspaper Co. v. Superior Court*, 457 U.S. 596, 613-14 (1982) (Burger, C.J., dissenting).
[267] *Id.* at 614. (Burger, C.J., dissenting).
[268] *Id.* at 619-20.

ability to frame cases and to use selective legal factors makes the law extremely malleable. Even when judges agree on how a question should be framed, the capacity to use a multitidue of legal factors beyond precedent allows them to support divergent conclusions.

The second dissent in *Globe Newspaper*, written by Justice Stevens, relied on factors similar to those used by the Southern District of New York in *Nation Magazine v. Department of Defense*.[269] Although he argued for a broad constitutional right of access in *Richmond Newspapers*, Stevens' *Globe Newspaper Co.* dissent argued that the case should be framed in terms of justiciability issues, noting the constitutional novelty of the access question presented in the case as well as the lack of facts presented by the case.[270] Stevens argued that the case should be dismissed as moot, an issue raised in *Nation Magazine*.[271] Stevens wrote, "We have only *recently* recognized the First Amendment right of access to newsworthy matter."[272] Because the right was so recently recognized and the Massachusetts Supreme Court's interpretation of the statute didn't cover the facts as they actually occurred,[273] Stevens counseled against deciding the case on its face.

> In developing constitutional jurisprudence, there is a special importance in deciding cases on concrete facts. Only in specific controversies can the Court decide how this right of access to criminal trials can be accommodated with other societal interests, such as the protection of victims or defendants. . . .

> The question whether the Court should entertain a facial attack on a statute that bears on the right of access cannot be answered simply by noting that the right has its source in the First Amendment. [274]

---

[269] 762 F. Supp. 1558 (S.D.N.Y. 1991).
[270] *Globe Newspaper, Co.*, 457 U.S. at 620-21 (Stevens, J., dissenting).
[271] *Nation Magazine*, 762 F. Supp. at 1568-69.
[272] *Globe Newspaper, Co.*, 457 U.S. at 620-21 (emphasis added).
[273] *Id.* at 620 (Stevens, J., dissenting).
[274] *Id.* at 621 (citations omitted).

Based on his conclusions, Stevens would have dismissed the appeal,[275] a result similar to the *Nation Magazine* court's decision that it was not pragmatic to decide a case with no concrete controversy.[276]

The Court continued to expand access to courtrooms in the 1980s, consistently framing the cases in terms of a First Amendment right to access or as a need to balance access with the proper functioning of the judicial system. In 1984, in *Press-Enterprise Co. v. Riverside County Superior Court*[277]—known as *Press-Enterprise I* to distinguish it from the 1986 case discussed below—the Court ruled that as an integral part of a criminal trial, jury selection was subject to the First Amendment presumption of openness. In the opinion of the Court,[278] Burger used both the historical arguments[279] he articulated in previous cases and Brennan's factors of democratic and First Amendment theories and the structural benefits openness brings to the justice system.[280]

Although Burger clearly framed the case as a First Amendment issue, perhaps the most detailed First Amendment argument came in Stevens' concurring opinion. Once again, the language of Stevens' opinion was not limited to the benefits of transparency in the judicial process. Returning to his focus on democratic theory and the benefits of open government, Stevens wrote that access to the judiciary was simply a part of a greater right of access to information held by the government.

> The focus commanded by the First Amendment makes it appropriate to emphasize the fact that the underpinning of our holding today is not simply the interest in effective judicial administration; the First Amendment's concerns are much broader. The "common core purpose of assuring freedom of communication on matters relating to the functioning of government" that underlies the decision of cases of this kind provides protection to all members of the public "from

---

[275] *Globe Newspaper, Co.*, 457 U.S. at 623 (Stevens, J., dissenting).

[276] *Nation Magazine*, 762 F. Supp at 1572.

[277] 464 U.S. 501 (1984).

[278] Justices Blackmun and Stevens filed concurring opinions and Marshall filed an opinion concurring in the judgment.

[279] *Press-Enterprise I*, 464 U.S. at 506-08.

[280] *Id.* at 508-10.

abridgment of their rights of access to information about the operation of their government, including the Judicial Branch."[281]

In 1986, in *Press Enterprise v. Riverside County Superior Court*[282]—or *Press-Enterprise II*—the Court held that a First Amendment-based presumption of openness extended to criminal pretrial hearings as well. After quickly dealing with mootness in a manner similar to *Richmond Newspapers*,[283] Burger returned to democratic theory to support the holding. Writing for the majority once again, he used both history and the democratic theory-based structural value of openness to establish a test for deciding when a particular type of judicial proceeding was presumptively open. Under the "experience and logic" test, if a court proceeding was traditionally open to the public and "public access play[ed] a significant positive role in the functioning of the particular process in question," the proceeding was presumptively open to the public.[284]

Interestingly, using the factors of historical analysis and First Amendment theory to support his arguments, Stevens once again dissented. Although Stevens again clearly stated his belief that "a proper construction of the First Amendment embraces a right of access to information about the conduct of public affairs,"[285] he disagreed that preliminary hearings in criminal trials should be open. Citing his own dissent in *Globe Newspaper Co.* as well as his own concurring opinion in *Richmond Newspapers, Inc.*, Stevens wrote, "[T]he freedom to obtain information that the government has a legitimate interest in not disclosing is far narrower than the freedom to disseminate information, which is 'virtually absolute' in most contexts."[286] Stevens contended

---

[281] *Id.* at 517 (Stevens, J., concurring) (quoting Richmond Newspapers, Inc. v. Virginia, 448 U.S. 555, 575 (1980) (plurality opinion); *id.* at 584 (Stevens, J., concurring)). In addition, Stevens cited two cases in which, according to Stevens, the Court had "implicitly endorsed" a right of access, Zemel v. Rusk, 381 U.S. 1, 17 (1966) and Branzburg v. Hayes, 408 U.S. 665, 681 (1972).

[282] 478 U.S. 1 (1986).

[283] *Id.* at 6.

[284] *Id.* at 8.

[285] *Id.* at 18 (Stevens, J., dissenting).

[286] *Id.* at 20.

that the majority's historical analysis did not support a constitutional right of access because Burger's discussion focused on common law access[287] while its structural analysis would go too far, requiring almost all judicial proceedings, including civil and grand jury proceedings, to be open to the public.[288]

Although Stevens identified a First Amendment issue as being the principle legal issue in the case,[289] his primary frame focused on balancing the competing claims of transparency and the defendant's rights to a fair trial and his reputation. Thus, although Stevens reaffirmed his belief in a constitutional right of access, he wrote that in the situation at hand "[t]he constitutionally grounded fair trial interests of the accused if he is bound over for trial, and the reputation interests of the accused if he is not, provide a substantial reason for delaying access to the transcript for at least the short time before trial."[290] Although Stevens again wrote that the First Amendment should be read to include a broad right of access to governmental information, he also noted the right was not absolute and had to be weighed against the defendant's rights. Thus, more than the opinions that simply focused on the history of openness, Stevens' opinion invoked the frame of how to weigh a defendant's rights against the public's rights.[291] To support his conclusion, Stevens relied upon originalism, discussing common law at the time of the ratification of the Constitution and framers' intent.[292]

In sum, the Court has held that the courtrooms are presumptively open, although this presumption may be overcome by a compelling or overriding government interest so long as the restrictions are narrowly tailored to serve that interest. Interestingly enough, however, with the exception of Burger's opinion in *Globe* and Stevens' opinion in *Press Enterprise II*, the opinions did not use a clear balancing frame, often focusing on the First Amendment or the history of openness or "logic" of openness of a particular proceeding. As recently as 2004 the Court

---

[287] *Id.* at 24-25.
[288] *Id.* at 26-28.
[289] *Id.* at 15.
[290] *Id.* at 29.
[291] *Id.* at 20.
[292] *Id.* at 21.

relied upon the experience and logic test to determine that Puerto Rico's requirement of a private preliminary hearing unless the defendant requested otherwise was unconstitutional.[293]   This differs from many of the national security and judiciary cases discussed previously, in which the courts specifically emphasized the need to balance competing interests.

In addition, it is important to note that in some of the opinions in these cases—particularly a number of Stevens' opinions—the justices suggested that there is at least a qualified First Amendment right of access to all information in the government's possession.   Thus, the Court has firmly grounded a right of access to the judiciary in the Constitution and continues to do so despite multiple changes on the Court.   Since abandoning the Sixth Amendment issues presented in the early judicial access cases, the justices have consistently held that the core principle in these cases is a First Amendment right of access.   This contrasts with many of the national security/transparency cases that have discussed the First Amendment issues presented by the cases, only to focus on frames of justiciability in order to avoid deciding cases.

Furthermore, cases involving access to the judiciary stand out from the national security cases discussed above for their in-depth discussions of multiple legal factors.   In contrast to cases involving national security and transparency, the cases discussed in this section have used a wide range of legal factors to reach their decisions, including historical analysis, framers' intent, democratic theory, First Amendment values and precedent.   The opinions in the cases— including the dissents—contain detailed discussions of framers' intent as well as First Amendment and democratic theory.   In contrast, although the national security/transparency cases include discussions of First Amendment theory, the courts have either relied on precedent to justify decisions, even when there was little precedent to guide these

---

[293] El Vocero de Puerto Rico (Caribbean International News Corp.) v. Puerto Rico, 508 U.S. 147 (2004).   The Supreme Court of Puerto Rico held that "closed hearings [we]re compatible with the unique history and traditions of the Commonwealth, which display a special concern for the honor and reputation of the citizenry, and that open hearings would prejudice defendants' ability to obtain fair trials because of Puerto Rico's small size and dense population." The U.S. Supreme Court held that the decision was "irreconcilable" with *Press-Enterprise II. Id.* at 149.

decisions or focused on the hypothetical nature of the facts of the case to decide not to decide. Even the courts' discussions of First Amendment theory in the national security cases discussed in this chapter were tied to the precedents established by the judicial access cases.

However, it is important to note that while the Court has established a strong line of cases supporting a right of access to the judiciary using a variety of arguments, it would have been easy to do otherwise, as evidenced by the dissents in the cases as well as the national security cases. For example, although Burger eventually adopted Brennan's focus on democratic structure, had Burger's opinion in *Globe Newspaper Co.* attracted a majority of justices, judicial access cases might look very similar to national security access cases. As noted, many of the cases demonstrate how justices are able to use different factors to reach divergent conclusions, even when they agree on the frame or key legal issue presented in the case. Additionally, had a majority of the Court been drawn to Stevens' focus on the lack of concrete facts available for analysis in *Globe Newspapers*, the Court would not have advanced a First Amendment right of access in the case.

It is also important to note that there is one area of judicial access that might follow a different path than the judicial access cases discussed above. After the September 11, 2001, terrorist attacks, the U.S. government claimed a need to conduct numerous judicial proceedings in secret. Although the Supreme Court has yet to review any of these cases, it has denied certiorari in at least one terrorism-related case in which all pleadings were sealed, every hearing was conducted in a closed courtroom, and the case did not appear on any docket.[294] In 2004, Mohamed Kamel Bellaouel, an Algerian man married to a U.S. citizen, was detained in Miami, Florida, for overstaying his student visa. Bellaouel was held for five months, during which time he was transferred to Virginia to testify at the trial of 9/11 conspirator Zacarias Moussaoui.[295] Bellahouel filed a habeas corpus petition challenging his detention, but there was no public

---

[294] M.K.B. v. Warden, 540 U.S. 1213 (2004).

[295] See Meliah Thomas, *The First Amendment Right of Access to Docket Sheets*, 94 CAL. L. REV. 1537 (2006), for a discussion of the case.

record the case existed.[296] The case was made public only after a clerk for the Eleventh Circuit Court of Appeals inadvertently listed the case on the public oral argument calendar, after which reporters published stories about the case. When the Eleventh Circuit upheld the secret proceedings, Bellaouel appealed. Although a coalition of twenty-three media organizations, including the Reporters Committee for Freedom of the Press, moved for leave to intervene, the Supreme Court denied the motion, granted the government's motion for leave to file a brief in opposition under seal, and denied Bellaouel's petition for a writ of certiorari.[297] Although, the Supreme Court has ruled that neither U.S. citizens nor aliens can be denied the right of habeas corpus,[298] the scope of terrorists suspects' constitutional rights and the First Amendment right of access to these cases remain unclear. It is possible that the combination of judicial access and national security concerns will lead to a new line of cases that differ from the other judicial access cases and more closely resemble the national security cases discussed above.

To date, however, the Supreme Court has treated access to the judiciary fundamentally differently than other access cases. While a majority of the U.S. Supreme Court has framed access to judiciary cases in terms of the First Amendment, few courts have found even a limited constitutional right of access when national security is involved. Furthermore, many of the few courts that have found a limited right of access have decided the cases on other grounds. Possible reasons for these differences and the overall framework these individual cases have created are addressed in the final chapter of this book.

---

[296] Petition for Writ of Certiorari at 23-24, *M.K.B.*, 540 U.S. 1213 (No. 03-6747).

[297] *M.K.B.*, 540 U.S. at 1213. While the Court kept the government's brief in opposition secret, it granted a motion to release a heavily redacted version of Bellaouel's petition to the public.

[298] *See* Hamdi v. Rumsfeld, 542 U.S. 507 (2004); Rasul v. Bush, 542 U.S. 466 (2004).

CHPATER FIVE

Conclusion

As noted in the introductory chapter, although recent events have drawn attention to the conflict between national security, freedom of expression and transparency, the tension between these principles is nothing new. As discussed, as early as 1644, John Locke's writings advanced the idea that a democratic government's central purpose is to protect each individual's rights against invasion *and* to protect "the entire society from having the rights of its members robbed from them by another nation's war-launching invasion."[1] Yet, despite this long history, it was not until the 1950s that a United States federal court first considered how to balance these two important interests when the executive's ability to classify national security information was first reviewed in *Greene v. McElroy*.[2] Despite this late start, in the years following *Greene* federal courts have consistently and repeatedly been called upon to balance national security with freedom of expression and transparency. As recently as 2007 a federal court examined the constitutionality of the non-disclosure provisions of the Patriot Act,[3] and some commentators have called the federal government's prosecution of the two former lobbyists for disseminating national security information in *United States v. Rosen*[4] a dangerous attempt by the government to prosecute individuals who behave much like journalists who cover national security do.[5] As Fred Kaplan noted, the individuals were charged with distributing information "*not* to foreign governments or spies but rather '*to persons not entitled to receive it*'"

---

[1] Thomas B. McAffee, *Restoring the Lost World of Classical Legal Thought: The Presumption in Favor of Liberty Over Law and the Court Over the Constitution*, 75 U. CIN. L. REV. 1499, 1507 (2007).
[2] 360 U.S. 474 (1959).
[3] Doe v. Gonzales, 500 F. Supp. 2d 379 (S.D.N.Y. 2007).
[4] United States v. Rosen, 445 F. Supp. 2d 602 (E.D. Va. 2006).
[5] *See, e.g.*, Jonathon H. Adler & Michael Berry, *A Troubling Prosecution*, NAT'L REV. ONLINE, Aug. 21, 2006, http://article.nationalreview.com/?q=NjkyM2E5ZGE0ODdmNGViZjhhMDBi NWRlMWJmZTUxYTQ=; Fred Kaplan, *You're a Spy*, SLATE, Feb. 15, 2006, *at* http://www.slate.com/id/2136324.

and "this is what journalists do routinely."[6]   Thus, for almost fifty years, courts have shaped the way this country controls national security information, and it is certain they will continue to do so long into the future.

The primary purpose of this book is to examine the legal, theoretical, and public policy arguments used by federal courts when they address the conflict between government secrecy and transparency in order to understand the overall structure that currently governs national security information in this country. To achieve this, the book examined a broad swath of cases dealing with prior restraints, post-publication punishments and access to national security information and locations. By analyzing such a wide range of cases, an overall approach to national security information could be explored. The goal was to move beyond the level of examining an individual legal complaint—or even a series of complaints about a particular aspect of national security information such as prior restraints *or* post-publication punishments *or* access—to begin to create a picture of the underlying relationships and power structures that govern the control of national security information across these categories. In addition, in order to provide a contrast that would help illuminate any specific approaches courts are taking to national security cases, the book compared national security cases to a group of "control" cases—the judiciary cases discussed at the end of each chapter. By comparing prior restraint, post-publication punishment and access cases that have dealt with the judicial system to those dealing with national security information, the book was able to explore when courts dealt with similar issues in a similar fashion and when they did not. While it would be impossible to determine if national security cases are unique, this approach provided valuable insight into how national security is—and is not—different from other cases dealing with prior restraints, post-publication punishments and access.

National Security and Transparency Frames

While the individual cases examined record a fascinating history of our courts' national security jurisprudence, the issues they attempt to resolve, the way the courts' have framed those issues and the modes of

---

[6] Kaplan, *supra* note 5 (emphasis in original).

legal analysis used in the opinions are the truly interesting aspect. As Kevin T. McGuire and Barbara Palmer wrote, individual cases simply provide the vehicle, framework or "legal architecture" for the principle of law they represent.[7] By examining a large body of cases and looking for the underlying principles shared among them, it is possible to understand the broader, re-occurring legal issues the cases represent and see the social structures created by the rulings.

In the national security and prior restraint cases, the major frames judges used were straight First Amendment or national security frames that did not analyze the strength of the other interest, frames that highlighted the need to balance freedom of expression with national security, and those that focused on separation of powers issues. There were only three opinions that invoked freedom of expression without expressly stating it needed to be balanced with national security. The opinions that focused on the First Amendment without discussing national security, such as Justice William Brennan's opinion in *New York Times v. United States*,[8] discussed the role freedom of expression plays in a democracy or emphasized the high standard the First Amendment places on the government to justify a prior restraint. In addition to Brennan's concurrence in *Pentagon Papers*, the only other opinions to frame a case in solely terms of the First Amendment without attempting to balance freedom of expression with national security were Justice Potter Stewart's dissent in *United States v. Snepp*[9] and Judge Janet C. Hall's opinion in *Doe II*.[10] Similarly, there were only two opinions that invoked the government's need for secrecy without also discussing the First Amendment implications of a case. Only the Supreme Court's opinions in *Snepp* and the D.C. District Court's opinion in *Stillman v. CIA*[11] referenced the need to protect national security information without discussing the First Amendment, freedom of expression or government transparency. The opinions issued in *United States v. Progressive Magazine*,[12] *United States v.*

---

[7] Kevin T. McGuire & Barbara Palmer, *Issue Fluidity on the U.S. Supreme Court*, 89 AM. POL. SCI. REV. 691, 692 (1995).

[8] 403 U.S. 713, 727 (1971) (Brennan, J., concurring).

[9] 444 U.S. 507, 519-22 (1980) (Stewart, J., dissenting).

[10] Doe v. Gonzales, 386 F. Supp. 2d 66 (D. Conn. 2005) (hereinafter *Doe II*).

[11] 517 F. Supp. 2d 32, 33 (D.D.C. 2007).

[12] 467 F. Supp. 990 (W.D. Wis. 1979).

Marchetti,[13] *McGehee v. Casey*,[14] *National Federation of Federal Employees v. United States*,[15] *Doe I*,[16]*Doe III*,[17] and Stewart's concurrence,[18] Chief Justice Warren Burger's dissent[19] and Justice Harry Blackmun's dissent[20] in *Pentagon Papers* focused on balancing First Amendment or freedom of expressions claims with national security.

As noted in chapter two, in addition to freedom of expression and national security issues, the national security/prior restraint cases discussed focused extensively on separation of power issues. There were two distinct frames related to separation of power concerns that emerged in a number of the opinions, as well as a third that was found only in *Doe II*. The first framed focused on the relative powers of the courts and Congress. The most prominent opinions to feature this frame were the concurring *Pentagon Paper* opinions by Justices Hugo Black,[21] William O. Douglas,[22] Stewart,[23] Byron White[24] and Thurgood Marshall[25] that discussed Congress' role in creating laws that might be used to prevent the *New York Times* and *Washington Post* from publishing. In addition, *Doe III* contained a long and detailed discussion of the limits of congressional power, taking the legislative branch to task for overstepping its authority.[26] The second frame involving separation of powers issues focused on balancing the judiciary's and executive's power to control and/or review national security information decisions. These opinions included Douglas',

---

[13] 446 F.2d 1309 (4th Cir. 1972).
[14] 718 F.2d 1137 (D.C. Cir. 1983).
[15] 695 F. Supp. 1196 (D.D.C. 1988).
[16] Doe v. Ashcroft, 334 F. Supp. 2d 471 (S.D.N.Y. 2004) (hereinafter *Doe I*).
[17] Doe v. Gonzales, 500 F.Supp. 2d 379 (S.D.N.Y. 2007) (hereinafter *Doe III*).
[18] New York Times, Co., 403 U.S. at 728 (Stewart, J., concurring).
[19] *Id.* at 748 (Burger, C.J., dissenting).
[20] *Id.* at 761 (Blackmun, J., dissenting).
[21] *Id.*at 718. (Black, J., concurring).
[22] *Id.* at 721 (Douglas, J., concurring).
[23] *Id.* at 728 (Stewart, J., concurring).
[24] *Id.* at 731 (White, J., concurring).
[25] *Id.* at 742 (Marshall, J., concurring).
[26.] 500 F.Supp. 2d 379, 409-15 (S.D.N.Y. 2007).

Stewart's, White's and Marshall's concurrences[27] and John Marshall Harlan II's dissent in *Pentagon Papers*,[28] *Marchetti, Alfred A. Knopf, Inc. v. Colby*,[29] *McGehee* and *Stillman*. The majority of the discussion about separation of powers in these opinions focused on the need to defer decisions to the executive branch or, in the case of *McGehee*, to the CIA. A final frame dealing with the power of a branch of government was found in *Doe II*, which discussed the power of the courts to intervene in national security cases without explicitly referencing a need to balance the court's power with the power of the executive branch.

In the national security and post-publication punishment cases discussed in chapter three, similar frames were used by the courts. As in chapter two, the two most frequently discussed legal issues were the need to balance national security with freedom of expression and separation of powers issues. Separation of powers issues were discussed in every opinion except for the Fourth Circuit's majority opinion in *Morison v. United States*,[30] which framed the case entirely in terms of the government's ability to punish employees for disseminating national security information, and Judge T.S. Ellis' opinion in *United States v. Rosen*,[31] which framed the case as a need to balance national security and freedom of expression. The need to balance national security concerns with freedom of expression was discussed in every opinion except the Supreme Court's majority opinion in *Haig v. Agee*,[32] which framed the case entirely in terms of separation of powers, and Justice Harry Blackmun's opinion in the *Agee*[33] and Judge James Phillips' opinion in *Morison*,[34] which both discussed the First Amendment without examining the need for national security, and the Fourth Circuit's majority opinion in *Morison*.

---

[27] *New York Times Co.*, 403 U.S. at 721 (Douglas, J., concurring); *id.* at 728-30 (Stewart, J., concurring); *id.* at 732 (White, J., concurring); *id.* at 741-42 (Marshall, J., concurring).
[28] *Id.* at 756 (Harlan, J., dissenting).
[29] 509 F.2d 1362 (4th Cir. 1975).
[30] 844 F.2d 1057 (4th Cir. 1988).
[31] 445 F. Supp. 2d 602 (E.D. Va. 2006).
[32] 453 U.S. 280 (1980).
[33] *Id.* at 310 (Blackmun, J., concurring).
[34] *Morison*, 844 F.2d at 1087 (Phillips, J., concurring).

In the access cases, not only was there a continued focus on separation of powers issues, the opinions discussed the power of courts at even greater length. As noted, in the forty-four years between the Supreme Court's decision in *Greene v. McElroy*[35] and the D.C. District Court's opinion in *Flynt v. Rumsfeld*,[36] the courts consistently engaged in discussions of a First Amendment right of access, but ultimately most of the courts focused on the justiciability of the cases, the power of courts to intervene in national security information cases, or separation of powers issues. While this trend was also seen in many of the opinions examined in chapters two and three, in chapter four cases many of the courts were reluctant to inject themselves into disputes about access and found other ways to decide the cases. In many ways, this made the opinions in chapter four the most complex of those identified by the research, and it was often difficult to identify exactly how the opinions were framing the primary legal issues presented by the cases. Many opinions discussed multiple frames, hinting at a First Amendment or national security frame only to decide the case on a frame related to separation of powers, the political question doctrine or practical considerations related to the specific facts of the case.

The most frequently discussed frame in the national security and access cases was separation of powers. *Zemel v. Rusk*,[37] *United States v. AT&T*,[38] both the majority opinion and White's dissent in *Department of Navy v. Egan*,[39] *Stehney v. Perry*,[40] *Nation Magazine v. Department of Defense*[41] and *Flynt* all discussed the issue in one context or another. While some of the cases specifically framed the issues in terms of justiciability, mootness or the political question doctrine, others engaged in discussions of the need to balance the powers of the separate branches of government that were similar to those in chapters two and three.

While there was more discussion of separation of powers issues, there was less focus on the need to balance freedom of expression with

---

[35] 360 U.S. 474 (1959).
[36] 245 F. Supp. 2d 94 (D.D.C. 2003).
[37] 318 U.S. 1 (1965).
[38] 567 F.2d 121 (D.C. Cir. 1977).
[39] 484 U.S. 518 (1988); *id.* at 534 (White, J., dissenting).
[40] 907 F. Supp. 806 (D.N.J. 1995).
[41] 762 F. Supp. 1558 (S.D.N.Y. 1991).

national security. Only three of the access opinions discussed in the chapter—the majority opinion and White's dissent in *Egan*, and the Southern District of New York's decision in *Nation Magazine*—specifically framed the cases as dealing with the need to balance national security with the First Amendment and transparency concerns. As noted, the *Nation Magazine* court was particularly clear that the case was about balancing the two issues. While *Sherrill v. Knight*,[42] *Getty Images v. Department of Defense*,[43] and *Flynt* all balanced transparency with another factor, as discussed below, the opinions relied on practical considerations rather than on straight discussions of the importance of keeping national security information secret. Two opinions discussed the First Amendment without explicitly also discussing a need to balance it with national security concerns or the government's "right" to keep information secret. These included Douglas' dissent in *Zemel*[44] and the D.C. District Court's opinion in *Brunnenkant v. Laird*.[45] Furthermore, although he did not support such a right, Tom C. Clark's dissent in *Greene* clearly framed the case as dealing with a constitutional right of access to information.[46] It is important to note that the discussions of the First Amendment were often focused on whether there was a constitutionally based right of access or a "right to know."

In addition to separation of powers issues, a First Amendment-based right to know and the need to balance national security with transparency, there were a few frames unique to this line of cases. First, *Greene*, *Egan* and *Zemel* focused extensively on due process and/or procedural questions, legal issues that were not discussed at great length in the other cases in this book with the exception of *Morison* and *Rosen*. Second, because *Sherrill*, *Nation Magazine*, *Getty Images* and *Flynt* all discussed practical problems associated with making a decision in the case as factors that led to or supported their decisions, it was difficult to determine which legal issue the courts were truly focusing on. While the *Sherrill* court discussed the practical

---

[42] 569 F. 2d 124 (D.C. Cir. 1977).
[43] 193 F. Supp. 2d 112 (D.D.C. 2002).
[44] 318 U.S. 1, 23 (1965).
[45] 360 F.Supp. 1330 (D.D.C. 1973).
[46] 360 U.S. 474, 524 (1959).

needs of the Secret Service to keep the president safe, *Nation Magazine*, *Getty* and *Flynt* all discussed the practical problems related to a court considering largely hypothetical claims related to the undeveloped constitutional doctrine of the right to know. Thus, as noted, it was not totally clear what legal frame the courts were most focused on.

In sum, it appears as if the courts are framing the cases in a variety of ways. While balancing national security and freedom of expression/transparency and balancing the roles of the different branches of government appear to be the most common frames, the individual judges have been able to frame similar cases—or even the same case—in a variety of ways. Unfortunately, because frames can be introduced during oral arguments, by the litigants in briefs, or by third parties in amici briefs, and these documents were not always readily available for the lower court cases identified by this research, it was difficult to determine the origin of some of these frames. While some of the opinions clearly stated they were taking their frames from arguments presented by one of the litigants[47] or were addressing issues not present at the lower court level or argued by either side,[48] it was beyond the scope of this project to track each individual frame through the litigation process to determine where the frame originated.

National Security and Transparency Factors

In addition to the different frames the opinions cited, there were a number of legal factors or modes of legal interpretations judges used to reach and/or justify conclusions. As noted in chapter one, it is

---

[47] As noted in chapter two, in *New York Times v. United States*, 403 U.S. 713 (1971), Alexander Bickel's deliberate attempt to frame the case in terms of the First Amendment and separation of powers was adopted by the courts. *See supra* pp. 73-74. In addition, as discussed in chapter four, in *Greene v. McElroy*, 360 U.S. 474 (1959), although the majority credited Justice Tom Clark for framing the cases "colorfully," Clark in fact took the frame directly from the solicitor general, while in *Department of Navy v. Egan*, 484 U.S. 518 (1988), the majority of the Court adopted a frame advanced by the solicitor general.

[48] In *Nixon v. Warner Commc'n*, 435 U.S. 589 (1978), discussed in chapter four, the Supreme Court clearly stated it was deciding the case based on a "element that was neither advanced by the parties nor given appropriate consideration by the courts below." *Id.* at 602-03.

important to remember in any discussion of the law that judges and the lawyers who argue before them are trained to approach problems in a specific way and to find solutions to those problems by thinking about the law. In addition, judicial opinions are acts of persuasion and legitimization, and the law is the primary way this is done. That is, "legalism" is the primary way judges structure and explain their opinions. Thus, legal factors, such as precedent, original intent, and texualism exert a unique influence on the mindset of judges and work as a constraint on policy making as well as serve as a way to ex post facto justify their policy preferences, sway colleagues and legitimize decisions.

In the national security and prior restraint cases discussed in chapter two, the most frequently discussed factors were precedent (16 opinions), followed by originalism/framers' intent (6), democratic theory (6), statutory textual analysis (5), First Amendment theory (5), legislative history/intent (5) and constitutional textualism (3). The high number of references to democratic theory was primarily accounted for by opinions that discussed the important role national security played even in democratic systems of government. In addition to these more common factors, two other factors were relied upon by courts to reach and/or justify their conclusions. First, in *Alfred A. Knopf, Inc. v. Colby*,[49] Chief Judge Clement Haynsworth cited the practical problems associated with the judiciary and national security information as reasons the court should not exercise its right to review national security information decisions. Rather than rely upon precedent or interpretations of the constitutional power of courts, Haynsworth simply concluded that courts were "ill-equipped" to deal with national security information.[50] Second, the Supreme Court's majority opinion in *Snepp* relied upon a blend of the law of contracts and trusts to support its conclusion that Snepp had violated his confidentiality agreement and a trust could be set up for the government's benefit.[51]

A majority of the cases relied upon multiple factors to support their conclusions. Fifteen of the twenty-one opinions relied upon at least two factors. Douglas' opinion in *Pentagon Papers* relied upon the

---

[49] 509 F.2d 1362 (4th Cir. 1975).
[50] *Id.* at 1369.
[51] 444 U.S. 507 (1980).

most, discussing six different factors—statutory textual analysis, legislative intent, precedent, constitutional text, framers' intent and democratic theory. Interestingly, the six opinions that primarily relied upon one factor all relied upon precedent. They were a combination of Supreme Court and lower court decisions. The Supreme Court opinions included Brennan's, Blackmun's and Burger's opinions in *Pentagon Papers* and Stewart's dissent in *Snepp*.

Although there were only a few cases identified by the research that considered post-publication punishments and national security information, the opinions were notably complex, many relying on a multitude of factors. In the cases discussed, precedent was relied on to reach a decision in all seven opinions; however, only Blackmun's concurrence in *Agee* focused exclusively on precedent, accusing the majority of diverting from precedent without expressly acknowledging it.[52] All of the other opinions relied on a variety of factors to support their arguments. In addition to precedent, the opinions relied on statutory textual analysis (4 opinions), legislative history/intent (3), First Amendment theory (3), originalism/framers' intent (2) and democratic theory (2). Judge Ellis' opinion in *Rosen* was particularly wide-ranging in the factors it discussed.[53] Ellis cited democratic theory, First Amendment theory, original intent, statutory textual analysis, legislative history/intent and precedent.

In the national security and access cases discussed in chapter four, all thirteen opinions written in the ten cases relied heavily on precedent to justify or support their conclusions. Precedent was followed by First Amendment theory (5 opinions), constitutional textual analysis (4), practical or pragmatic reasons related to the undeveloped nature of a case (4), legislative history/intent (3), statutory textual analysis (3), and framers' intent/originalism (1). As noted, the cases that discussed pragmatic or practical concerns— *Nation Magazine v. Department of Defense*,[54] *Getty Images v. Department of Defense*[55] and *Flynt v. Rumsfeld*[56]—all focused on the undeveloped nature of the claims or on

---

[52] 453 U.S. 280, 310 (1980) (Blackmun, J., concurring).
[53] 445 F. Supp. 2d 602 (E.D. Va. 2006).
[54] 762 F. Supp. 1558 (S.D.N.Y. 1991).
[55] 193 F. Supp. 2d 112 (D.D.C. 2002).
[56] 245 F. Supp. 2d 94 (D.D.C. 2003).

pragmatic concerns related to deciding an important constitutional question based on speculative claims without the clear guidance of a Supreme Court precedent.

The cases differed from those in chapters two and three in that First Amendment theory and constitutional textual analysis were relied upon more heavily. This is perhaps because many of the cases were discussing a constitutionally based right of access or "right to know." Because the right to know has not been as well defined by the Supreme Court as the standards associated with prior restraints or post-publication punishments, the lower courts were left to define the existence or extent of a constitutional right to know through means other than precedent. It is interesting to note, however, that this did not lead the judges to focus on framers' intent/originalism. It appears the judges did not look to historical evidence to shed light on the existence of a right to know. The only case to discuss framers' intent was *United States v. AT&T,*[57] which did so to illuminate its discussion of separation of powers.

As could be expected, in all three types of cases, precedent was the legal factor the opinions most frequently used to justify or reach decisions. Precedent was cited in thirty-six opinions, followed by First Amendment theory (13), statutory textual analysis (12), legislative history/intent (11), originalism/framers intent (9), democratic theory (8), constitutional textualism (7), and pratical/pragmatic issues (5). These findings are consistent with the writings of Jeffery A. Segal and Harold J. Spaeth. As discussed in chapter one, Segal and Spaeth argued that precedent is often a powerful predictor of judicial decisions and that the frequency with which courts base decisions on precedent far surpasses any other aspect of the legal model.[58] This was true of Supreme Court cases as well as lower court cases, a finding consistent with the writings of Erwin Chemerinsky. While the Supreme Court is arguably less tied to precedent than lower courts, as Chemerinsky wrote, "A significant portion of almost every Supreme Court opinion is

---

[57] 567 F.2d 121 (D.C. Cir. 1977).

[58] JEFFERY A. SEGAL & HAROLD J. SPAETH, THE SUPREME COURT AND THE ATTITUDINAL MODEL REVISITED 76 (2002).

about how the decisions fit within, and flow from, the earlier case."[59] As they do in many cases, the judges in these cases often spent part of an opinion discussing why the present case was similar to or different from preceding cases or alternative lines of precedent. It is important to note, however, that precedent included discussions of precedents being improperly used. As discussed throughout the book, concurring and/or dissenting opinions were often critical of the majorities' uses of or reliance on precedent.

Significantly, although references did not reach the frequency of precedent, a number of opinions discussed First Amendment theory, and it appears that theory is an important way courts determine and/or justify exactly what conduct or actions are supported by the First Amendment. In chapters two and three, these discussions most frequently focused on the role of a free press or freedom of expression in self-government or as a check on government abuse while in chapter four they often focused on the possible existence of a constitutional right to know. It appears, then, that in addition to relying on precedent, many of the courts were also attempting to use First Amendment and democratic theory to determine for themselves and/or justify for others to what extent the Amendment protected a specific act or compelled the government to allow access to information or a location. This suggests that First Amendment theory is an important component of a jurist's toolbox of legal factors, a finding supported by previous research.

In First Amendment cases, judges often rely on rhetorical devices to justify decision making. For example, in a 1996 study, legal scholar W. Wat Hopkins found that when the "marketplace of ideas" metaphor was used as part of the rationale in a majority or plurality opinion as opposed to dicta or hyperbole, the U.S. Supreme Court consistently ruled in favor of the free speech interest.[60] Individual justices referred to the marketplace concept in seventy majority or plurality opinions and ruled in favor of free speech interests in all thirty-one cases in which the metaphor was part of the rationale for the Court's ruling.[61]

---

[59] Erwin Chemerinsky, *The Rhetoric of Constitutional Law*, 100 MICH. L. REV. 2008, 2019 (2002).

[60] W. Wat Hopkins, *The Supreme Court Defines the Marketplace of Ideas*, 73 JOURNALISM & MASS COMM. Q. 40, 41 (1996).

[61] *Id.* at 42.

This was true despite the fact that the justices consistently referred to the metaphor without a citation or cited a reference to a previous case that, in turn, provided no citation for the metaphor.[62]

The role of the press in a democracy—or the lack of a special role for the press—can also be used as a judicial tool to support or justify a decision. Law professor David A. Anderson has also written of the importance of the Supreme Court's rhetorical shifting between protecting "free speech," "free expression," and "free press."[63] Although a majority of the Supreme Court has never interpreted the Press Clause to have a meaning independent of the Speech Clause, the existence of the Press Clause influences interpretations and can serve to justify extending protections to the press.[64] For example, Anderson argued that in cases such as *Near v. Minnesota*,[65] *Lovell v. City of Griffin*,[66] and *Branzburg v. Hayes*,[67] sections of opinions that reference "the press" and its unique role in our society do so to signal strong protection for the press as an institution, which is not the case when the Court refers to freedom of expression.[68] Anderson has also contended that the "insidious" substitution of the term "the media" for "the press" in legal discourse is an indication of diminished protection. Anderson argued that the substitution of the media for the press "may have begun merely as an acknowledgement that the press had outgrown its print origins, but it has had the effect of stripping away the historical and rhetorical reverences that attached to 'the press' and replacing it with the more neutral, or perhaps even negative, connotations of 'the media.'" [69] This special role for the press was cited several times in the access cases discussed in chapter four, although it was never a powerful enough tool to justify a right of access for the press based on the First Amendment.

---

[62] *Id.* at 42-43.

[63] David A. Anderson, *Freedom of the Press*, 80 TEX. L. REV. 429 (2002).

[64] David A. Anderson, *Freedom of the Press in Wartime*, 77 U. COLO. L. REV. 49, 66 (2005).

[65] 283 U.S. 697 (1931).

[66] 303 U.S.444 (1938).

[67] 408 U.S. 665 (1972).

[68] Anderson, *supra* note 63, at 506-07.

[69] *Id.* at 506.

A final factor related to the time in which a decision was made—or the "context" of the decision—was referenced in several cases throughout the book and deserves mention. This reference to time and/or events was found in a number of opinions and suggests that courts are aware of historical factors that may impact or limit the power of their decisions. In both *Doe I* and *Doe II* Marrero's opinions were careful to reference the temporal and geographic proximity of the events of 9/11.[70]   While the weight of 9/11 did not stop Marrero from ruling against the government, the "critical time of national emergency" brought about by the Cold War was clearly on Clark's mind when he ruled for the government in *Greene*.[71]

Comparing National Security Cases to Judiciary Cases
There were a number of significant similarities *and* differences between the national security cases and judiciary cases discussed in this book. As all the courts did in the national security cases, the Supreme Court often framed judiciary cases in terms of balancing the First Amendment with another important value, often the effective operation of the judicial system.   However, in the judiciary cases, there were a fair number of opinions that either emphasized that there was no conflict presented in the case or that any conflict was heavily outweighed by First Amendment concerns.   Justice William Brennan's opinion in *Nebraska Press Association v. Stuartt* is perhaps the best example of an argument that there was no conflict between the issues[72] while Justice William Francis Murphy's and Justice Wiley Rutledge, Jr.'s opinions in *Pennekamp v. Florida* were good examples of opinions that suggested balance but stressed the importance of the First Amendment, the need for transparency in a democracy and the immediate nature of the danger needed to justify a post-publication punishment under the clear and present danger standard.[73]

As in the national security cases, the most frequently relied upon legal factor was precedent.   Twenty-one of the opinions focused at least

---

[70] *Doe I*, 334 F. Supp. 2d 471, 477-78 (S.D.N.Y. 2004); *Doe III*, 500 F.Supp. 2d 379, 415 (S.D.N.Y. 2007).
[71] 360 U.S. 474, 515 (1959) (Clark, J., dissenting).
[72] 427 U.S. 539, 572-73 (1976) (Brennan, J., concurring).
[73] 328 U.S. 331, 376 (1946) (Murphy, J., concurring); *id.* at 372 (Rutledge, J., concurring).

partially on precedent to reach or justify a decision. Precedent was followed by originalism/framers' intent and First Amendment theory, both of which were discussed in thirteen of the opinions, and democratic theory, which was discussed in six of the opinions. A number of the originalist arguments, though, were in the context of discussions of the history of judicial proceedings, rather than discussions of framers' intent. Interestingly the Court did not rely upon constitutional or statutory textualism (1 opinion each), or legislative intent (1 opinion) nearly as much as in the national security cases.

As noted above, while it is no surprise that the Court relied heavily on precedent, perhaps the most interesting finding is the extent to which the justices discussed the role of freedom of expression in self-government, the checking function and the right to know. Although, as noted above, the national security courts used First Amendment theory quite a bit, in comparison, it appears as if the Supreme Court has spent a great deal of time discussing First Amendment theory and the role of transparency in the judicial process. In several of the chapter four access to the judiciary opinions, such as Burger's opinion in *Richmond Newspapers v. Virginia*,[74] the justices specifically rejected constitutional textualism in favor of originalism, framers' intent and/or First Amendment theory to find a right of access, which was obviously not specifically mentioned in the text of the Constitution. These cases were then relied on as precedents by the national security and access courts in their exploration of the existence of a right of access.[75]

Overall, the national security and judiciary opinions involving prior restrains were the most similar to each other. As noted, the most significant difference between the two categories of cases was the focus in the national security cases on what level of deference the courts should give the executive when determining if publication of classified information would be harmful. The vast majority of opinions in both categories of cases framed the key legal issue as the need to balance the

---

[74] 448 U.S. 555 (1980).
[75] As mentioned in chapter four, *Nation Magazine v. Dep't of Defense*, 762 F. Supp. 1558, 1572 (S.D.N.Y. 1991), specifically relied upon *Richmond Newspapers* and *Globe Newspaper Co. v. Superior Court*, 457 U.S. 596 (1982), to determine there was a right to know based on the checking function of the First Amendment.

First Amendment with some other constitutional mandate. As discussed, many of the cases relied on similar precedents to reach or justify their conclusions. Indeed, many of the national security cases cited the judiciary cases and vice versa.

The national security and judiciary cases involving post-publication punishment were somewhat similar in that almost every opinion spent at least some time discussing the cases in terms of the First Amendment. As noted, however, the two sets of cases relied on different factors. While the national security cases tended to focus on textualism, legislative intent and history and a variety of factors, the judicial cases primarily relied on the clear and present danger precedents and First Amendment theory to support their conclusions. Interestingly, in the judiciary cases, even justices who issued dissenting opinions did not deviate from using the same precedents as the majority opinion. They merely disagreed with the application of the precedents. In addition, unlike the prior restraint cases, there was very little intersection between the two sets of cases in chapter three, and the national security cases rarely cited the judiciary cases.

In many ways, the two categories of access cases discussed in chapter four provided the most interesting comparisons. While the two sets of cases were very similar in terms of how the courts framed and discussed the key legal issues, they showed many differences in terms of outcomes. Although some justices have ruled against courtroom closures based on their interpretation of the strength of the government's arguments or their use of divergent legal justifications, the vast majority of justices have acknowledged a First Amendment-based right of access to the judiciary. This stands in contrast to the national security cases where, at best, the courts have found a qualified or tentative right of access. Interestingly, however, as opposed to the cases discussed in chapter three, those discussed in chapter four did cite each other. In the national security cases, the opinions often turned to the judiciary cases to look for evidence of a constitutionally based right to know or right of access. While they were unwilling to totally embrace the notion that a right of access exists outside of the judicial context, the opinions certainly used the judiciary precedents to support their arguments that there might be some sort of universal qualified right of access guaranteed by the First Amendment. Much of this can be explained by the courts' focus on separation of power issues and, as discussed below, lead to interesting conclusions about the judiciary's willingness to exert power over another branch of government.

Perhaps the starkest difference between the two categories of cases was the heavy reliance on separation of powers frames in the national security cases across prior restraint, post-publication punishment and access national security cases. Although some of the judiciary cases mentioned peripheral issues, such as federalism or the inherent power of courts,[76] the only judiciary case to explicitly frame a case in terms of a separation of powers concern was Justice Lewis Powell's opinion for the Court in *Nixon v. Warner Communications, Inc.*[77] Of course, that is not surprising given the facts of that case, which involved a request to copy the White House tapes of a former President. In the other judiciary cases, there simply was no separation of powers issue because they involved the Supreme Court reaching decisions that affected only the judicial branch.

In contrast, the national security cases are as much—if not more—about separation of powers and balancing powers as they are about balancing the First Amendment with national security. As noted, a great number of the opinions discussed the inherent power of the courts vis-à-vis the executive or legislative branch or grappled with how much deference the courts should give to the executive branch in determining what information should be classified. There are a number of explanations for this. First, it is possible that this emphasis is related to constitutional questions and concerns. Several of the cases outlined in the research focused on which branch of government was given the power to control national security information by the Constitution or focused on framers' intent to determine who should have the power. For example, in *Department of Navy v. Egan*, Justice Harry Blackmun wrote that the authority to protect national security information flowed directly from the Constitution and fell on the President "as head of the

---

[76] As noted, Justice Felix Frankfurter discussed federalism issues in *Bridges v. California,* 314 U.S. 252, 280 (1941) (Frankfurter, J., dissenting), and *Craig v. Harney,* 331 U.S. 367, 385 (1947) (Frankfurter, J., dissenting).

[77] 435 U.S. 589 (1978). In addition to using a separation of powers frame, the *Nixon* Court also discussed the judiciary's lack of practical ability to deal with the dispute at hand, an argument used by several of the national security and transparency opinions.

Executive Branch and as Commander in Chief." [78]   Second, it could be related to practical concerns with the ability and/or expertise of the courts to deal with national security information.   Several of the opinions focused on the judiciary's inability to know what information might be dangerous to national security or the inability of courts to properly control and house national security information. [79]   Finally, it is possible that it is related to inter-institutional constraints placed on the judiciary.   As noted in chapter one, scholars who advance the "strategic account" of judicial decision making have argued that justices are strategic actors who must consider the preferences of other actors and institutions and the institutional and historical context in which they act. [80]

Regardless of why the focus on separation of powers, it is clear from this research that it remains a concern for judges at all levels of the judiciary. Citing a number of Supreme Court precedents, Blackmun concluded, "[U]nless Congress specifically has provided otherwise, courts traditionally have been reluctant to intrude upon the authority of the Executive in military and national security affairs." [81]   In his concurring opinion in *United States v. Morison*, Judge Wilkinson summed up this idea: "In short, questions of national security and foreign affairs are 'of a kind for which the Judiciary has neither aptitude, facilities nor responsibility and which has long been held to belong in the domain of political power not subject to judicial intrusion or inquiry.'" [82]

---

[78] 484 U.S. 518, 527 (1988).

[79] *See, e.g.*, Alfred A. Knopf, Inc. v. Colby, 509 F.2d 1362, 1369 (4th Cir. 1975).

[80] *See, e.g,* LEE EPSTEIN & JACK KNIGHT, THE CHOICES JUSTICES MAKE (1998); Robert Lowry Clinton, *Game Theory, Legal History, and the Origins of Judicial Review: A Revisionist Analysis of* Marbury v. Madison, 38 AM. J. POLI. SCI. 285 (1994); Lori Hausegger & Lawrence Baum, *Inviting Congressional Action: A Study of Supreme Court Motivations in Statutory Interpretation*, 43 AM. J. POLI. SCI. 162 (1999); Jack Knight & Lee Epstein, *On the Struggle for Judicial Supremacy*, 30 LAW & SOC. REV. 87 (1996).

[81] *Egan*, 484 U.S. at 530.

[82] 844 F.2d 1057, 1083 (4th Cir. 1988) (Wilkinson, J., concurring) (quoting Chicago & Southern Air Lines, Inc. v. Waterman S.S. Corp., 333 U.S. 103, 111 (1948)).

Conclusion

In addition to answering questions related to the frames/legal issues and modes of legal analysis the courts used in these cases, one of the primary purposes of this book was to catalog the overall structure created by the cases. As Professor Cathy Packer wrote, it is only by studying the societal implications of a body of case law that scholars can "fully comprehend the impact of . . . [individual] disputes on both individuals and society."[83] In addition to the conclusions outlined above related to the frames and factors used in these cases, a number of broader theoretical observations about the structure that the courts have created can be made.

First, the analysis identified a great deal of similarity in the treatment of prior restraints across national security and judiciary cases, early signs of national security access cases adopting the approach of judiciary access cases, and a lack of similarity across post-publication punishment cases. This indicates that while the courts have a well-developed approach to prior restraint cases, they are struggling to develop a consistent approach to post-publication punishment and access cases. As noted in chapter one, Mark J. Richards and Herbert M. Kritzer used the term "jurisprudential regime" to refer to a key precedent, or a set of related precedents, that structure the way courts evaluate key elements of cases in a particular legal area.[84] This research suggests that the judiciary's antipathy toward prior restraints—established in cases such as *Near v. Minnesota*,[85] *Organization for a Better Austin v. Keefe*,[86] and *New York Times Co. v. United States*[87]—has become well enough established that lower courts are easily applying the standard, even when the governmental interest at stake is as important as national security. The right to know appears at best to be a developing regime—well-established in the judicial access cases, but undeveloped elsewhere. Thus, while the national

---

[83] Cathy Packer, *Don't Even Ask! A Two-Level Analysis of Government Lawsuits Against Citizen and Media Access Requestors*, 13 COMM. L. & POL'Y 29, 32 (2008).

[84] Mark J. Richards & Herbert M. Kritzer, *Jurisprudential Regimes in Supreme Court Decision Making*, 96 AM. POLI. SCI. REV. 305, 315-16 (2002).

[85] 283 U.S. 697 (1931).

[86] 402 U.S. 415 (1971).

[87] 403 U.S. 713 (1971).

security access courts frequently cited the key precedents that would establish a "right to know regime," the lower courts are currently struggling to apply that regime outside of the judicial context. In contrast, post-publication punishment cases, perhaps because of the limited number of cases the Supreme Court has considered, instead relied on a case-by-case determination. While the Court has a regime for judiciary cases—consistently turning to the clear and present danger precedents[88]—this regime has not crossed over to other areas of the law. This conclusion comes with an important caveat, however. The ability to selectively frame cases and use divergent legal factors does allow judges and litigants to find ways around jurisprudential regimes.[89] That is, while a judge might be more constrained by the strength of the Court's prior restraint jurisprudential regime, the ability to frame cases and selectively use some factors over others left them with at least some room to maneuver.

Second, the research demonstrates that First Amendment and democratic theory are important rhetorical tools that can be used in conjunction with legal factors such as precedent or originalism to help jurists reach and justify conclusions. In addition, it appears as if there was a heavy reliance on First Amendment and democratic theory when breaking new legal ground. That is, judges can rely on First Amendment or democratic theory to establish new jurisprudential regimes or in combination with precedent to justify a decision that might not be specifically supported by the precedent, textualism or orginalism. For example, it is noteworthy that the court access cases relied heavily on theory, both First Amendment and democratic, when establishing a constitutional right to attend and report on trials. The justices certainly could not turn to textualism or precedent and instead needed to justify why a right to attend trials was inherent in the First Amendment. Future research would be greatly informed by looking for

---

[88] As noted, the main difference in the post-publication punishment cases was not whether the clear and present danger test applied, but rather what kind of expression qualified as a "clear and present danger."

[89] For example, as discussed in chapter two, the dissenting justices in the Pentagon Papers case retained the ability to selectively argue the case was about the power of the executive branch, whereas the government in the Patriot Act cases had the ability to argue the restrictions were not truly prior restraints.

such rhetorical devices in opinions in addition to textualism, orginialism, and precedent.

Third, the research both does and does not support the contention that national security is a different area of the law. While some of the opinions treated national security information in a very different way than other types of information, it appears that national security is not a "trump card" that can be used by the government to achieve its objectives while avoiding judicial scrutiny. While some opinions, such as Clark's dissent in *Greene*[90] or Haynsworth's opinion in *Marchetti,*[91] went to great lengths to express the need to defer almost entirely to the executive branch in matters of national security, the majority of judges were unwilling to abdicate their judicial function and took their duty to protect civil liberties seriously, often attempting to balance the two competing concerns. There are, however, at least two ways in which national security cases are very different from the judiciary cases identified by this research.

As noted, one area that is different in national security information cases is that they consistently invoke separation of powers concerns. The national security cases thus serve as an important reminder that the judiciary is but one part of our governmental structure that must take into account the desires and powers of the other branches of government. While the ratification of the Constitution set out the powers of each branch, as scholars have noted, this was only the beginning of a long process by which political institutions take shape.[92] Rather than being static, the powers of our political institutions are defined through "sequences of events . . . either unanticipated by the framers or unspecified in the [Constitution]."[93] Under this analysis, it is clear that in national security cases the courts are being mindful of the desires and powers of other political institutions.

Such a finding should not come as a surprise to observers of the court system. The courts of today are not far removed from the constitutional battles between President Franklin D. Roosevelt and the Supreme Court, which resulted in the President's Court-packing plan

---

[90] 360 U.S. 474, 510 (1959) (Clark, J., dissenting).
[91] 446 F.2d 1309 (4th Cir. 1972).
[92] Knight & Epstein, *supra* note 80, at 88.
[93] *Id.*

and cast doubt on the future of the Court as a powerful political institution.[94] Undoubtedly, all of the jurists who issued opinions analyzed in this book were well aware of Roosevelt's Court-packing plan and other battles.[95] Thus, it is totally understandable that separation of powers would play a key role in national security cases but simply are not relevant in the judicial cases when judges are effectively making rules to govern their own house. In the judicial cases, the justices were free to rely upon First Amendment and democratic theory to create a system of access and dissemination without worrying about overextending their power.

An additional factor in the national security cases that is unlikely to been seen elsewhere was the consideration the courts gave to the dangers of making a "wrong" decision involving national security information. Although few of the opinions stated the stakes as bluntly as District Judge Robert Willis Warren's opinion in *United States v. Progressive Magazine*,[96] all of the jurists had to be aware of the potential results of allowing national security information to be disseminated. As Warren wrote:

> A mistake in ruling against *The Progressive* will seriously infringe cherished First Amendment rights. . . . It will curtail defendants' First Amendment rights in a drastic and substantial fashion. It will infringe upon our right to know and to be informed as well.
>
> A mistake in ruling against the United States could pave the way for thermonuclear annihilation for us all. In that event, our right to life is extinguished and the right to publish becomes moot.[97]

---

[94] See generally Gregory Caldeira, *Public Opinion and the U.S. Supreme Court: FDR's Court Packing Plan*, 81 AM. POL. SCI. REV. 1139 (1987), for an analysis of the battles between FDR and the Supreme Court.

[95] The first—and one of the most widely written about—confrontations between the executive and the Supreme Court was, of course, *Marbury v. Madison* 5 U.S. 137 (1803).

[96] 467 F. Supp. 990 (W.D. Wis. 1979).

[97] *Id.* at 995-96.

Taking these two issues together—separation of power frames and the consequences of making a "wrong decision"—it is no surprise that the question courts have not answered is just how much deference to the executive branch is appropriate. Cases currently working their way through the judicial system, such as *Doe III* and *United States v. Rosen*, will certainly have to deal with the question in one form or another. This, of course, is true of all cases involving national security, not simply those that deal with information policy. Any case that calls for balancing national security with a civil liberty, be it privacy, habeas corpus, or the right to a public trial of terrorists suspects, will have to focus on what level of deference to give the executive branch. Yet, as noted, some courts are willing to at least address the question. As discussed throughout this book, even after determining the judicial branch did indeed have some role to play in national security information cases, many of the opinions then spent a great deal of time attempting to determine what level of deference to give the executive branch. As Judge Victor Marrero wrote in *Doe III*, the Constitution was designed so that even in dangerous times both civil liberties and "the judiciary's unique role under our governmental system in protecting those liberties and upholding the rule of law" would not be circumscribed.[98]

Finally, this research has demonstrated that the law concerning information—like all law—is malleable. Through their ability to focus on specific frames while ignoring others, as well as their capacity to reach or ex post facto justify decisions based on different legal factors, courts do more than just apply the law, they mold the law. In the area of national security information, it is apparent that through framing and the selective use of precedent, framers' intent, First Amendment and democratic theory, or even practical issues related to the undeveloped nature of a case, judges have the ability to shape and manage the way our society controls information. While this is certainly not a new finding—the legal realists first advanced the idea that the law is vague, internally inconsistent, and revisable in the early twentieth century— the area of information control is a particularly important place to study it. As Packer wrote, disputes about the distribution of information are about "the fundamental relationship among the government, the media

---

[98] 500 F.Supp. 2d 379, 415 (S.D.N.Y. 2007) (citation and footnotes omitted).

and the public" because "[i]nformation is power, and the proper sharing of this power source is critical to the proper operation of a democratic government."[99] In addition, because the courts must strike a balance between national security and transparency *as well as* between the separate branches of government in national security information cases, it is obvious that although opinions are written in the legal formalist tradition, the law alone does not decide cases. Justice Oliver Wendell Holmes was one of the first jurists to suggest that law was not a formal process of neutral application or logical deduction but a process of choosing among competing values.[100] This book has demonstrated that when courts are asked to balance national security with freedom of expression, they not only must apply the law but also choose among the competing core democratic values of security and transparency, always a difficult task.

---

[99] Packer, *supra* note 83 at 33.
[100] *See, e.g.,* Oliver Wendell Holmes, *The Path of Law*, 10 HARV. L. REV. 457 (1897).

References

Anderson, David A. "The Origins of the Press Clause." *UCLA Law Review* 30 (1983): 455-541.

——. "Freedom of the Press." *Texas Law Review* 80 (2002): 429-530.

——. "Freedom of the Press in Wartime." *University of Colorado Law Review* 77 (2005): 49-100.

Arrington, Theodore S., and Saul Brenner. "Strategic Voting for Damage Control on the Supreme Court." *Political Research Quarterly* 57 (2004): 565-573.

Bailey, Michael, Brian Kamoie, and Forrest Maltzman. "Signals from the Tenth Justice: The Political Role of the Solicitor General in Supreme Court Decision Making." *American Journal of Political Science* 49 (2005): 72-85.

Ballou, Eric E., and Kyle E. McSlarrow. "Plugging the Leak: The Case for a Legislative Resolution of the Conflict Between the Demands of Secrecy and the Need for an Open Government." *Virginia Law Review* 71 (1985):801-868.

Baum, Lawrence. "Measuring Policy Change in the U.S. Supreme Court." *American Political Science Review* 82 (1988): 905-912.

Best, Paul. "The Fundamental Rights Controversy: The Essential Contradictions of Normative Constitutional Scholarship." *Yale Law Journal* 90 (1982): 1063-1109.

BeVier, Lillian R. "The First Amendment and Political Speech: An Inquiry into the Substance and Limits of the Principle." *Stanford Law Review* 30 (1978): 299-358.

——. "An Informed Public, an Informing Press: The Search for a Constitutional Principle." *California Law Review* 68 (1980): 482-517.

Blasi, Vincent. "The Checking Value in First Amendment Theory." *American Bar Foundation Research Journal* 1977 (1977): 521-649.

Bobbitt, Philip. *Constitutional Interpretation.* New York: Oxford University Press, 1991.

Bork, Robert. "Neutral Principles and Some First Amendment Problems." *Indiana Law Journal* 47 (1971): 1-35.

Boucher, David, & Paul Kelly. "The Social Contract and Its Critics: An Overview." In *The Social Contract from Hobbes to Rawls*, edited by David Boucher & Paul Kelly, 1-34. New York: Routledge, 1994.

Brennan, Jr., William J. "Speech to the Text and Teaching Symposium." In *Originalism: A Quarter Century of Debate*, edited by Steven G. Calabresi, 55-70. Washington, D.C.: Regnery Publishing, 2007.

Caldeira, Gregory. "Public Opinion and the U.S. Supreme Court: FDR's Court Packing Plan." *American Political Science Review* 81 (1987): 1139-1153.

———. "Review of the Supreme Court and the Attitudinal Model." *American Political Science Quarterly* 88 (1994): 485-486.

Caldeira, Gregory A., and John R. Wright. "Organized Interests and Agenda Setting in the U.S. Supreme Court." *American Political Science Review* 82 (1988): 1109-1128.

Chemerinsky, Erwin. "The Jurisprudence of Justice Scalia: A Critical Appraisal." *University of Hawai'i Law Review* 22 (2000): 385-402.

———. "The Rhetoric of Constitutional Law." *Michigan Law Review* 100 (2002): 2008-2035.

Clinton, Robert Lowry. "Game Theory, Legal History, and the Origins of Judicial Review: A Revisionist Analysis of *Marbury v. Madison*." *American Journal of Political Science* 38 (1994): 285-302.

Copeland, David A. *The Idea of a Free Press*. Evanston, IL: Northwestern University Press, 2006.

Corley, Pamela C., Robert M. Howard, and David C. Nixon. "The Supreme Court and Opinion Content: The Use of the Federalist Papers." *Political Research Quarterly* 58 (2005): 329-340.

Cornell, Saul. "The Original Meaning of Original Understanding: A Neo-Blackstonian Critique." *Maryland Law Review* 67(2007):150-165.

Cross, Frank. "Political Science and the New Legal Realism: A Case of Unfortunate Interdisciplinary Ignorance." *Northwestern University Law Review* 92 (1997): 251-326.

Cross, Frank B. and Blake J. Nelson. "Strategic Institutional Effects on Supreme Court Decisionmaking." *Northwestern Law Review* 95(2001): 1437-1494.

Dorf, Robert, and Saul Brenner. "Conformity Voting on the United States Supreme Court." *Journal of Politics* 54 (1992): 762-776.

Dumain, Ian M. "Seminal Issues as Viewed Through the Lens of the Progressive Case: No Secret, No Defense: *United States v. Progressive.*" *Cardozo Law Review* 26 (2005): 1323-1336.

DuVal, Jr., Benjamin S. "The Occasions of Secrecy." *University of Pittsburgh Law Review* 47 (1986): 579-674.

Edgar, Harold and Benno C. Schmidt Jr. "The Espionage Statutes and Publication of Defense Information." *Columbia Law Review* 73 (1973): 929-1087.

Emerson, Thomas I. "Legal Foundations of the Right to Know." *Washington University Law Quarterly* 1976 (1976): 1-24.

——. "Toward a General Theory of the First Amendment." *Yale Law Journal* 72 (1963): 877-956.

Entman, Robert M. "Framing: Toward a Clarification of a Fractured Paradigm." *Journal of Communication* 43 (1993): 51-58.

Epstein, Lee, and Jack Knight. *The Choices Justices Make.* Washington, D.C.: CQ Press, 1998.

Epstein, Lee, and Joseph F. Kobylka, *The Supreme Court and Legal Change: Abortion and the Death Penalty.* Chapel Hill: University of North Carolina Press, 1992.

Eskridge Jr., William N. "The New Textualism." *UCLA Law Review* 37(1990): 621-692.

Fenster, Mark. "The Opacity of Transparency." *Iowa Law Review* 91 (2007): 885-950.

Foerstel, Herbert M. *Freedom of Information and the Right to Know.* Santa Barbara, CA: Greenwood Publishing Group, 1999.

Forsyth, Murray. "Hobbes's Contractarianism." In *The Social Contract from Hobbes to Rawls*, edited by David Boucher & Paul Kelly, 35-50. New York: Routledge, 1994.

Gates, John B., and Glenn A. Phelps. "Intentionalism in Constitutional Opinions." *Political Research Quarterly* 49 (1996): 245-262.

George, Tracey E., and Lee Epstein. "On the Nature of Supreme Court Decision Making." *American Political Science Review* 86 (1992): 323-338.

Gillman, Howard. "What's Law Got to Do With It? Judicial Behavorialists Test the 'Legal Model' of Judicial Decision Making." *Law and Social Inquiry* 26 (2001): 465-504.

Gitlin, Todd. *The Whole World is Watching: Mass Media in the Making and Unmaking of the New Left.* Berkley: University of California Press, 1980.

Gorman, Brian J. "Biosecurity and Secrecy Policy: Problems, Theory, and a Call for Executive Action." *I/S: A Journal of Law and Policy for the Information Society* 2 (2006): 53-102.

Greenawalt, Kent. *Law and Objectivity.* New York: Oxford University Press, 1992.

Gutmann, Amy, and Denis Thompson. *Democracy and Disagreement.* Cambridge, MA: Harvard University Press, 1996.

Hausegger, Lori, and Lawrence Baum. "Inviting Congressional Action: A Study of Supreme Court Motivations in Statutory Interpretation." *American Journal of Political Science* 43 (1999): 162-186.

Haynie, Stacia L. "Leadership and Consensus on the U.S. Supreme Court." *Journal of Politics* 54 (1992): 1158-1170.

Held, David. *Models of Democracy.* Stanford: Stanford University Press, 2006.

Henkin, Louis. "The Right to Know and the Duty to Withhold: The Case of the Pentagon Papers." *University of Pennsylvania Law Review* 120 (1971): 271-280.

Hobbes, Thomas. *Leviathan.* Edited by Edwin Curley. Indianapolis: Hackett Publishing Company, Inc., 1994.

Hoffman, Daniel. *Governmental Secrecy and the Founding Fathers.* Santa Barbara, CA: Greenwood Publishing Group, 1981.

Holmes, Oliver Wendell. "The Path of Law." *Harvard Law Review* 10 (1897): 457-478.

Hopkins, W. Wat. "The Supreme Court Defines the Marketplace of Ideas." *Journalism and Mass Communication Quarterly* 73 (1996): 40-52.

Horwitz, Morton J. *The Transformation of American Law, 1870-1960.* Cambridge, MA: Harvard University Press, 1992.

Ivers, Gregg, and Karen O'Connor. "Friends or Foes: The Amicus Curiae Participation and Effectiveness of the American Civil Liberties Union and the Americans for Effective Law Enforcement in Criminal Cases, 1969-1982." *Law and Policy* 9 (1987): 161-178.

Johnson, Timothy R., Paul J. Wahlbeck, and James F. Spriggs, II., "The Influence of Oral Arguments on the U.S. Supreme Court." *American Political Science Review* 100 (1998): 99-113.

Katz, Steven L. "Ground Zero: The Information War in the Persian Gulf." *Government Information Quarterly* 9 (1992): 380-408.

Kirtley, Jane E. "Transparency and Accountability in a Time of Terror: The Bush Administration's Assault on Freedom of Information." *Communication Law and Policy* 11 (2006): 479-509.

Klein, Anthony R. "National Security Information: Its Proper Role and Scope in a Representative Democracy." *Federal Communications Law Journal* 42(1990): 433-462.

Knight, Jack, and Lee Epstein. "On the Struggle for Judicial Supremacy." *Law and Society Review* 30 (1996): 87-120.

Kotlowski, Dean J. "Trial by Error: Nixon, the Senate, and the Haynsworth Nomination." *Presidential Studies Quarterly* 1 (1996): 71-91.

Kramer, Larry. "Panel on Originalism and Pragmatism." In *Originalism: A Quarter Century of Debate*, edited by Steven G. Calabresi, 151-200. Washington, D.C.: Regnery Publishing, 2007.

Kitrosser, Heidi. "Secrecy and Separated Powers: Executive Privilege Revisited." *Iowa Law Review* 92 (2007): 489-544.

Kesavan, Vasan and Michael Stokes Paulsen. "The Interpretive Force of the Constitution's Secret Drafting History." *Georgetown Law Journal* 91 (2003): 1113-1214.

Lee, William E. "The Supreme Court and the Right to Receive Expression." *Supreme Court Review* (1987): 303-344.

———. "The Unusual Suspects: Journalists as Thieves." *William and Mary Bill of Rights Journal* 8 (2000): 53-134.

Levy, Leonard W. *Emergence of a Free Press.* New York: Oxford University Press, 1985.

Llewellyn, Karl N. "Some Realism About Realism—Responding to Dean Pound." *Harvard Law Review* 44 (1931): 1222-1264.

———. "A Realistic Jurisprudence—The Next Step." *Columbia Law Review* 30 (1930): 431-465.

Locke, John. *Second Treatise of Government.* Edited by C.B. Macpherson. Indianapolis: Hackett Publishing Co., 1980.

Maltese, John Anthony. "National Security v. Freedom of the Press: *New York Times v. United States.*" In *Creating Constitutional Change: Clashes over Power and Liberty in the Supreme Court*, edited by Gregg Ivers and Kevin T. McGuire, 233-248. Charlottesville: University of Virginia Press, 2004.

Maltzman, Forrest, and Paul J. Wahlbeck. "May it Please the Chief? Opinion Assignments in the Rehnquist Court." *American Journal of Political Science* 40 (1996): 421-443.

———. "Strategic Policy Considerations and Voting Fluidity on the Burger Court." *American Political Science Review* 90(1996): 581-592.

Maltzman, Forrest, James F. Spriggs and Paul J. Wahlbeck, *Crafting Law on the Supreme Court: The Collegial Game.* New York: Cambridge University Press, 2000.

Markovits, Richard S. *Matters of Principle: Legitimate Legal Argument and Constitutional Interpretation.* New York: New York University Press, 1998.

McAffee, Thomas B. "Restoring the Lost World of Classical Legal Thought: The Presumption in Favor of Liberty Over Law and the Court Over the Constitution." *University of Cincinnati Law Review* 75 (2007): 1499-1594.

McGuire, Kevin T. "Obscenity, Libertarian Values, and Decision Making in the Supreme Court." *American Politics Quarterly* 18 (1990): 47-68.

McGuire, Kevin T., and Barbara Palmer. "Issue Fluidity on the U.S. Supreme Court." *American Political Science Review* 89 (1995): 691-703.

McGuire, Kevin T., and James A. Stimson. "The Least Dangerous Branch Revisited: New Evidence on Supreme Court Responsiveness to Public Preferences." *Journal of Politics* 66 (2004): 1018-1035.

McLeod, Douglas M., and Benajmin H. Detenber. "Framing Effects of Television News Coverage of Social Protest." *Journal of Communication* 49 (1999): 3-23.

Meese, III, Edwin. "Speech Before the American Bar Association." In *Originalism: A Quarter Century of Debate*, edited by Steven G. Calabresi, 47-54. Washington, D.C.: Regnery Publishing, 2007.

Meiklejohn, Alexander. *Political Freedom: The Constitutional Power of the People.* New York: Oxford University Press, 1965.

———. *Free Speech and Its Relation to Self-Government.* New York: Harper and Brother Publishers, 1948.

Murphy, Walter F. *Elements of Judicial Strategy.* Chicago: University of Chicago Press, 1964.

Nimmer, Melville B. "National Security Secrets v. Free Speech: The Issues Left Undecided in the Ellsberg Case." *Stanford Law Review* 26 (1974): 311-334.

Packer, Cathy. "Don't Even Ask! A Two-Level Analysis of Government Lawsuits Against Citizen and Media Access Requestors." *Communication Law and Policy* 13 (2008): 29-62.

Pallitto, Robert M., and William G. Weaver. *Presidential Secrecy and the Law.* Baltimore: The Johns Hopkins University Press, 2007.

Phelps, Glenn A., and John B. Gates. "The Myth of Jurisprudence: Interpretive Theory in the Constitutional Opinions of Justices Rehnquist and Brennan." *Santa Clara Law Review* 31(1991): 567-597.

Posner, Richard A. *Not a Suicide Pact: The Constitution in a Time of National Emergency.* New York: Oxford University Press, 2006.

Prados, John, and Maragret Pratt Porter, eds. *Inside the Pentagon Papers.* Lawrence, KS: The University Press of Kansas, 2004.

"Recent Case: Constitutional Law-Due Process and Free Speech-District Court Holds That Recipients of Government Leaks Who Disclose Information 'Related to the National Defense' May Be Prosecuted Under the Espionage Act." *Harvard Law Review* 120 (2007): 821-828.

Richards, Mark J., and Herbert M. Kritzer. "Jurisprudential Regimes in Supreme Court Decision Making." *American Political Science Review* 96 (2002): 305-321.

Roberts, Alasdair. "National Security and Open Government." *Georgetown Public Policy Review* 9 (2004): 69-85.

Rosenberg, Gerald. "Symposium: The Supreme Court and the Attitudinal Model." *Law and Courts* 4 (1994): 3-11.

Rohde, David W., and Harold J. Spaeth. *Supreme Court Decision Making*. San Francisco: W.H. Freeman & Co., 1976.

Rozell, Mark J. *Executive Privilege: Presidential Power, Secrecy, and Accountability*. Lawrence, KS: The University Press of Kansas, 2002.

Samaha, Adam M. "Government Secrets, Constitutional Law, and Platforms for Judicial Intervention." *UCLA Law Review* 53 (2006): 909-976.

Scalia, Antonin. *A Matter of Interpretation: Federal Courts and the Law*. Princeton: Princeton University Press, 1997.

Schauer, Frederick. *Free Speech: A Philosophical Enquiry*. New York: Cambridge University Press, 1982.

——. "Statutory Construction and the Coordinating Function of Plain Meaning." *Supreme Court Review* (1990): 231-256.

Schubert, Glendon. *The Judicial Mind Revisited*. New York: Oxford University Press, 1974.

Segal, Jeffery A. "Predicting Supreme Court Cases Probability: The Search and Seizure Cases, 1962-1981." *American Political Science Review* 78 (1984): 891-900.

Segal, Jeffery A., and Albert D. Cover. "Ideological Values and the Votes of U.S. Supreme Court Justices." *American Political Science Review* 83 (1989): 557-565.

Segal, Jeffery A., and Harold J. Spaeth. "The Influence of Stare Decisis on the Votes of U.S. Supreme Court Justices." *American Journal of Political Science* 40 (1996): 971-1003.

——. *The Supreme Court and the Attitudinal Model Revisited*. New York: Cambridge University Press, 2002.

Shaman, Jeffery. "The Constitution, the Supreme Court and Creativity." *Hastings Constitutional Law Quarterly* 9 (1982): 257-278.

Shane, Peter M. "Social Theory Meets Social Policy: Culture, Identity and Public Information Policy After September 11." *I/S: A Journal of Law and Policy for the Information Society* 2 (2006): i-xxiii.

Shapiro, Martin. *Law and Politics in the Supreme Court*. New York: Free Press, 1964.

Siebert, Fredrick Seaton. *Freedom of the Press in England 1476-1776*. Urbana, IL: University of Illinois Press, 1965.

Silver, Derigan A. "National Security and the Press: The Government's Ability to Prosecute Journalists for the Possession or Publication of National Security Information." *Communication Law and Policy* 13 (2008): 447-483.

Simon, Larry G. "The Authority of the Framers of the Constitution: Can Originalist Interpretation Be Justified?" *California Law Review* 73 (1985): 1482-1539.

Spaeth, Harold J., and Jeffrey A. Segal. *Majority Rule or Minority Will: Adherence to Precedent on the U.S. Supreme Court.* New York: Cambridge University Press, 1999.

Stein, Laura. "Understanding Speech Rights: Defensive and Empowering Approaches to the First Amendment." *Media, Culture and Society* 26 (2004): 102-120.

Steinberg, Jules. *Locke, Rousseau, and the Idea of Consent.* Santa Barbara, CA: Greenwood Publishing Group, 1978.

Sunstein, Cass R. "Probability Neglect: Emotions, Worst Cases, and Law." *Yale Law Journal* 112 (2002): 61-108.

Thomas, Meliah. "The First Amendment Right of Access to Docket Sheets." *California Law Review* 94 (2006): 1537-1580.

Thompson, Dennis F. "Democratic Secrecy." *Political Science Quarterly* 114 (1999): 181-193.

Topol, David H. "*United States v. Morison*: A Threat to the First Amendment Right to Publish National Security Information." *South Carolina Law Review* 43 (1992): 581-616.

Trudell, Jereen. "The Constitutionality of Section 793 of the Espionage Act and its Application to Press Leaks." *Wayne Law Review* 33 (1986): 205-228.

Ulmer, S. Sidney. "Issue Fluidity in the U.S. Supreme Court." In *Supreme Court Activism and Restraint*, edited by Stephen C. Halpern and Charles M. Lambe, 691-725. Lexington, MA: Lexington Books, 1982.

Venable, Barry E. "The Army and the Media." *Military Review* (Jan.-Feb. 2002): 66-71.

Weaver, William G., and Robert M. Pallito. "State Secrets and Executive Power." *Political Science Quarterly* 120 (2005): 85-112.

Wells, Christina E. "'National Security' Information and the Freedom of Information Act." *Administrative Law Review* 56 (2004): 1195-1222.

Wilson, James G. "The Most Sacred Text: The Supreme Court's Use of the Federalist Papers." *Brigham Young University Law Review* 1985 (1985): 65-136.

Case Index

Subject Index